Architecting Microsoft Azure Solutions Study & Lab Guide
Harinder Kohli

All progress happens outside the comfort zone
Michael John Bobak

Architecting Microsoft Azure Solutions Study & Lab Guide Part 2
Exam 70-535

Harinder Kohli

Published by:

kindle | direct publishing

This edition has been published by arrangement with **Kindle Direct Publishing**.

ISBN
ISBN: 9781983006197

Edition: 1st Edition May 2018

Contents at a Glance

Architecting Microsoft Azure Solutions Study & Lab Guide Part 2: Exam 70-535

Contents

Case Studies

1. Design a Business Continuity Solution for Web/App tier and Database Tier
2. Choosing a Database tier
3. Azure Web App High Availability
4. Real Time Prediction of breakdown of Industrial Machinery using Stream Analytics and Machine Learning
5. Visualize real-time IoT Device Data using Power BI
6. Visualize real-time IoT Device Data using Azure Web App

Lab Exercises

Chapter 1 Azure SQL Database
1. Creating and Connecting to Azure SQL Database
2. Geo-Replication. Creating Replica of Primary Database in different region

Chapter 2 Azure MySQL and PostgresSQL
3. Creating and Connecting to MySQL Database in 4 Steps
4. Creating and Connecting to PostgreSQL Database in 4 Steps
5. Restoring a Server from backup

Chapter 3 Azure Web App
6. Creating Web App
7. Exploring Application Settings
8. Exploring Deployment options
9. Exploring Authentication/Authorization options
10. Exploring Manual scale out
11. Exploring Autoscaling
12. Website Performance Test
13. Exploring creating Backup

Chapter 4 Mobile Apps
14. Create Mobile App Backend & Download Android Project (Android Example)
15. Add Authentication to App (Android)

Chapter 6 Azure Analytics Solutions
16. Create, Connect and Query SQL Data Warehouse using Sample Database
17. Create Data Lake Analytics Account with associated Data lake Store
18. Perform Analytics on Data stored in Data Lake Store using U-SQL Script
19. Adding Azure Storage as Data Source
20. Create an Azure Analysis Services server and add a data source
21. Create and Query HDInsight Hadoop Cluster

Chapter 7 Azure Data Services
22. Create Data Lake Store account and upload Data
23. Create Hadoop Cluster with Data Lake as Primary Storage
24. Create Data lake Analytics Cluster with Data Lake as Primary Storage

Chapter 8 Azure IOT Solutions
25. Deploy Stream Analytics Job to Process Real Time Data
26. Deploying IOT Hub
27. Add & Connect IoT Device to IoT Hub
28. Sending output of IOT Hub to Stream Analytics
29. IOT Hub Device Provisioning Service Setup
30. Link the IoT Hub with Device Provisioning service

Architecting Microsoft Azure Solutions Study & Lab Guide Part 2: Exam 70-535

Chapter 19 Monitoring Solutions

Chapter 20 Azure Automation

Introduction

Architecting Microsoft Azure Solutions Study & Lab Guide Part 2: Exam 70-535 is being published after a delay of 7 Months. Originally to be published in Oct 2017 was delayed because of multiple reasons including MS changing the exam from 70-534 to 70-535.

70-535 Exam is targeted toward Azure Architects who can design Cloud Solutions using Azure Services. 70-535 Exam focuses both on **Infrastructure Topics** such as Virtual Servers, Networks, Storage, Azure Active Directory, Azure CDN and **Database & PaaS Topics** such as SQL Database, Web Apps, IoT Solutions & Service Bus. One of the key success points to pass the exam is to work with Azure portal and practice configuring various Azure services.

Architecting Microsoft Azure Solution Lab & Study Guide helps you prepare for 70-535 Exam. It contains Topic lessons, Design Case Studies & Lab Exercises. It is being published in 2 separate Books.
Part 2 (Which is this book) focuses on Databases & PaaS Topics
Part 1 Focuses on Infrastructure Topics and is being published separately.

The twin focus of this book is to get your fundamental on Azure Services on strong footing and prepares you to design cloud solutions using Azure Services. Topic lessons, Design case studies and lab exercises are all geared towards making you understand Azure fundamentals. 70-535 Exam heavily focuses on fundamentals of Azure Services.

Best of Luck for 70-535 Exam.

I would be pleased to hear your feedback and thoughts on the book. Please comment on Amazon or mail to: harinder-kohli@outlook.com.

Harinder Kohli

How to contact Author

Email: harinder-kohli@outlook.com
Linkedin: https://www.linkedin.com/in/harinderkohli/
Azure Blog @ https://mykloud.wordpress.com

Updates about the book will be published on my blog site.

Register and get bonus full scale case study

Send your Amazon e-mail as proof of purchase of the book and receive full scale case study.

Download TOC and Sample Chapter from Box.com

https://app.box.com/s/guqzrxzxnh4euc8c10qnmzzltfmeeu4y

Chapter 1 Azure SQL Database

This Chapter covers following

- Azure SQL Database
- Azure SQL Database v/s SQL Server
- Comparing Azure SQL Database (PaaS) to SQL Server running on Azure VM (IaaS)
- Azure SQL Database - Single Database Model
- Azure SQL Database – Elastic Pool Model
- Azure SQL Database service tiers (DTU Model)
- Azure SQL Database service tiers (vCore Model)
- Azure SQL Database High Availability Using Active Geo-Replication
- High availability using Active Geo-Replication and Failover groups
- Azure SQL Database Backup and Restore
- Business continuity options with Azure SQL Database
- Scaling up or scaling down a single database
- In-Memory technologies in SQL Database
- Azure SQL Database access control
- Protecting SQL Data
- Azure SQL Database Threat Detection & Auditing
- SQL Database dynamic data masking
- Azure SQL Pricing

This Chapter Covers following Case Studies

- Design a Business Continuity Solution for Web/App tier and Database Tier
- Choosing a Database tier

This Chapter Covers following Lab Exercises

- Creating and Connecting to Azure SQL Database
- Geo-Replication. Creating Replica of Primary Database in different region

Chapter Topology

In this chapter we will add Azure SQL Database to the topology.

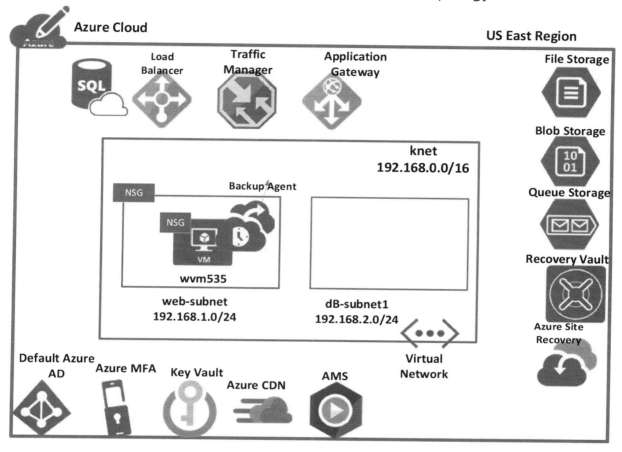

Following Topology will be used in Geo-Replication Exercise lab to replicate Primary Database in US East Region to US West Central Region.

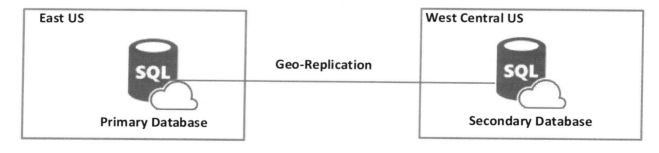

Azure SQL Database

Azure SQL Database is a relational database-as-a-service (DBaaS) in the cloud built on the Microsoft SQL Server platform. Azure SQL Database is a managed resource which means we don't have to install, upgrade or patch the database. You also don't have to manage the underlying infrastructure – Hardware and Operating System.

Benefits of Azure SQL Database

1. The benefit of using the Azure SQL Database service is the ability to spin up and consume a relational database in minutes; it can then easily be replicated for geo redundancy without all the infrastructure deployment and management normally required.
2. SQL Database supports existing SQL Server tools, libraries, and APIs. As a result, it is easy to develop new solutions, to move your existing SQL Server solutions, and to extend your existing SQL Server solutions to the Microsoft cloud without having to learn new skills.
3. Third we don't have to manage any upgrade or patching or underlying hardware and operating system.
4. You can Scale up or scale down a database at any time without downtime.

Azure SQL Database v/s SQL Server

SQL Database can be used in two ways- Azure SQL Database or SQL Server as a VM.

Azure SQL Database is a managed resource. We don't have to install the database or patch it. Scale out requires no downtime. Geo Replication can be configured in just 3-4 steps.

In case of SQL Server we need to install SQL server on a windows VM. This option requires more operational overhead and skilled resources are required for administration, installation and deployment. Replication configuration is complex and requires skilled resources for deployment.

Comparing Azure SQL Database (PaaS) to SQL Server running on Azure VM (IaaS)

Feature	Azure SQL	SQL Server on Azure VM
Feature	Not all features are supported.	Supports all SQL Server Features.
PaaS vs IaaS	This is a PaaS (Platform as a service) also referred to as DBaaS.	This is IaaS. SQL Server Installed on a Windows Server VM.
Administrative Overhead	There are very less Admin overhead required to maintain the database.	This requires specialized IT resources to Install and maintain the database and underline OS.
High Availability and Business Continuity	Built in High Availability and DR features. Features include Geo-Replication and Automated Backups.	You need to plan for all HA & DR. This requires very specialized IT resources for implementation.
Scalability	Very easy to scale up and down. You can add or remove resources when required without anytime.	You have to Plan for scalability and will require downtime.
Upgrades	You get all new features free of cost. They are implemented without any admin overhead.	You need to Plan for upgrades/patches which requires downtime. For next Major version of the database you need to pay the upgrade cost. Minor upgrades are free.
Max Database Size	4 TB	64 TB
License	License is included in PaaS. On-premise license cannot be ported	License is included as part of IaaS Marketplace. On-premise license can be ported
Use Case	New cloud-designed applications that have time constraints in development and marketing.	Existing applications that require fast migration to the cloud with minimal changes.
Use Case	Building Software-as-a-Service (SaaS) applications.	Migrating and building enterprise and hybrid applications.

Azure SQL Database - Single Database Model

Single databases are individual and fully isolated databases optimized for workloads when performance demands are somewhat predictable.

Azure SQL Database offers three tiers in Single Database Model – Basic, Standard, Premium. Within each tier there are multiple performance levels.

Each database tier is distinguished primarily by performance, which is measured in Database Transaction/Throughput Units (DTUs). There are Multiple Performance levels within a tier to handle different workloads.

Database Transaction Units (DTUs) determine the performance tier of the database. A DTU is a blended measure of CPU, memory, and data I/O and transaction log I/O that are guaranteed to be available to a standalone Azure SQL database at a specific performance level.

The figure below shows various service Tiers and performance level within each tier and their associated DTUs.

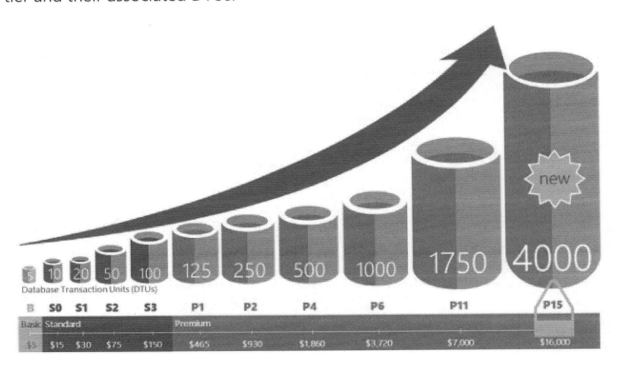

You can change service tiers at any time with minimal downtime to your application.

Architecting Microsoft Azure Solutions Study & Lab Guide Part 2: Exam 70-535

Azure SQL Database – Elastic Pool Model

SQL Database elastic pools are used for managing and scaling **multiple databases that have varying and unpredictable usage demands**. The databases in an elastic pool are on a single Azure SQL Database server and share a set number of resources at a set price.

Elastic pools solve the problem of unpredictable usage patterns by allocating performance resources to a pool rather than an individual database, and pay for the collective performance resources of the pool rather than for single database performance.

Elastic Database Transaction Units (eDTUs) determine the performance tier of the databases in an elastic pool. A eDTU is a blended measure of CPU, memory, and data I/O and transaction log I/O that are guaranteed to be available to a Azure SQL database Elastic pool..

Individual Databases in the elastic pool can consume varying level of eDTU but Pooled databases consumption don't exceed the limits of the pool, so your **cost remains predictable even if individual database usage doesn't.**

The figure below various services tiers and their associated eDTUs limits.

Auto-scale up to 5 eDTUs per DB — Basic

Auto-scale up to 100 eDTUs per DB — Standard

Auto-scale up to 1000 eDTUs per DB — Premium

An elastic pool is given a set number of eDTUs, for a set price. Within the pool, individual databases are given the flexibility to auto-scale within set parameters. Under heavy load, a database can consume more eDTUs to meet demand. Databases under light loads consume less, and databases under no load consume no eDTUs.

Azure SQL Database offers three tiers in Elastic Pool Model – Basic, Standard, Premium. Within each tier there are multiple performance levels.

Each database tier is distinguished primarily by performance, which is measured in elastic Database Transaction/Throughput Units (DTUs).

Databases best suited for pools

Databases with varying activity over time are great candidates for elastic pools because they are not active at maximum level at the same time and can share eDTUs.

Advantage of Elastic Pool Model

One of the advantage of Pools is that you can reduce the cost of Databases as the pool eDTUs are shared by many databases.

For the same value, eDTU is priced 1.5 Times that of DTU.

Azure SQL Database service tiers (DTU Model)

Azure SQL Database offers **Basic**, **Standard**, and **Premium** service tiers. Service tiers are primarily differentiated by a range of performance level and storage size.

Basic Tier: Basic Tier is best suited for a Test/Dev or low end application environment, supporting typically one single active operation at a given time.
Standard Tier: Best suited for cloud applications with low to medium IO performance requirements, supporting multiple concurrent queries.
Premier Tier: Designed for IO-intensive production workloads with high-availability and zero downtime, supporting many concurrent users. Examples are databases supporting mission critical applications.

Single Database Model

	Basic Tier	Standard	Premium
Maximum DTUs	5	3000	4000
Max Database size	2 GB	1 TB	4 TB
Backup retention	7 days	35 days	35 days
IO throughput	2.5 IOPS/DTU	2.5 IOPS/DTU	48 IOPS/DTU
IO latency	5ms (read), 10ms (write)	5ms (read), 10ms (write)	2ms (read/write)
Performance Levels within tiers	1	S0, S1, S2, S3, S4, S6, S7, S9 & S12	P1, P2, P4, P6, P11 & P15
In-memory OLTP	NA	NA	Supported

Elastic Pool Model

	Basic Tier	Standard	Premium
Maximum eDTUs per database	5	3000	4000
Maximum eDTUs per pool	1600	3000	4000
Maximum storage size per database	2 GB	1 TB	1 TB
Maximum storage size per pool	156 GB	4 TB	4 TB
Max Number of Databases/pool	500	500	100
Backup retention	7 days	35 days	35 days
IO throughput	Low	Medium	Higher
IO latency	> Premium	> Premium	< Basic & Std
Performance Levels within tiers	Multiple	Multiple	Multiple
Max in-memory OLTP storage (GB)	NA	NA	Supported

Azure SQL Database service tiers (vCore Model)

In vCore mode Azure SQL Database offers **General Purpose** and **Business Critical** Service tiers for both Single Database and Elastic Pool Model.

vCore model allows you to independently scale compute and storage resources based upon your workload needs. It also allows you to use Azure Hybrid Benefit for SQL Server to gain cost savings.

With Azure Hybrid Benefit for SQL Server you can save up to 30 percent on Azure SQL Database by using your existing SQL Server licenses.

	General Purpose	**Business Critical**
Compute	1 to 16 vCore	1 to 16 vCore
Memory	7 GB per core	7 GB per core
Storage	Premium remote storage, 5 GB – 4 TB	Local SSD storage, 5 GB – 1 TB
I/O	500 IOPS per vCore with 7500 maximum IOPS	5000 IOPS per core
Availability	1 replica, no read-scale	3 replicas, 1 read-scale, zone redundant HA
Backups	RA-GRS, 7-35 days (7 days by default)	RA-GRS, 7-35 days (7 days by default)
In-Memory	NA	Supported
Use Case	Most business workloads. Offers budget oriented balanced and scalable compute and storage options.	Business applications with high IO requirements. Offers highest resilience to failures using several isolated replicas.

Exercise 1: Creating and Connecting to Azure SQL Database

There are 3 steps involved in this: Create SQL Database, Create server level firewall rule and Connect to SQL Database using SQL Server Management Studio (SSMS) from a client machine.

Step 1 Create Azure SQL Database

1. Log on to Azure portal @ https://portal.azure.com
2. In Azure Portal Click +create a resource>Databases>SQL Database>Create SQL Database Blade open. Fill the following as per your requirement.

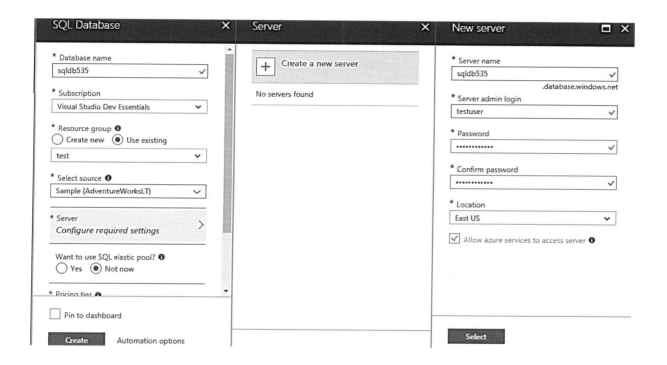

Step 2: Create SQL Database server level firewall rule

Firewall service on newly created Azure SQL Database server prevents external applications and tools from connecting to the server unless a firewall rule is created to open the firewall for specific client IP addresses.

1. Go the newly created SQL Database Dashboard.

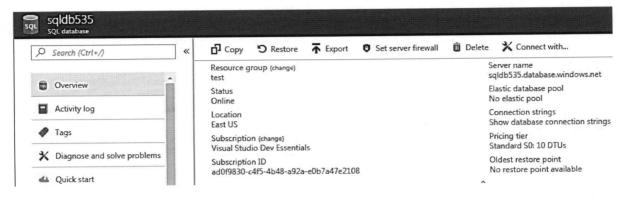

2. Click Set Server Firewall in top pane>Firewall Setting Blade opens>Here enter the client IP address which will connect to Azure SQL Database>Click Save.

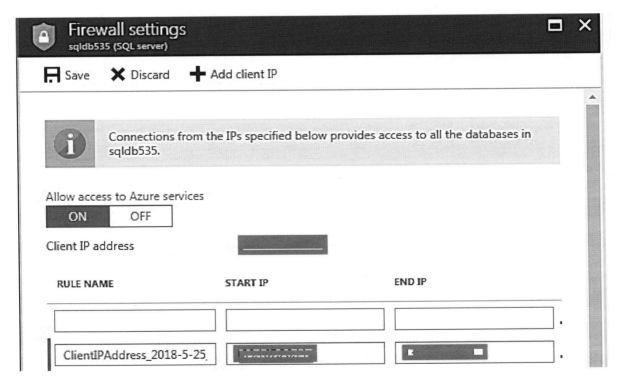

Step 3 Connect to SQL Database using SQL Server Management Studio (SSMS): On the client machine whose IP was entered in step 2, open SSMS and enter Azure SQL database server name, username and password.

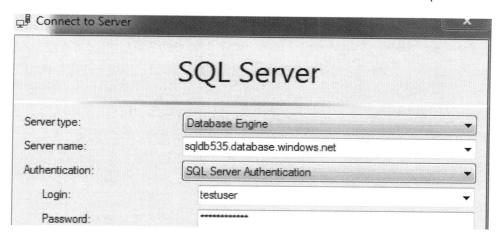

SSMS opens. You can see Azure SQL Database sqldb535 created in step 1. Here you can create database instance to be used by application.

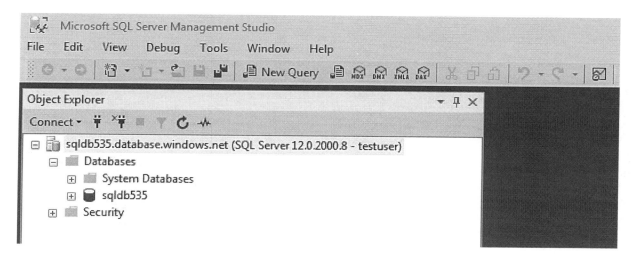

Step 4: For your application to access SQL database you need to add connection strings in the application code. In SQL Database dashboard click connection string in left pane>In Right pane you can see connection strings for your application type.

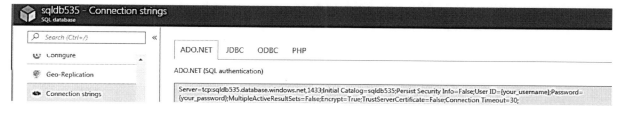

Architecting Microsoft Azure Solutions Study & Lab Guide Part 2: Exam 70-535

Azure SQL Database High Availability Using Active Geo-Replication

Geo-Replication replicates a database to have up to four readable secondary databases in the same or different regions of your choice.

These secondary databases are kept synchronized with the primary database using an asynchronous replication mechanism. Active geo-replication leverages the Always On technology of SQL Server to asynchronously replicate committed transactions on the primary database to a secondary database using read committed snapshot isolation (RCSI). At any given point, the secondary database might be slightly behind the primary database, the secondary data is guaranteed to never have partial transactions.

Secondary databases are available for querying and for failover in the case of a data center outage or the inability to connect to the primary database. The failover must be initiated manually by the application of the user.

Figure below shows Primary SQL database being replicated to secondary regions using Active Geo-Replication.

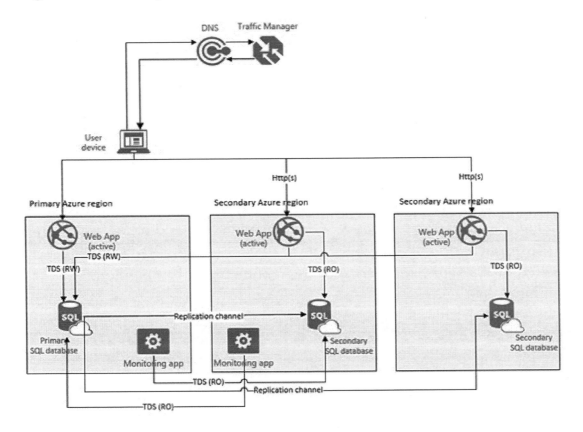

Architecting Microsoft Azure Solutions Study & Lab Guide Part 2: Exam 70-535

High availability using Active Geo-Replication and Failover groups

With Geo-Replication failover to secondary is manual operation. Geo-Replication with auto-failover groups results in automatic failover.

Auto-failover groups works on top of active geo-replication but the same asynchronous replication mechanism is used.

Auto-failover groups support replication of all databases in the group to only one secondary server in a different region. Active geo-replication, without auto-failover groups, allows up to four secondaries in any region.

Auto-failover groups provide read-write and read-only listener end-points that remain unchanged during failovers. Additionally, they can use the readable secondary databases to offload read-only workloads.

Figure below shows Traffic Manager using Priority Routing is sending all Traffic to Primary Region. If Primary Region fails TM will direct all traffic to Secondary Region. Database failover will be automatic because of failover groups.

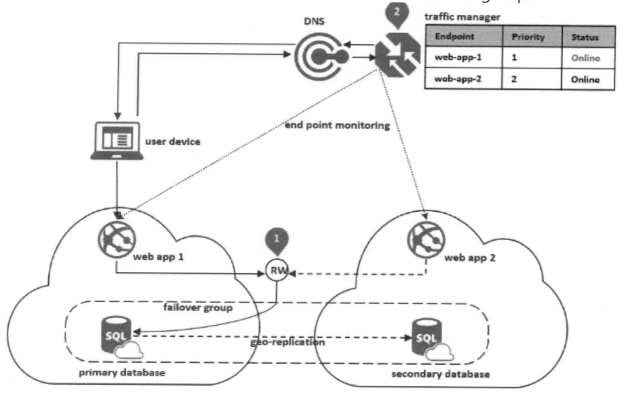

Exercise 2: Geo-Replication. Creating Replica of Primary Database in different region

1. In Azure Portal go to Primary SQL Database Dashboard created in **Exercise 1** > Click Geo-Replication in left Pane> In Right pane select secondary region > Create Secondary Blade opens> specify following and click ok.

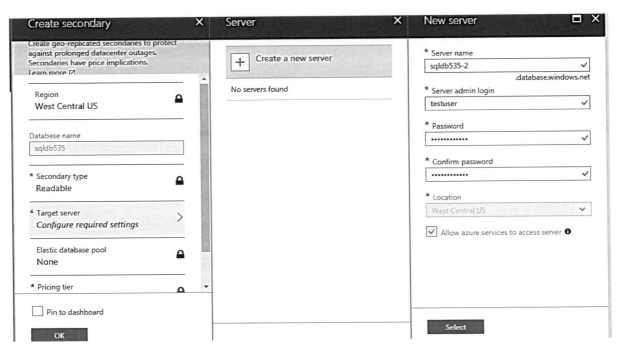

2. Click Geo-Replication in dashboard again> you can see both primary and secondary Database which is readable only.

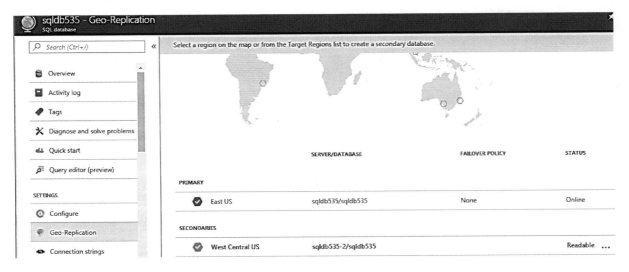

Azure SQL Database Backup and Restore

Azure SQL Database has built-in provision to take Automatic backups for up to 35 days. These backups are created automatically and at no additional charge. Backups are stored Geo-Redundant storage (RA-GRS). If you want to keep backups in your own storage container you can configure a long-term backup retention policy.

Backups are used to restore your server to a **Point-in-time Restore**. You can also use **Geo-Restore** to restore your server to a different region or same region.

Backup Retention

Automated Backups retention in the Geo-Redundant Storage is based on Service Tier of the database. All backups are encrypted using AES 256-bit encryption.

Basic service tier is 7 days.
Standard service tier is 35 days.
Premium service tier is 35 days.

Backup Frequency: Azure SQL Database takes full, differential and transaction log backups. Full backups occur weekly, differential backup happens every few hours and transaction log backup occur every 5-10 minutes.

Point in Time Restore

Point-in-time restores an existing database to a specified point in time within the retention period as a new database on the same logical server.

Geo-Restore

Geo-restore recovery option is used when your database is unavailable because of an incident in the region where the database is hosted.

You can restore a SQL database to a new server in any Azure region from the most recent geo-replicated full and differential backups. Geo-restore uses a geo-redundant backup as its source and can be used to recover a database even if the database or datacenter is inaccessible due to an outage.

Business continuity options with Azure SQL Database

SQL Database provides several business continuity features including automated backups, Long- term backup retention and database replication.

Point-in Time Restore from Automated Database Backups: SQL Database automatically performs a combination of full database backups weekly, differential database backups hourly, and transaction log backups every five minutes to protect your business from data loss. These backups are stored in geo-redundant storage for 35 days for databases in the Standard and Premium service tiers and seven days for databases in the Basic service tier.

Long-Term Backup Retention: The Long-Term Backup Retention feature enables you to store your Azure SQL Database backups in an Azure Recovery Services vault for up to 10 years. Long-Term Backup Retention is used for applications that have regulatory, compliance, or other business purposes that require you to retain the automatic full database backups beyond the 7-35 days provided by SQL Database automatic backups.

Geo-Restore: With Geo-Restore you restore database to a new server in any Azure region from the most recent geo-replicated full and differential backups. Recovery usually takes place within 12 hours - with data loss of up to one hour determined by when the last hourly differential backup with taken and replicated.

Active Geo-Replication: Geo-Replication replicates a database to same or another region. You can configure an automatic failover policy or use manual failover to promote the secondary to become the new primary.

Comparing RTO and RPO of various backup and replication options

Capability	RPO/RTO
Point in Time Restore from backup	Any restore point within 7 days for Basic and 35 days for Standard and Premier tiers
Restore from Azure Backup Vault	RTO < 12h, RPO < 1 week
Geo-Restore from geo-replicated backups	RTO < 12h, RPO < 1h
Geo-Replication	RTO < 30s, RPO < 5s

RTO is the time required to bring database back online.
RPO is the Data loss within the defined period.

Scaling up or scaling down a single database

You can change the service tier manually or programmatically at any time without downtime to your app.

Changing the service tier and/or performance level of a database creates a replica of the original database at the new performance level, and then switches connections over to the replica. No data is lost during this process but during the brief moment when we switch over to the replica, connections to the database are disabled, so some transactions in flight may be rolled back.

In-Memory technologies in SQL Database

In-memory Database relies on computer memory (RAM) instead of slower hard disks for storage.

In-Memory technologies in Azure SQL Database, improve performance of various workloads: transactional (online transactional processing (OLTP)), analytics (online analytical processing (OLAP)), and mixed (hybrid transaction/analytical processing (HTAP)) by processing Data in memory instead of Slower hard Disk.
In-Memory technologies reduces cost by eliminating the need to upgrade the pricing tier of the database to achieve performance gains.

In-Memory technologies are available in the Premium tier only.

In-Memory technologies available with Azure SQL Database are as follows:

1. **In-Memory OLTP** increases throughput and reduces latency for transaction processing.
2. **Clustered columnstore indexes** reduce your storage footprint (up to 10 times) and improve performance for reporting and analytics queries.
3. **Non-clustered columnstore indexes** allow very fast execution of analytics queries on the OLTP database, while reducing the impact on the operational workload.

You can also combine In-Memory OLTP and columnstore indexes. This allows you to both perform very fast transaction processing and run analytics queries very quickly on the same data.

Azure SQL Database access control

Database access control is done both at server level and at database level.
Database access control at server level is done with Firewall.
Database access control at database level is done with Authentication.

Firewall

Firewalls prevent all access to your database server until IP address of the connecting computer is specified in Azure SQL Database Server.
The firewall grants access to databases based on the originating IP address of each request.

Authentication

SQL Database supports two types of authentication – SQL Authentication and Azure Active Directory Authentication.

SQL Authentication - SQL Authentication uses a username and password which were specified during database creation.

Azure Active Directory Authentication - Azure Active Directory Authentication, uses identities managed by Azure Active Directory.

Authorization

Authorization refers to what a user can do within an Azure SQL Database, and this is controlled by your user account's database role memberships and object-level permissions.

Protecting SQL Data

SQL Database secures you data by providing encryption for data in motion using Transport Layer Security, for data at rest using Transparent Data Encryption, and for data in use using Always Encrypted.

Transparent Data Encryption

Azure SQL Database transparent data encryption performs real-time encryption and decryption of the database, associated backups, and transaction log files at rest without requiring changes to the application.

TDE encrypts the storage of an entire database by using a symmetric key called the database encryption key. In SQL Database the database encryption key is protected by a built-in server certificate. The built-in server certificate is unique for each SQL Database server.

Enabling Transparent Data Encryption

On the database dashboard>Click Transparent encryption> click on

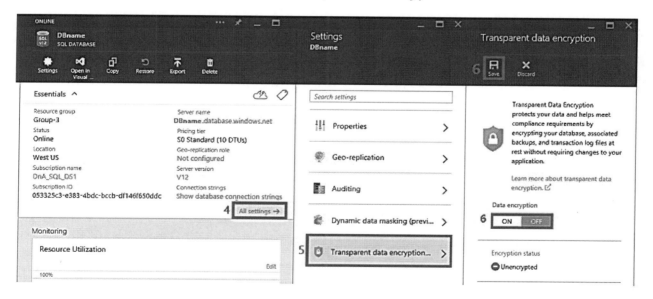

Always Encrypted

Always Encrypted protect data by allowing clients to encrypt sensitive data inside client applications and never reveal the encryption keys to the Database Engine (SQL Database or SQL Server).

Always Encrypted provides a separation between those who own the data (and can view it) and those who manage the data (but should have no access). Always Encrypted ensures that on-premises database administrators, cloud database operators, or other high-privileged cannot access the encrypted data. Always Encrypted enables customers to confidently store sensitive data outside of their direct control.

Always Encrypted makes encryption transparent to applications. An Always Encrypted-enabled driver installed on the client computer achieves this by automatically encrypting and decrypting sensitive data in the client application. The driver encrypts the data in sensitive columns before passing the data to the Database Engine, and automatically rewrites queries so that the semantics to the application are preserved. Similarly, the driver transparently decrypts data, stored in encrypted database columns, contained in query results.

Always Encrypted is available in SQL Server 2016 and SQL Database.

Azure SQL Database Threat Detection & Auditing

SQL Threat Detection enables customers to detect and respond to potential threats as they occur by providing security alerts on anomalous activities. Users will receive an alert upon suspicious database activities, potential vulnerabilities, SQL injection attacks, as well as anomalous database access patterns.

SQL Threat Detection alerts provide details of suspicious activity and recommend action on how to remediate those threats.

SQL Database Auditing

Azure SQL Database Auditing tracks database events and writes them to an audit log in your Azure Storage account.

Auditing can help you maintain regulatory compliance, understand database activity, and gain insight into discrepancies and anomalies that could indicate business concerns or suspected security violations.

Enabling Auditing & Threat Detection

In SQL Database Dashboard Click auditing and threat detection in left pane> in right pane click enable Threat detection.

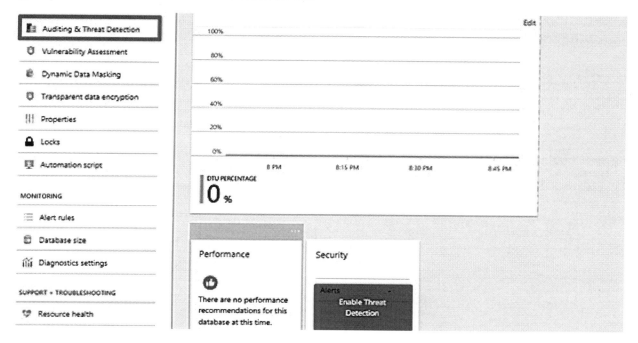

Exploring threat detection alerts in Security Center

SQL Database Threat Detection integrates alerts with Azure Security Center. Clicking on the SQL security alert tile in Azure SQL Dashboard launches Azure Security Center alerts blade and provides an overview of active SQL threats detected on the database.

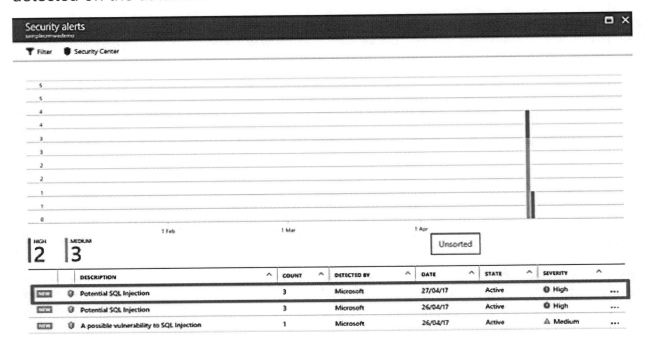

Clicking on a specific alert provides additional details on the threat and how to remediate the threat.

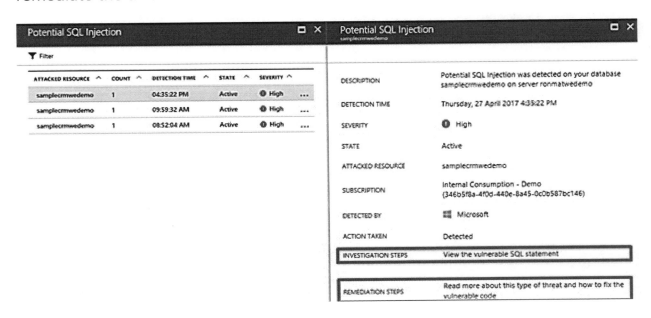

SQL Database Dynamic Data Masking

SQL Database dynamic data masking limits sensitive data exposure by masking it to non-privileged users.

It's a policy-based security feature that hides the sensitive data in the result set of a query over designated database fields, while the data in the database is not changed.

Dynamic Data Masking Example

Call center agent of a Bank are provided access to customer credit card details to resolve customer queries when they call. A masking rule can be defined that masks all but the last four digits of any credit card number in the result set of any query.

Azure SQL Pricing (Standard Tier)

For the same value, eDTU is priced 1.5 Times that of DTU. But with eDTU you can put multiple Databases in the pool which then reduces the price.
Note: I will just put Pricing for Standard Tier for both Single Database and Elastic Pool so that you can compare the prices of both models.

Single Database Model: Standard Tier Pricing

Tier	DTUs	Max Storage Per DB	Price
S0	10	250	$0.0202/hr
S1	20	250	$0.0404/hr
S2	50	250	$0.1009/hr
S3	100	250	$0.2017/hr

Elastic Pool Model: Standard Tier Pricing

eDTU per Pool	Max storage Per Pool	Max DBs per pool	Max eDTUs per Database	Price
50	50 GB	100	50	$0.1511/hr
100	100 GB	200	100	$0.3021/hr
200	200 GB	500	200	$0.6042/hr
300	300 GB	500	300	$0.9063/hr
400	400 GB	500	400	$1.2084/hr
800	800 GB	500	800	$2.4167/hr
1200	1.2 TB	500	1200	$3.625/hr
1600	1.6 TB	500	1600	$4.8334/hr
2000	2 TB	500	2000	$6.0417/hr
2500	2.4 TB	500	2500	$7.5521/hr
3000	2.9 TB	500	3000	$9.0625/hr

Active Geo-Replication Pricing: Secondary active geo-replication databases are priced at 1x of primary database prices. The cost of geo-replication traffic between the primary and the online secondary is included in the cost of the online secondary.

SQL Database Threat Detection: Cost of each protected SQL Database server will be billed at the same price as Azure Security Center Standard tier, at $15/node/month.

Architecting Microsoft Azure Solutions Study & Lab Guide Part 2: Exam 70-535

Design Case study 1: Design a Business Continuity Solution for Web/App tier and Database Tier.

An Automobile giant is running a 2-tier Dealer application – web/app tier running on Azure Web App and Database Tier running on Azure SQL Database. Recently they had a regional outage and had to face a downtime of 3 hours. They want to have a Disaster recovery solutions hosted in different region which can be activated in case of an outage or a regional disaster. They want DR site should be up and running within 30 minutes of outage or disaster at primary site.

They have constraint that Cross-region connectivity between the application and the Primary database is not acceptable due to latency. This was confirmed during a pilot test.

Design a solution which satisfies the above requirement.

Solution

Designing Web/App Tier

For web/app tier we will have active-passive deployment of Azure Web App as cross region connectivity between the application and the Primary database is not acceptable due to latency. Web App in Primary Region will be active and Web App in secondary will be passive.

Azure Traffic Manager (TM) will be used to Load balance traffic between web apps in Primary and secondary regions. As it is Active-Passive deployment, Traffic Manager should be set up to use failover routing.

Web App in each region will be connected to Azure SQL Database in there region only.

Designing Database Tier

Primary Region already has Azure SQL Database running. Using Active Geo-Replication a secondary Database will be created in secondary Region. Database in each region will be paired to the Web App in there region only.
Azure SQL Database in Primary Region is active and is Primary Database.

Active Traffic and Disaster Recovery to Secondary Site

All Traffic will be served through primary region. In case of outage Traffic will be shifted to Secondary Region. Secondary Database will be promoted to Primary Database manually or automatically using a monitoring app.

Figure below shows the Business Continuity solution for 2-tier Dealer Application.

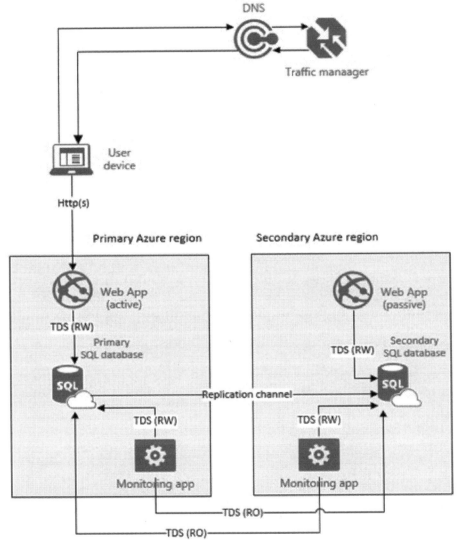

Note: MS is now recommending failover groups to be used with Geo-Replication. With Geo-Replication, failover to secondary is manual operation.
Geo-Replication with auto-failover groups results in automatic failover.

Design Case study 2: Choosing a Database tier

A corporate company is deploying a 2 tier application - Web/App tier and Database tier in Azure. They have chosen Azure SQL Database as there backend.

The application team has given there requirement for Database tier. Database size will be 400 GB and they want Database performance DTU of upto 50.

Based on above Requirement choose the appropriate Database tier.

Solution

Standard S2 Tier gives a DTU of 50. Maximum Database size in S2 is 250 GB. Premium P1 Tier gives a DTU of 125. Maximum Database size in P1 is 500 GB.

Premium P1 Tier will be chosen as it satisfies both DTU and Size requirements. Whereas Standard S2 Tier satisfies only DTU Requirement.

SQL Server Stretch Database

SQL Server Stretch Database feature migrates warm & cold data from on-premises SQL Server transparently and securely to the Microsoft Azure cloud.

Stretch Database is a feature of SQL Server 2016.

Figure below shows the architecture of SQL Server Stretch Database.

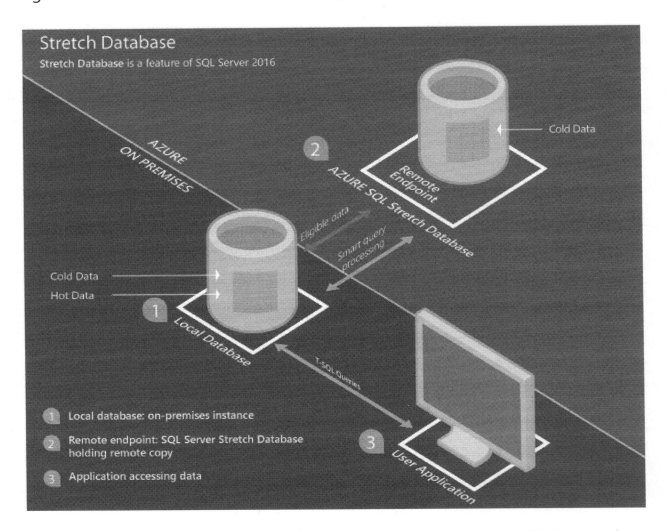

When you enable Stretch Database feature on your on-premises SQL Server, then an Azure SQL instance is created in Azure cloud. Secondly cold data is migrated to Azure cloud and is always available for querying.

Stretch Database lets you provide longer retention times for large amounts of data without scaling up enterprise storage.

Architecting Microsoft Azure Solutions Study & Lab Guide Part 2: Exam 70-535

Benefits of Stretch Database

1. Cold data migrated to Azure is always online and available to query.
2. Benefit from the low cost of Azure rather than scaling expensive on-premises storage. Azure storage can be 80% less expensive than adding to on-premises SSD.
3. Stretch Database doesn't require any changes to existing queries or applications – the location of the data is completely transparent to the application. SQL Server handles the data movement in the background.
4. Reduction in on-premises maintenance and storage for your data. Backups for your on-premises data run faster and finish within the maintenance window. Backups for the cloud portion of your data run automatically.
5. SQL Server's Always Encrypted provides encryption for your data in motion. Row Level Security (RLS) and other advanced SQL Server security features also work with Stretch Database to protect your data.

Enabling SQL Server Stretch Database

1. In SQL Server Management Studio, in Object Explorer, select the database on which you want to enable Stretch> Right-click and select **Tasks**, and then select **Stretch**, and then select **Enable** to launch the wizard.

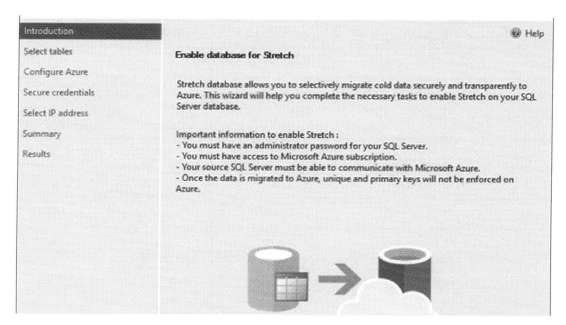

SQL Server Stretch Database Pricing

SQL Server Stretch Database has following pricing components:

Compute

Compute usage is represented with Database Stretch Unit (DSU) and customers can scale up and down the level of performance/DSUs they need at any time.

PERFORMANCE LEVEL (DSU)	PRICE
100	$1,825/month
200	$3,650/month
300	$5,475/month
400	$7,300/month
500	$9,125/month
600	$10,950/month
1000	$18,250/month
1200	$21,900/month
1500	$27,375/month
2000	$36,500/month

Storage

Data storage is charged based at $0.16/GB/month. Data storage includes the size of your Stretch DB and backup snapshots. All Stretch databases have 7 days of incremental backup snapshots.

Note: Storage transactions are not billed. You only pay for stored data and not storage transactions.

Geo-Backup (Optional): Storage for geo-redundant copies is billed at $0.12/GB/Month.

Outbound Data Transfer

Outbound data transfers are charged at regular data transfer rates.

Chapter 2 Azure MySQL & PostgreSQL Database

This Chapter covers following

- Azure MySQL Database
- Azure MySQL Database v/s MySQL Server
- MySQL Service Tiers
- Azure MySQL High Availability
- Azure MySQL Backup and Restore
- Azure PostgreSQL Database
- Azure PostgreSQL Database v/s PostgreSQL Server
- PostgreSQL Service Tiers
- Azure PostgreSQL High Availability
- Azure PostgreSQL Backup and Restore

This Chapter Covers following Lab Exercises

- Creating and Connecting to MySQL Database in 3 Steps
- Creating and Connecting to PostgreSQL Database in 3 Steps
- Restoring a Server from backup

Chapter Topology

In this chapter we will add Azure MySQL and PostgreSQL database to the topology.

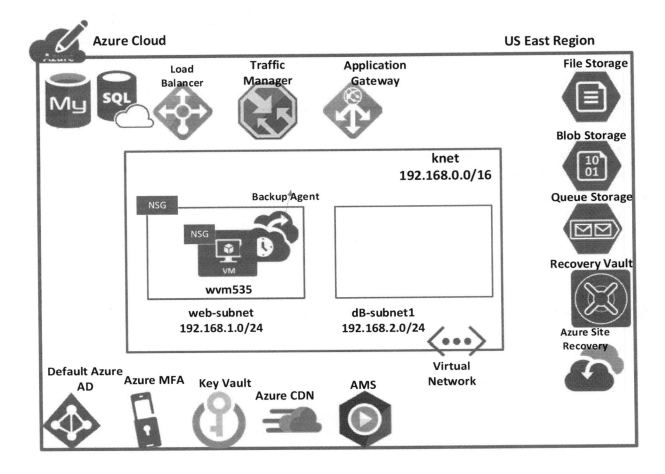

Azure MySQL Database

MySQL is an open-source relational database management system.

Azure MySQL Database is a relational database-as-a-service (DBaaS) in the cloud built on open source MySQL Server engine. Azure MySQL Database is a managed resource which means we don't have to install, upgrade or patch the database. You also don't have to manage the underlying infrastructure – Hardware and Operating System.

Features of Azure MySQL Database

1. Built-in high availability with no additional cost.
2. Automatic backups and point-in-time-restore for up to 35 days.
3. Secured to protect sensitive data at-rest using Storage encryption and Data in-motion using SSL.
4. Dynamically change compute in seconds and scale storage independently.
5. Enterprise-grade security and compliance.

Benefits of Azure MySQL Database

1. The benefit of using the Azure MySQL Database service is the ability to spin up and consume a relational database in minutes.
2. You don't have to manage any upgrade or patching of underlying hardware and operating system.
3. You can Scale up or scale down a database at any time.
4. You can use existing MySQL Server tools & libraries. As a result, it is easy to develop new solutions, to move your existing MySQL Server solutions to the Microsoft cloud without having to learn new skills.

Azure MySQL Database v/s MySQL Server

MySQL can be used in two ways- Azure MySQL Database or MySQL as a VM. Azure SQL Database is a managed resource. We don't have to install the database or patch it. Scale out requires no downtime.
In case of MySQL Server we need to install MySQL server on a VM. This option requires more operational overhead and skilled resources for deployment.

MySQL Service Tiers

Azure MySQL Database offers **Basic**, **General Purpose** and **Memory Optimized** service tiers.

Basic Tier: Basic Tier is for Workloads requiring light compute and I/O performance. The Compute instance for Basic Tier can be provisioned with Maximum of 2 vCore.

General Purpose: General Purpose Tier is for workloads requiring balanced compute and memory with scalable I/O throughput. The Compute instance for General Purpose Tier can be provisioned with Maximum of 32 vCore.

Memory Optimized: Memory Optimized is for High performance database workloads requiring in-memory performance for faster transaction processing and higher concurrency. The Compute instance for Memory Optimized Tier can be provisioned with Maximum of 16 vCore.

	Basic Tier	General Purpose	Memory Optimized
Compute	Upto 2 vCore	Upto 32 vCore	Upto 16 vCore
Storage	1 TB	2 TB	2 TB
Backup Retention	Upto 35 Days	Upto 35 Days	Upto 35 Days
Backup Redundancy options	Locally Redundant	Locally & Geo Redundant	Locally & Geo Redundant
Point-in-time-restore	Yes	Yes	Yes
Geo-restore	NA	Yes	Yes

Exercise 3: Creating and Connecting to MySQL Database in 4 Steps

Step 1 Create Azure SQL Database: In Azure Portal Click +create a resource>Databases>Azure Database for MySQL >Create MySQL Database Blade opens> Fill the following as per your requirement.

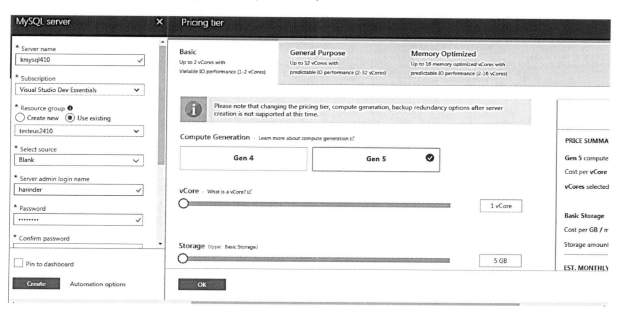

Step 2 Create MySQL Database server level firewall rule: This will open the MySQL Server firewall for specific client IP addresses. In MySQL Dashboard Click Connection Security>Click +Add MY IP>Save.

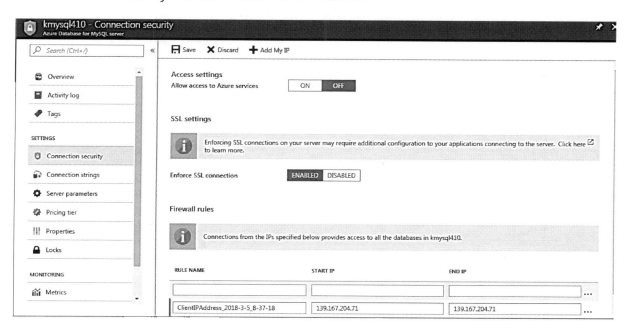

Architecting Microsoft Azure Solutions Study & Lab Guide Part 2: Exam 70-535

Step 4 Connection Strings

For your application to access MySQL database you need to add connection strings in the application code.
Connection String tab in left pane shows various connection strings for your application type.

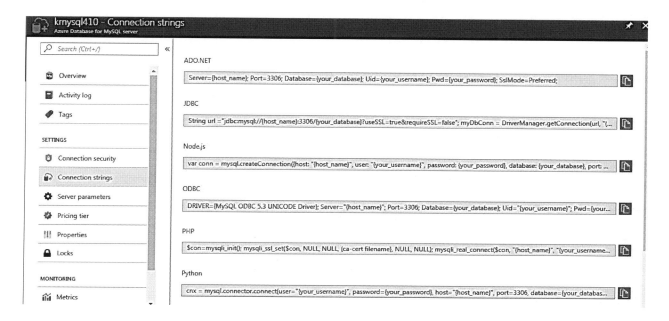

Azure MySQL High Availability

Azure MySQL database has Built-in high-availability without requiring any extra configuration, replication or cost.

Azure MySQL database high availability (HA) is based on built-in fail-over mechanisms when a node-level interruption occurs. A node-level interruption could occur because of a hardware failure or in response to a service deployment.

During normal time changes made to an Azure Database are recorded synchronously in Azure storage when the transaction is committed. If a node-level interruption occurs, the database server automatically creates a new node and attaches data storage to the new node. Any active connections are dropped and any inflight transactions are not committed.

Azure MySQL Backup and Restore

Azure MySQL Database has built-in provision to take Automatic backups and point-in-time-restore for up to 35 days. Backups are stored either in Locally Redundant or Geo-Redundant storage. Backups are used to restore your server to a point-in-time.

Azure Database for MySQL takes full, differential and transaction log backups. These backups allow you to restore a server to any point-in-time within your configured backup retention period. The default backup retention period is seven days. You can optionally configure it up to 35 days. All backups are encrypted using AES 256-bit encryption.

Backup Frequency: Full backups occur weekly, differential backups occur twice a day, and transaction log backups occur every five minutes.

Backup redundancy options: Azure MySQL Database provides the option to choose between locally redundant or geo-redundant backup storage in the General Purpose and Memory Optimized tiers. The Basic tier only offers locally redundant backup storage. With geo-redundant backup storage, backups are stored not only in region in which MySQL Database server is hosted but are also replicated to a paired data center.

Restore: Performing a restore creates a new server from the original server's backups. There are two types of restore available: Point-in-time restore & Geo Restore.
Point-in-time restore creates a new server in the same region as your original MySQL Database server.
Geo Restore allows you to restore your server to a different region. Geo Restore is available only if you configured your server for geo-redundant backup storage

Backup storage cost: Azure MySQL Database provides up to 100% of your provisioned server storage as backup storage at no additional cost. Any additional backup storage used is charged in GB-month.

Azure PostgreSQL Database

PostgreSQL is free and open-source relational database management system. PostgreSQL is developed by the PostgreSQL Global Development Group.

Azure PostgreSQL Database is a relational database-as-a-service (DBaaS) in the cloud built on the community version of open-source PostgreSQL database engine. PostgreSQL Database is a managed resource which means we don't have to install, upgrade or patch the database. You also don't have to manage the underlying infrastructure – Hardware and Operating System.

Features of Azure PostgreSQL Database

1. Built-in high availability with no additional cost.
2. Automatic backups and point-in-time-restore for up to 35 days.
3. Secured to protect sensitive data at-rest using Storage encryption and Data in-motion using SSL.
4. Dynamically change compute in seconds and scale storage independently.
5. Enterprise-grade security and compliance.

Benefits of Azure PostgreSQL Database

1. The benefit of using the Azure PostgreSQL Database service is the ability to spin up and consume a relational database in minutes.
2. You don't have to manage any upgrade or patching of underlying hardware and operating system.
3. You can Scale up or scale down a database at any time.
4. You can use existing PostgreSQL Server tools & libraries. As a result, it is easy to develop new solutions, to move your existing PostgreSQL Server solutions to the Microsoft cloud without having to learn new skills.

Azure PostgreSQL Database v/s PostgreSQL Server

PostgreSQL can be used in two ways- PostgreSQL Database or PostgreSQL VM. Azure PostgreSQL Database is a managed resource. We don't have to install the database or patch it. Scale out requires no downtime. In case of PostgreSQL Server we need to install PostgreSQL server on a VM. This option requires more operational overhead and skilled resources for deployment.

PostgreSQL Service Tiers

Azure PostgreSQL Database offers **Basic**, **General Purpose** and **Memory Optimized** service tiers.

Basic Tier: Basic Tier is for Workloads requiring light compute and I/O performance. The Compute instance for Basic Tier can be provisioned with Maximum of 2 vCore.

General Purpose: General Purpose Tier is for workloads requiring balanced compute and memory with scalable I/O throughput. The Compute instance for General Purpose Tier can be provisioned with Maximum of 32 vCore.

Memory Optimized: Memory Optimized Tier is for High performance database workloads requiring in-memory performance for faster transaction processing and higher concurrency. The Compute instance for Memory Optimized Tier can be provisioned with Maximum of 16 vCore.

Table below shows comparison between various Azure PostgreSQL tiers.

	Basic Tier	General Purpose	Memory Optimized
Compute	Upto 2 vCore	Upto 32 vCore	Upto 16 vCore
Storage	1 TB	2 TB	2 TB
Backup Retention	Upto 35 Days	Upto 35 Days	Upto 35 Days
Backup Redundancy options	Locally Redundant	Locally & Geo Redundant	Locally & Geo Redundant
Geo-restore	NA	Yes	Yes

Exercise 4: Creating and Connecting to PostgreSQL Database in 4 Steps

Step 1 Create Azure **PostgreSQL** Database: In Azure Portal Click +create a resource>Databases>Azure Database for PostgreSQL >Create PostgreSQL Database Blade opens> Select Parameters as per your req and click create.

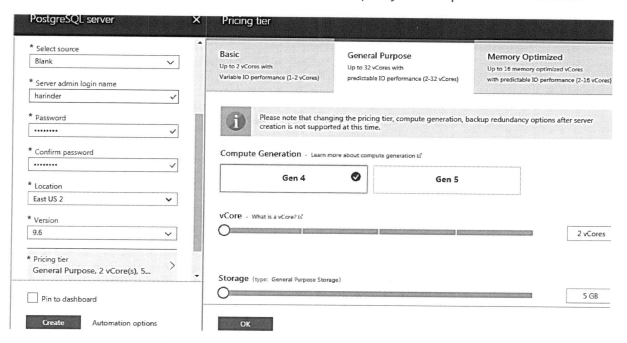

Step 2 Create **PostgreSQL** Database server level firewall rule: In PostgreSQL Dashboard Click Connection Security>Click +Add MY IP>Save.

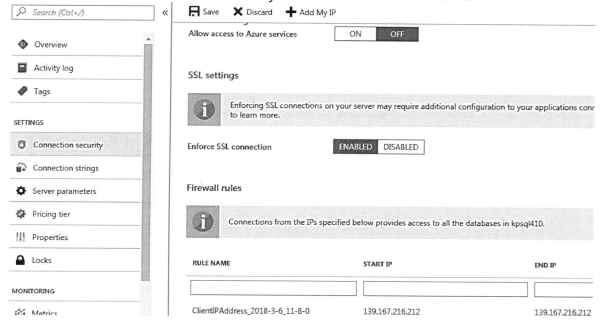

Step 3 Connect to the server by using PgAdmin GUI tool: On the client machine whose IP was entered in step 2, open PgAdmin GUI tool and enter Azure PostgreSQL database server name, username and password. You can find Hostname from PostgreSQL Dashboard.

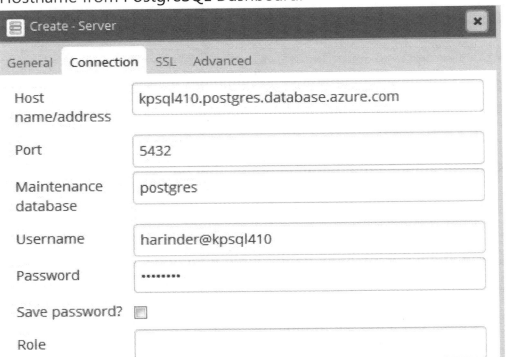

Figure below shows PgAdmin GUI tool connected to PostgreSQL Database

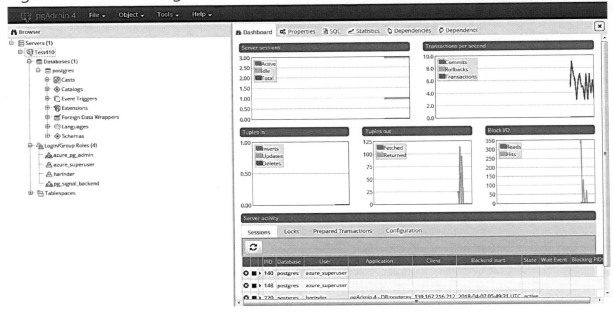

Step 4 Connection Strings:

For your application to access PostgreSQL database you need to add connection string and Database Username & Password in the application code.

Connection String tab in left pane shows various connection strings for your application type.

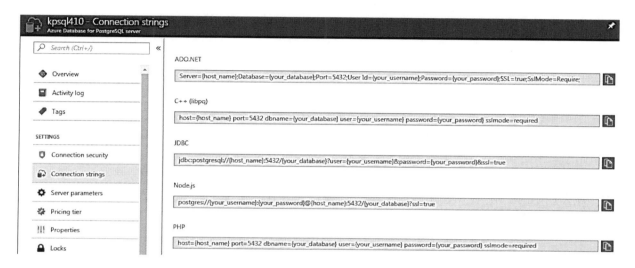

Azure PostgreSQL High Availability

Azure PostgreSQL database has Built-in high-availability without requiring any extra configuration, replication or cost.

Azure PostgreSQL database high availability (HA) is based on built-in fail-over mechanisms when a node-level interruption occurs. A node-level interruption could occur because of a hardware failure or in response to a service deployment.

During normal time changes made to an Azure PostgreSQL Database are recorded synchronously in Azure storage when the transaction is committed. If a node-level interruption occurs, the database server automatically creates a new node and attaches data storage to the new node. Any active connections are dropped and any inflight transactions are not committed.

Azure PostgreSQL Backup and Restore

Azure PostgreSQL Database has built-in provision to take Automatic backups and point-in-time-restore for up to 35 days. Backups are stored either in Locally Redundant or Geo-Redundant storage. Backups are used to restore your server to a point-in-time.

Azure Database for PostgreSQL takes full, differential and transaction log backups. These backups allow you to restore a server to any point-in-time within your configured backup retention period. The default backup retention period is seven days. You can optionally configure it up to 35 days. All backups are encrypted using AES 256-bit encryption.

Backup Frequency: Full backups occur weekly, differential backups occur twice a day, and transaction log backups occur every five minutes.

Backup redundancy options: Azure PostgreSQL Database provides the option to choose between locally redundant or geo-redundant backup storage in the General Purpose and Memory Optimized tiers. The Basic tier only offers locally redundant backup storage. With geo-redundant backup storage, backups are stored not only in region in which MySQL Database server is hosted but are also replicated to a paired Data Centre.

Restore: Performing a restore creates a new server from the original server's backups. There are two types of restore available: Point-in-time restore & Geo Restore.
Point-in-time restore creates a new server in the same region as your original PostgreSQL Database server.
Geo Restore allows you to restore your server to a different region. Geo Restore is available only if you configured your server for geo-redundant backup storage.

Backup storage cost: Azure PostgreSQL Database provides up to 100% of your provisioned server storage as backup storage at no additional cost. Any additional backup storage used is charged in GB-month.

Exercise 5: Restoring a Server from backup

You can initiate Point in time restore by clicking Restore from overview Tab.

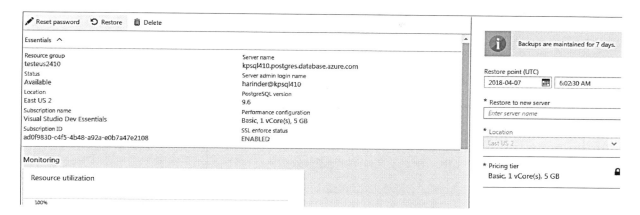

Chapter 3 Azure Web App

This Chapter covers following

- Azure Web App
- Comparing Windows VM and Web Apps
- Web App Tiers using App Service Plan
- Application Platform
- Deployment Slot
- Continuous Integration and Deployment
- Website Authentication with identity providers
- Web App Scale out (Manual or Autoscaling)
- Website Performance Test
- Web App Backup
- WebJobs
- Web App IP Restriction
- App Service Push
- MySQL in Web App
- Web App VNET Integration Option
- Web App Hybrid Connection
- App Service Environment (ASE)
- App Service Plan Tiers and Pricing

This Chapter Covers following Lab Exercises

- Azure Web App High Availability

This Chapter Covers following Lab Exercises

- Creating Web App
- Exploring Application Settings
- Exploring Deployment options
- Exploring Authentication/Authorization options
- Exploring Manual scale out
- Exploring Autoscaling
- Website Performance Test
- Exploring creating Backup

Architecting Microsoft Azure Solutions Study & Lab Guide Part 2: Exam 70-535

Chapter Topology

In this chapter we will add Web App to the topology.

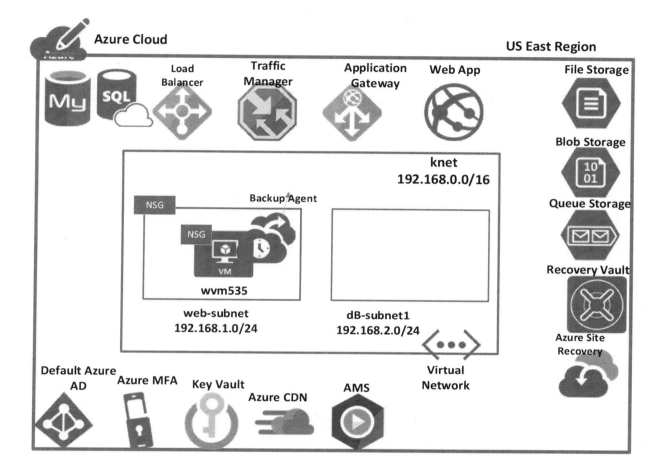

Azure Web Apps

Web Apps is a fully managed compute platform that is optimized for hosting websites and web applications.

Web Apps is a managed Windows VM with pre-installed IIS web server with a option to choose application framework (You can choose from Dot Net, PHP, Node.js, Python & Java) at Web App creation time.

(Note: In this chapter we will discuss web app for windows only and not WebApp for linux).

The Diagram below shows the difference between Azure IaaS VM and Azure Web App.

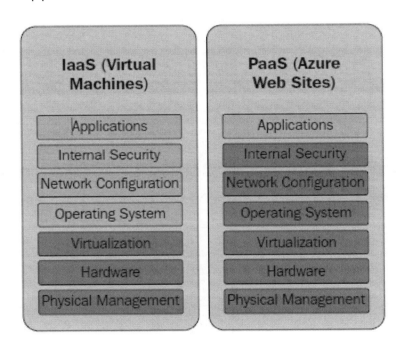

The boxes with Dark grey color are managed by Azure Cloud.

Using Web App you can develop in your favorite language, be it .NET, .NET Core, Java, Ruby, Node.js, PHP, or Python. Web Apps adds the power of Microsoft Azure services to your application, such as security, load balancing, autoscaling, and automated management. You can also take advantage of its DevOps capabilities, such as continuous deployment from VSTS, GitHub & Docker Hub.

Comparing Windows VM and Web Apps

Feature	Windows Azure VM	Web Apps
Deployment time	10-15 minutes	Within a minute
Pre-installed IIS Web Server and Application Framework	No	Yes
Available Option to choose for Application Framework	None	Dot Net, PHP, Node.js, Python & Java
Automatic OS updates, patches and security update by Azure team	No	Yes
DNS name provided by Azure	No	Yes
Scale out without configuring any load balancer	No	Yes
Built in additional Features available with Web App only.		continuous integration and deployment, User authentication with Multiple identity providers, Staging slot, Built in Website Performance Test, Built in Load Balancer

Web App Features

1. **Multiple languages and frameworks** - Support for ASP.NET, Node.js, Java, PHP, and Python.
2. **DevOps optimization** - Set up continuous integration and deployment with Visual Studio Team Services, GitHub, or BitBucket. Promote updates through test and staging environments.
3. **Global scale with high availability** - Scale-out manually or automatically.
4. **Connections to SaaS platforms and on-premises data** - Choose from more than 50 connectors for enterprise systems (such as SAP, Siebel, and Oracle), SaaS services (such as Salesforce and Office 365), and internet services (such as Facebook and Twitter). Access on-premises data using Hybrid Connections and Azure Virtual Networks.
5. **Security and compliance** - App Service is ISO, SOC, and PCI compliant.
6. **Visual Studio integration** - Dedicated tools in Visual Studio streamline the work of creating, deploying, and debugging.

Web App Tiers using App Service Plan

Each Web App is associated with App Service Plan. An App Service plan defines a features and set of compute resources available for a Web App to run.

To host Web Apps, Six Pricing tiers are available in App Service Plan: **Free, Shared, Basic, Standard, Premium and Isolated.**

Apps in the same subscription, region, and resource group can share an App Service plan. But individual Web App can be part of only one service plan.

All applications assigned to an App Service plan share the resources defined by it. This sharing saves money when hosting multiple apps in a single App Service plan.

	Free	Shared	Basic	Standard	Premium	Isolated
Web, mobile, or API apps	10	100	Unlimited	Unlimited	Unlimited	Unlimited
Disk space	1 GB	1 GB	10 GB	50 GB	250 GB	1 TB
Maximum instances	NA	NA	3	10	20	100
Custom domain	NA	Supported	Supported	Supported	Supported	Supported
Auto Scale	NA	NA	NA	Supported	Supported	Supported
VPN Hybrid Connectivity	NA	NA	NA	Supported	Supported	Supported
Virtual Network	NA	NA	NA	NA	NA	Supported
Use Cases	Trying out or Dev/Test	Dev/Test	Dedicated Test/Dev and low volume traffic	Production Workloads	Enhanced Performance for workloads	Scale, Security and Isolation

Creating App Service Plan

You can create an empty App Service plan or create App Service Plan as part of App creation or use system created S1 App Service Plan.

Exercise 6: Creating Web App

Click +Create a New Resource>Web+Mobile>Web App.>Specify following according to your needs in create Web App Blade. For App Service Plan select the system created App Service Plan>Click create.

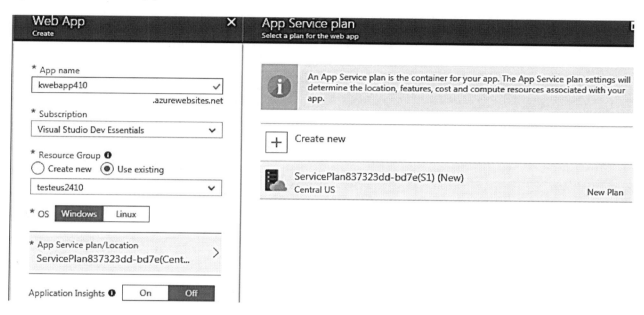

Figure below shows the dashboard of Web App. Note DNS of the Web App in right pane.

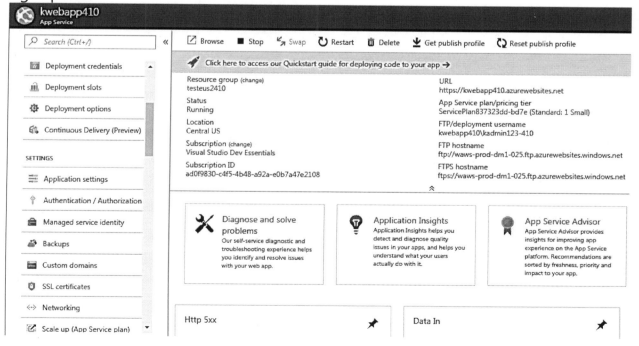

Application Platform

By default Web App (Windows) is created with dot net framework and PHP Application development platform. You have the option to choose Java Platform.

Exercise 7 Exploring Application Settings: In Web App Dashboard Click Application Settings in left pane>In Right pane select your Platform and Application options as per your requirement.

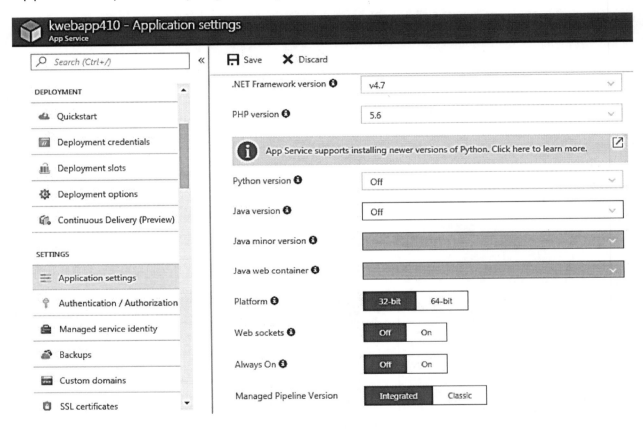

Deployment Slot (Important Concept)

Web apps have a deployment slot where you can also deploy websites for testing website features. You can validate websites changes in a staging deployment slot before swapping it with the production slot without any downtime.

Deployment slots are live apps with their own DNS hostnames.

Deployment Slot feature is only available with Standard or Premium app Plans. You need to add deployment slot from Web App dashboard before you can use it.

Benefits of Deployment Slot

1. Validate app changes in a staging deployment slot before swapping it with the production slot.
2. If the changes swapped into the production slot are not as expected, you can perform the same swap immediately to get your "last known good site" back.
3. Deploying app to staging slot first and swapping it into production ensures that all instances of the slot are warmed up before being swapped into production. This eliminates downtime when you deploy your app. The traffic redirection is seamless, and no requests are dropped as a result of swap ops.

Figure below shows the Web App deployed in the staging deployment Slot. Note the swap icon on top which can be used to swap staging slot with production slot.

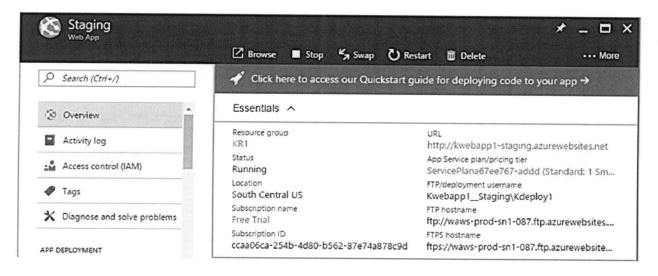

Continuous Integration and Deployment

Continuous integration and deployment is available out of the box for Visual Studio Team Services, Local Git Repository, GitHub, One Drive, Dropbox or BitBucket.

With CI/CD any change in website code in VS, GitHub etc is immediately propogated to the live website.

Exercise 8 Exploring Deployment options: In Web App Dashboard Click Deployment Options in left Pane> In Right pane select your option as per your requirement.

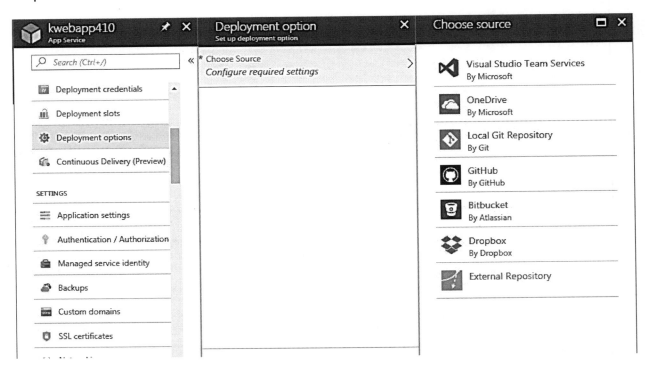

Best practice is to test updates through staging deployment slot.

You can validate websites changes in a staging deployment slot before swapping it with the production slot without any downtime.

Website Authentication with identity providers

You can add authentication to your website. Web App supports multiple authentication providers. App Service supports five identity providers out of the box: Azure Active Directory, Facebook, Google, Microsoft Account, and Twitter.

Exercise 9 Exploring Authentication/Authorization options: In Web App Dashboard Click Authentication/Authorization in left Pane> In Right pane select your option as per your requirement.

The biggest benefit of Web App authentication feature is that you don't have to add any code in the application.

Web App Scale out (Manual or Autoscaling)

Web Apps can be scaled out manually by setting the instance count or can automatically scale out (Autoscaling) based on pre-set metrics. Pre-set metrics can be based on CPU or Memory % or based on Schedule etc.

The important point here is load balancing between Web app instances is automatic and you don't have to set any load balancer.

Exercise 10 Exploring Manual scale out: In Web App Dashboard click Scale Out in left Pane> In Right pane enter the number of instances as per your requirement> Click Save.

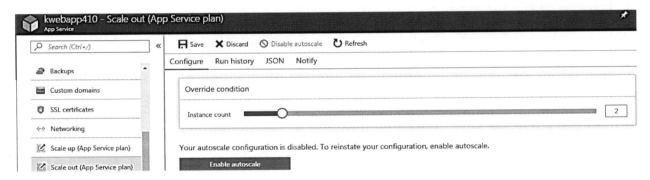

Exercise 11 Exploring Autoscaling: In Web App Dashboard click Scale Out in left Pane> In Right pane click Enable Autoscale>Select Scale based on Metric. We will use CPU metric.

Add Scale-Out Rule: Click + Add a Rule>Scale Rule blade opens> Select CPU % in Metric Box>In operation Box select increase count by> Leave other values as default.

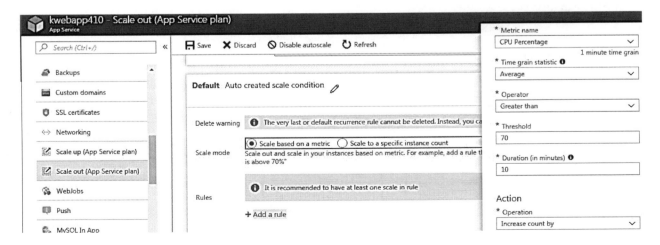

Architecting Microsoft Azure Solutions Study & Lab Guide Part 2: Exam 70-535

Website Performance Test

You can test your website response time, CPU and memory usage against varying user load **without setting elaborate testing infrastructure.** This can help you choose the right web app edition and to choose the right number of instances to deploy.

The fig below show creation of performance test with 250 user load.

Exercise 12 Configuring Performance Test: In App Dashboard Click Performance Test >+New>New Performance Test Blade opens>Choose option as per your Req.

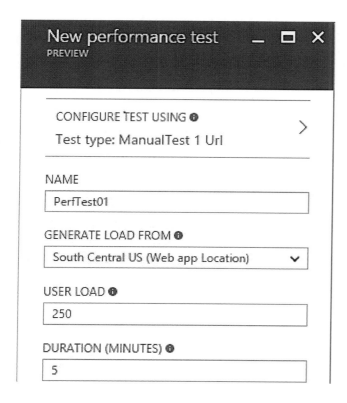

Figure below Shows website performance under 250 User load.

Architecting Microsoft Azure Solutions Study & Lab Guide Part 2: Exam 70-535

Web App Backup

The Backup and Restore feature in Azure App Service lets you easily create app backups manually or on a schedule. You can restore the app to a snapshot of a previous state by overwriting the existing app or restoring to another app. Backups can be up to 10 GB of app and database content.

Requirement for Backup

1. The Backup and Restore feature requires the App Service plan to be in the Standard tier or Premium tier. Premium tier allows a greater number of daily backups than Standard tier.
2. Azure storage account and container are required in the same subscription as the app that you want to backup.

What gets backed up

1. App configuration
2. File content
3. Database connected to your app

Exercise 13 Exploring creating Backup: In Web App Dashboard Click Backup.

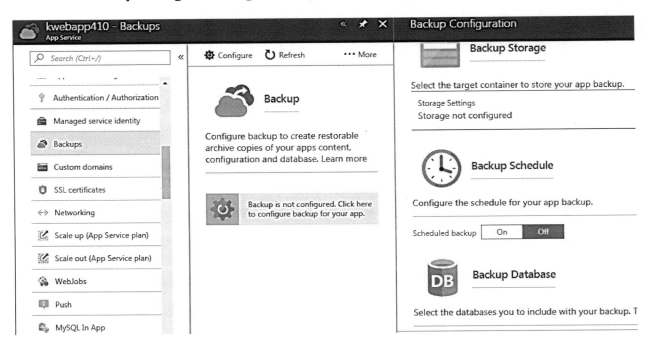

WebJobs

WebJobs enables you to run scripts or programs as background processes in the context of your app. WebJobs type can be Continuous or Triggered.

Continuous	Triggered
Starts immediately when the WebJob is created.	Starts only when triggered manually or on a schedule.
Runs on all instances that the web app runs on. You can optionally restrict the WebJob to a single instance.	Runs on a single instance that Azure selects for load balancing.

To add WebJobs: Click WebJobs in Left Pane> Click +Add> Add WebJob blade opens> Upload a file to run a script or program and choose other options as per your requirement and click ok.

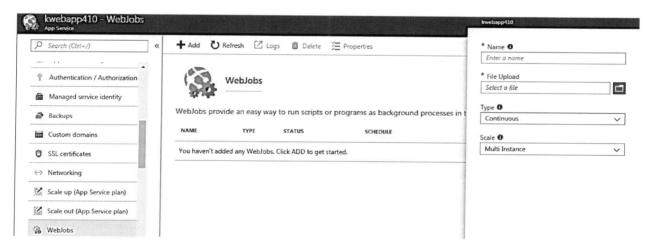

Supported file types for scripts or programs: The following file types are supported:
.cmd, .bat, .exe (using Windows cmd)
.ps1 (using PowerShell)
.sh (using Bash)
.php (using PHP)
.py (using Python)
.js (using Node.js)
.jar (using Java)

Web App IP Restriction

IP restrictions allow you to define a static list of IP addresses that are allowed access to your app.

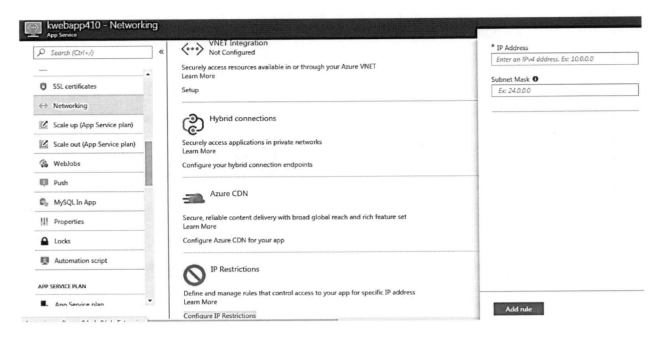

App Service Push

App Service Push enables you to send fast, scalable, and cross-platform mobile push notifications utilizing Notification Hubs.

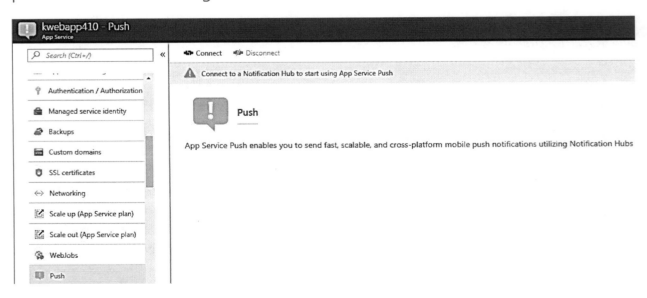

MySQL in Web App

MySQL In App runs a local MySQL instance with your app and shares resources from the App Service plan.

Note that apps using MySQL In App are not intended for production environments, and they will not scale beyond a single instance.

Add MySQL in the Instance: In Web App Dashboard Click MySQL in App> In Right Pane select on.

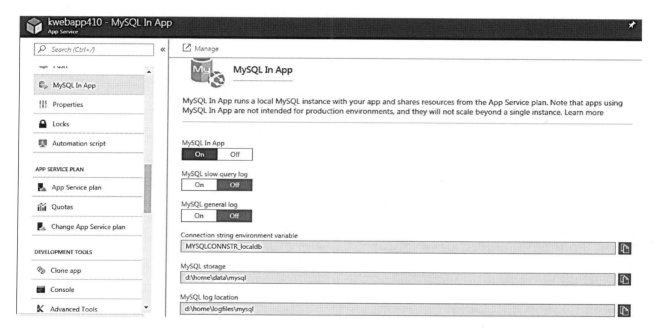

MySQL In App lets you import and export your data to and from an external MySQL database.

Web App VNET Integration Option

VNET Integration gives your web app access to resources in your virtual network. VNET Integration only works with apps in a Standard, Premium or Isolated plan. Target virtual network must have point-to-site VPN enabled with a Dynamic routing VPN gateway before it can be connected to an app. If your gateway is configured with Static routing, you cannot enable point-to-site Virtual Private Network (VPN).

Figure below shows how the system works. A VPN Gateway is created and attached to VNET. Azure Web App connect to VNET using VPN client software.

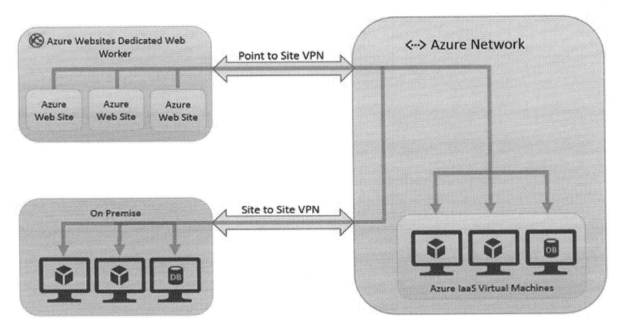

Configuring VNET Integration: In web App Dashbboard Click Networking >In Right Pane click Setup to add a Virtual Network.

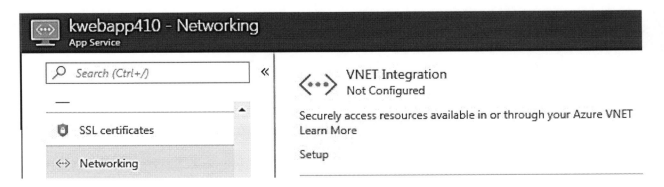

Web App Hybrid Connection

Using Hybrid Connections Web App can access application resources in other networks including on-premises network.
Web App Hybrid connection requires Azure Service Relay & Hybrid Connection Manager (HCM) installed on a windows server. The HCM is a relay service that you deploy within the network hosting the resource you are trying to access. The Hybrid Connections feature is available in Basic, Standard, Premium & Isolated plans.

Figure below shows how the system works. HCM Is installed on-premises. Azure Service Relay is created in Azure Cloud. The Hybrid Connections feature consists of two outbound calls to Azure Service Bus Relay. One from Web App and other from Hybrid Connection Manager.

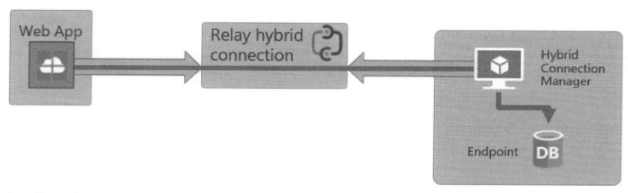

Configuring Hybrid Connection: Click Networking >In Right Pane click Configure your hybrid connection endpoints>Click + Add Hybrid Connection> click create new Hybrid connection> create new Hybrid connection blade opens> Enter as per your requirement and click Ok.

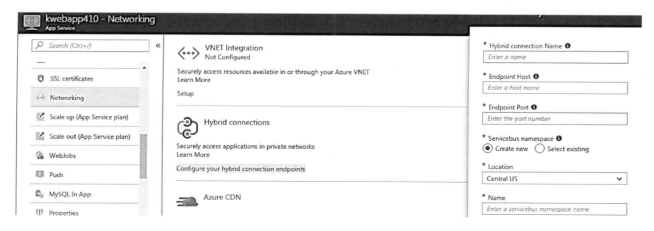

App Service Environment (ASE)

Azure App Service Environment (ASE) is a deployment of Azure App Service into a subnet in an Azure virtual network. You can use NSG features of virtual networks to control inbound and outbound network communications for your apps.

An ASE can be either internet-facing **(External ASE)** with a public IP address (VIP) or internal-facing **(Internal ASE)** with Azure internal load balancer (ILB) address. **ASE is created using App Service Isolated Plan.**

Note: ASE can be ASEv1 or ASEv2. This chapter focuses only on ASEv2.

Architecture

An ASE is composed of front ends and workers. Front ends are responsible for HTTP/HTTPS termination and automatic load balancing of app requests within an ASE. Workers are roles that host customer apps. Workers are available in three fixed sizes: I1, I2 & I3.

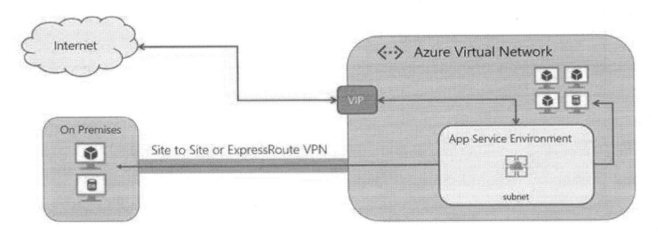

ASE Use Cases

1. Applications requiring large compute capacity. ASE supports upto 100 Instances. To add compute capacity beyond 100 instances you can scale horizontally by adding multiple ASE.
2. Isolation and secure network access.
3. High memory utilization.

ASE Horizontal Scaling

Application like Voting applications, sporting events and televised entertainment events require extremely large compute capacity.

High scale compute requirements can be met by horizontally scaling with multiple ASE deployments.

Figure below shows Multiple ASE deployments load balanced with Azure Traffic Manager.

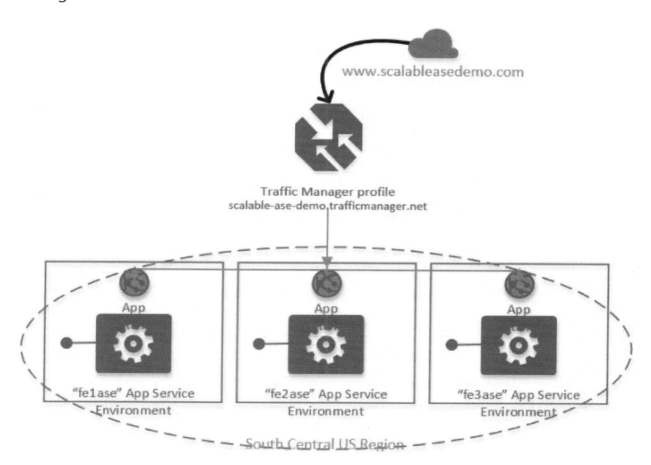

Note: Readers are requested to explore more features in web app dashboard such as custom domain name, SSL certificates etc.

Case Study 3: Azure Web App High Availability

A Global Multinational company is running dealer management application in Azure Web App. Azure Web App uses Azure SQL Database as backend.

They want to have a High Availability and DR solution in a different region. All traffic would be served from primary region. In case of outage in Primary region, Application traffic will be re-directed to Secondary region.

They want to minimize the cost of the HA & DR Setup. They have given a RTO of 30 minutes -60 minutes. There should be no data loss in Azure SQL Database. They want secondary region to be activated without any complicated procedures or operational & administrative overheads. Suggest a solution which satisfies the above requirement.

Solution

Options for High Availability across Primary and Secondary Regions

Active/passive with hot standby: Traffic goes to one region, while the other waits on hot standby. Hot standby means the Web App in the secondary region are running at all times.

Active/passive with cold standby: Traffic goes to one region, while the other waits on cold standby. Cold standby means the Web App in the secondary region are not running until needed for failover. This approach costs less to run, but will generally take longer to come online during a failure.

Active/active: Both regions are active, and requests are load balanced between them. If one region becomes unavailable, it is taken out of rotation.

We will choose **Active/passive with cold standby option** as cost of HA& DR setup is one of the main requirements given by the company.

Web App Setup: One Web App will be setup in each region. Primary Region Web App will be active and will serve all traffic. Secondary region Web App will be in **powered off mode** to save cost. In case of outage Web App in Secondary will be activated and will serve the application traffic. Each Web App will be connected to Azure SQL Database in their region only.

Azure SQL Database: Azure SQL Database in Primary region will be Geo-Replicated to Secondary region in read only mode. Each Azure SQL Database will be connected to Azure Web App in their region only. In case of outage in primary region, Azure SQL Database will be promoted as Primary Database.

Azure Traffic Manager: Traffic Manager will route incoming requests to the primary region. For the above scenario we will use **Priority** routing. With this setting, Traffic Manager sends all requests to the primary region unless the endpoint for that region becomes unreachable.

Steps to be taken for activating secondary region

1. Power-on Azure Web App in Secondary Region.
2. Promote Secondary region SQL Database as primary database.

Figure below shows the Architecture of the solution.

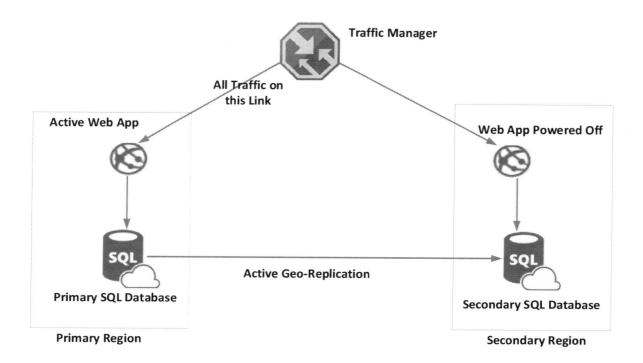

Important Note: Make sure to use Web App Standard Tier and above because Traffic Manager does not Basic/Shared/Free tier as endpoint.

App Service Plan Tiers and Pricing

Free & Shared Plan

The Free and Shared service plans run on the same Azure VMs as other apps. Some apps may belong to other customers.

The Free and Shared edition is ideal is ideal for experimenting with the platform and for development and test scenarios. The Shared edition further allows you to develop and test with features such as SSL & domain names and is suitable for low traffic sites.

Use the Free & Shared plan to quickly evaluate platform and convert the app at any time to one of the paid plans without delays or downtime.

Free and Shared plans are metered on a per App basis rather than per instance.

Instance	Cores	RAM	Storage	Max Instances	Autoscaling	Pricing
F1 (Free)	Shared (60 CPU Minutes/ Day)	1 GB	1 GB	NA	NA	$0
D1 (Shared)	Shared (240 CPU Minutes/ Day)	1 GB	1 GB	NA	NA	$0.013/hour

Basic Service Plan

It can be used as dedicated environment for Test & Dev. It can also be used for for apps that have lower traffic requirements. Built-in network load balancing support automatically distributes traffic across VM instances. No support for autoscaling and traffic management features.

Instance	Cores	RAM	Storage	Max Instances	Autoscaling	Pricing
B1	1	1.75 GB	10 GB	3	No	$0.075/hour
B2	2	3.5 GB	10 GB	3	No	$0.15/hour
B3	4	7 GB	10 GB	3	No	$0.30/hour

Standard Service Plan

Designed for production workloads. The Standard plan includes built-in autoscaling support that can automatically adjust the number of VM instances running to match your traffic needs.

Instance	Cores	RAM	Storage	Max Instances	Autoscaling	Pricing
S1	1	1.75 GB	50 GB	10	Yes	$0.10/hour
S2	2	3.5 GB	50 GB	10	Yes	$0.20/hour
S3	4	7 GB	50 GB	10	Yes	$0.40/hour

Premium Service Plan

The Premium service plan is designed to provide enhanced performance for production apps. Premium v2, features Dv2-series VMs with faster processors, SSD storage, and double memory-to-core ratio compared to Standard. The new Premium plan also supports increased instance count while still providing all the advanced capabilities found in the Standard plan.

Instance	Cores	RAM	Storage	Max Instances	Autoscaling	Pricing
P1v2	1	3.5 GB	250 GB	20	Yes	$0.25/hour
P2v2	2	7 GB	250 GB	20	Yes	$0.50/hour
P3v2	4	14 GB	250 GB	20	Yes	$1/hour

Isolated Service Plan

The Isolated plan allows customers to run their mission critical workloads in virtual network. The private environment used with an Isolated plan is called the App Service Environment. The plan can scale to 100 instances with more available upon request. In addition to the price per Isolated plan instance there is also a flat fee for each App Service Environment of $1.345/hour.

Instance	Cores	RAM	Storage	Max Instances	Autoscaling	Pricing
I1	1	3.5 GB	1 TB	100	Yes	$0.30/hour
I2	2	7 GB	1 TB	100	Yes	$0.60/hour
I3	4	14 GB	1 TB	100	Yes	$1.20/hour

Chapter 4 Azure Mobile App

This Chapter covers following

- Azure Mobile Apps
- Mobile App Features
- Mobile App Tiers and Pricing using App Service Plan

This Chapter Covers following Lab Exercises

- Create Mobile App Backend & Download Android Project (Android Example)
- Add Authentication to App (Android)

Chapter Topology

In this chapter we will add Azure Mobile App to the topology.

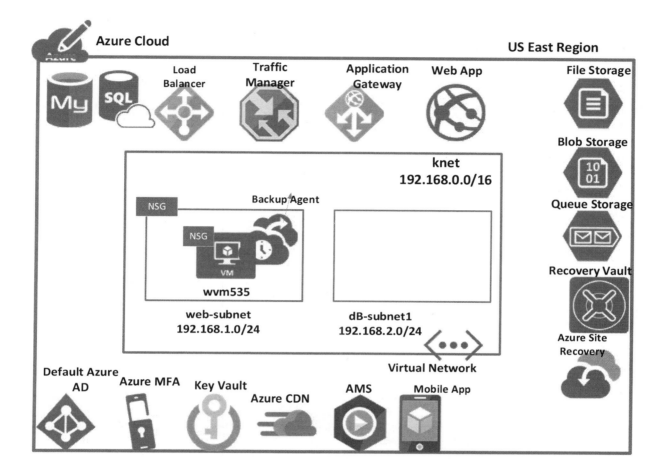

Azure Mobile Apps

Azure Mobile Apps is a fully managed platform as a service (PaaS) offering for the development and deployment Mobile applications across multiple platforms.

What does Azure Mobile App do?

1. Provides Mobile backend using Azure Hosted Services
2. Provides Project Application download (Android Project or IOS Project or Windows Project) which is pre- configured to work with Azure Hosted services in the backend.

Left side of Figure below shows Client Development Platforms SDKs (Android Studio on windows, Xcode for IOS on Mac, Windows App IDE etc) integrating with Mobile App backend in Azure cloud using Project Application (Not shown in figure).

Right side of Figure shows Mobile Backend. Backend Provides Development Platform which can be IOS, Android or Xamarin or Windows. It also provides additional functionality such as storage, Database, NoSQL, User authentication, Push Notification and Offline sync.

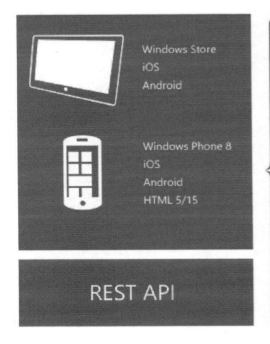

Mobile App Features

Build native and cross-platform apps: Whether you're building native iOS, Android, and Windows apps or cross-platform Xamarin or Cordova (PhoneGap) apps, you can take advantage of App Service by using native SDKs.

Authentication and authorization: Supports multiple identity providers, including Azure Active Directory for enterprise authentication, plus social providers such as Facebook, Google, Twitter, and Microsoft accounts.

Push notifications: The client SDKs integrate seamlessly with the registration capabilities of Azure Notification Hubs, so you can send push notifications to millions of users simultaneously.

Build offline-ready apps with data sync: Offline data sync is a client and server SDK feature of Azure Mobile Apps that makes it easy for developers to create apps that are functional without a network connection.
When your app is in offline mode, you can still create and modify data, which are saved to a local store. When the app is back online, it can synchronize local changes with your Azure Mobile App backend. The feature also includes support for detecting conflicts when the same record is changed on both the client and the backend. Conflicts can then be handled either on the server or the client.

Data access: Mobile Apps provides OData v3 data source that's linked to Azure SQL Database or an on-premises SQL server. You can easily integrate with other NoSQL and SQL data providers, including Azure Table storage, MongoDB, Azure Cosmos DB, and SaaS API providers such as Office 365 and Salesforce.com.

Client SDKs: There is a complete set of client SDKs that cover native development (iOS, Android, and Windows), cross-platform development (Xamarin.iOS and Xamarin.Android, Xamarin.Forms), and hybrid application development (Apache Cordova). Each client SDK is available with an MIT license and is open-source.

Exercise 14: Create Mobile App Backend & Download Android Project

1. In Azure Portal click +create a resource>Web + Mobile>Mobile App>create Mobile App Blade open>enter information as per your req and click ok.

2. **Create Development Platform for Your Mobile App (Android) using Azure Services**: In Mobile App Dashboard>Click Quickstart>Android.

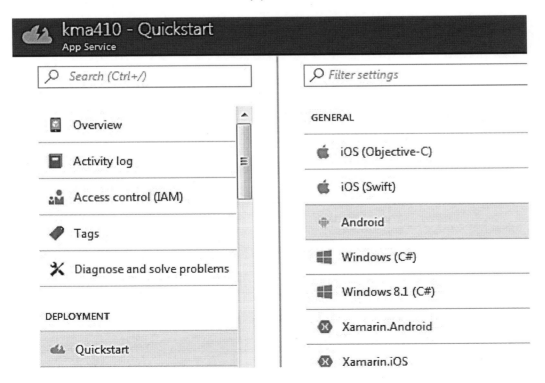

3. In Android Quickstart Blade you need to create and connect to a Database/storage and choose a Backend which can be Node.js or C#. You will also download Android Project app pre-configured to connect to Mobile backend on your PC where Android Studio is installed.

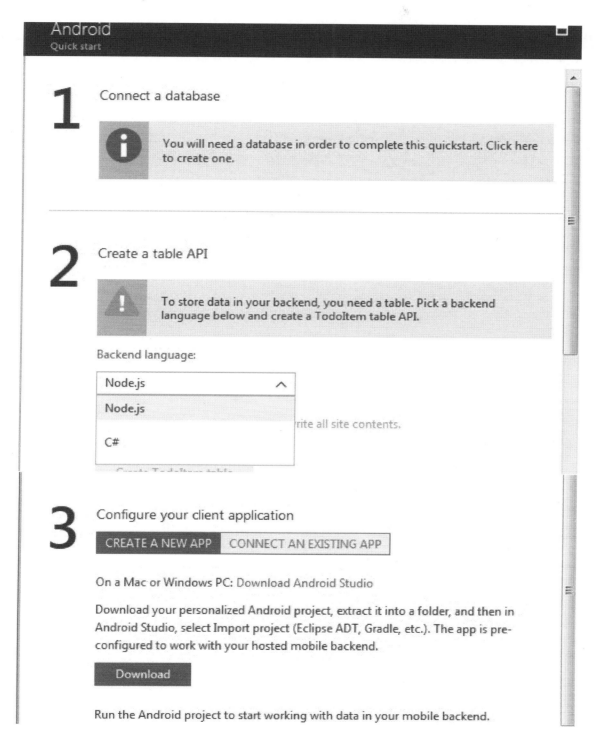

4. After you have created and connected to Database/storage and selected your application backend (node.js or C#) **download the Android Project app on your PC where Android Studio is installed.** Project App is pre-configured to work with Android Mobile Backend created in step 2.

5. In your PC open Android Studio where you have developed your Android App. Import the project which you downloaded and then run it to start the app in android simulator. It will connect to Azure Backend.

6. Similarly you can develop app for IOS.

From the above example you can infer that Mobile app provides backend for Apps and Client project Application to connect your Apps to Backend.

Exercise 15: Add Authentication to App (Android)

Adding Authentication to the App is a 2 Step Process.

Step 1: Register your App with one of the following Identity providers and generate app id and secret key. This step was shown in Azure B2C Exercise.

Azure Active Directory
Facebook
Google
Microsoft
Twitter

For example to register with Facebook go to https://developers.facebook.com/.

Step 2: In Mobile App dashboard click Authentication/Authorization in left pane> Choose your identity option in right pane and add the app id and secret key from step 1. You can add multiple identity providers to your app.

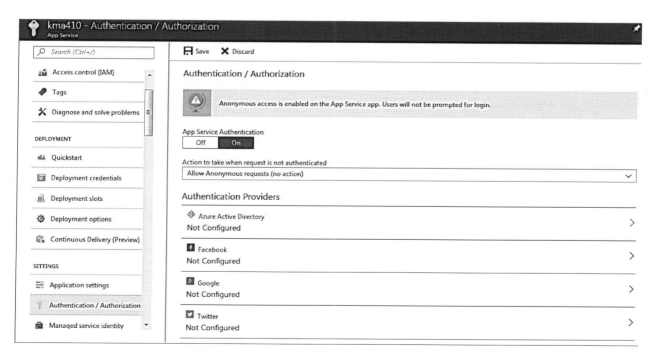

Mobile App Tiers and Pricing using App Service Plan

Each Mobile App is associated with App Service Plan. An App Service plan defines a features and set of compute resources available for a Web App to run.

To host Mobile Apps, Six Pricing tiers are available in App Service Plan: **Free, Shared, Basic, Standard, Premium and Isolated.**

Refer to Web App chapter to know more about App Service Plan Tiers and Pricing.

Chapter 5 Hybrid Applications

This Chapter covers following

- On-premises Data Gateway
- Data Management Gateway for Data Factory
- Identify Options to Join VM to domains
- Azure Relay Service
- Web App Hybrid and VPN Connection

On-premises Data Gateway

The on-premises data gateway **connects** on-premises data sources to Azure Services such as Azure Analysis Server, Logic Apps, Power BI & Microsoft Flow in the cloud.

Figure below show the Architecture and setup of on-premises data gateway.

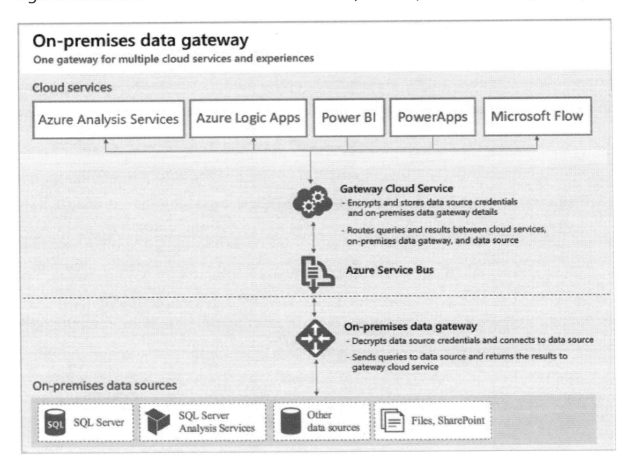

Component of the solutions: On-premises data gateway, Gateway Cloud Service & Azure Service Bus

Brief working: When Azure Resource requires access to on-premises data source it sends request to Gateway Cloud service. The gateway cloud service pushes the request to the Azure Service Bus. The on-premises data gateway polls the Azure Service Bus for pending requests and sends the request to the data source for execution. The results are sent from the data source, back to the gateway and then onto the cloud service and your server.

Data Management Gateway for Data Factory

The Data management gateway is installed in your on-premises environment to **copy** data between cloud and on-premises data stores.

Note: Data Management Gateway supports copy activity only. You cannot use Data Management Gateway to connect Azure resources to on-premises data sources.

Figure below shows the Architecture of Data Management Gateway.

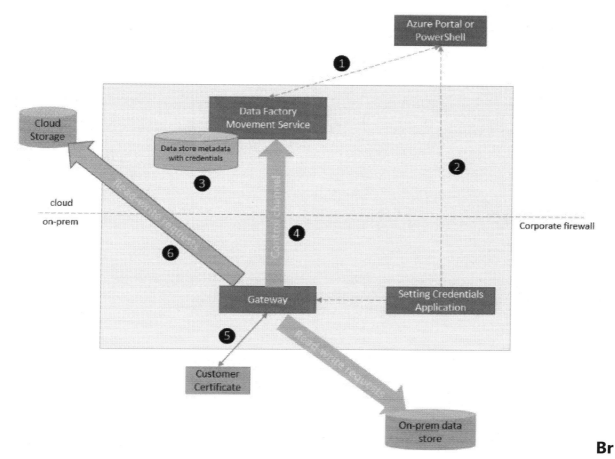

Brief Working: Data Management Gateway is installed on-premises and is registered with Data Factory. Azure Data Factory creates 2 linked services for connecting on-premises data store and Cloud Data store to Azure Data Factory. Data Factory service communicates with the gateway for scheduling & management of jobs via a control channel that uses a shared Azure service bus queue. The gateway copies data from an on-premises store to a cloud storage, or vice versa depending on how the Copy Activity is configured in the data pipeline.

Identify Options to Join VM to domains

To provide Active Directory services to workloads in cloud you have following options:

1. Deploy a stand-alone domain in Azure using domain controllers deployed as Azure virtual machines.
2. Extend the corporate AD domain/forest infrastructure by setting up replica domain controllers using Azure virtual machines.
3. Deploy a site-to-site VPN connection between workloads running in Azure Infrastructure Services and the corporate directory on-premises.
4. Azure AD Domain Services (Managed Read only Domain Controller).

Azure Relay Service

See Messaging Chapter

Web App Hybrid and VPN Connection

See Web App Chapter

Chapter 6 Azure Analytics Solutions

This Chapter covers following

- Azure SQL Data Warehouse
- Azure Data lake Analytics
- Azure Analysis Services
- Azure HDInsight

This Chapter Covers following Lab Exercises

- Create, Connect and Query SQL Data Warehouse using Sample Database
- Create Data Lake Analytics Account with associated Data lake Store
- Perform Analytics on Data stored in Data Lake Store using U-SQL Script
- Adding Azure Storage as Data Source
- Create an Azure Analysis Services server, add a data source, create a model from the data source and query the model database
- Create and Query HDInsight Hadoop Cluster

Chapter Topology

In this chapter we will add Azure SQL DW, Data Lake Analytics, Azure Analysis Services, Azure HDInsight to the topology.

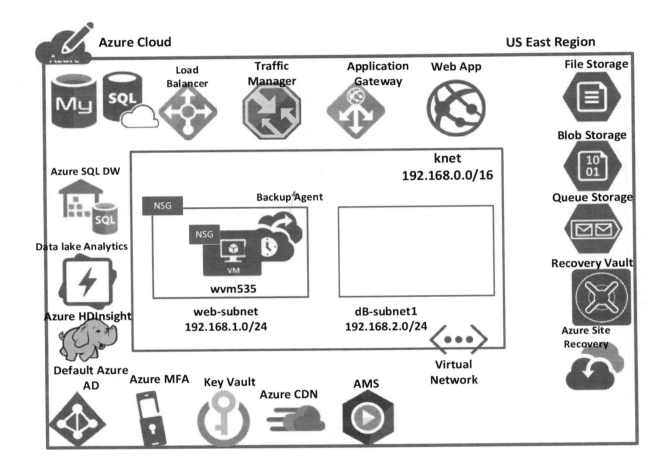

Data Warehouse Introduction

Data Warehouse integrates structured data from multiple sources. The combined data is then used for querying, reporting and analysis. Figure below shows Architecture of a Data Warehouse.

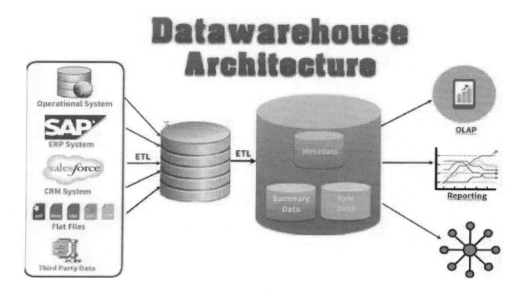

Note: To use unstructured data you need to transform it into structure dataset and then load into Data Warehouse.

Azure Data Warehouse

Azure SQL Data Warehouse is a fully managed Data Warehouse that analyses Structured Data using Business Intelligence tools.

Azure SQL Data Warehouse is a cloud-based, scale-out database that's capable of processing massive volumes of data, both relational and non-relational.

A SQL Data Warehouse database is designed for massively parallel processing (MPP). The database is distributed across multiple compute nodes and processes queries in parallel. SQL Data Warehouse has a control node that orchestrates the activities of all the compute nodes. The compute nodes themselves use SQL Database to manage your data.

The best way to load data into SQL Data Warehouse is to use Polybase. With PolyBase, the data loads in parallel from the data store (Blob Storage) to the compute nodes. PolyBase uses T-SQL commands to Load Data.

Figure below shows Data from Multiple sources being ingested into Data Store which can be Blob Storage or Data lake Store.

Structured Data can be directly loaded into Data Warehouse from Data Store.

Whereas unstructured data will be first transformed into structured Dataset using Data Lake Analytics or Hadoop etc and then loaded into Azure SQL DW.

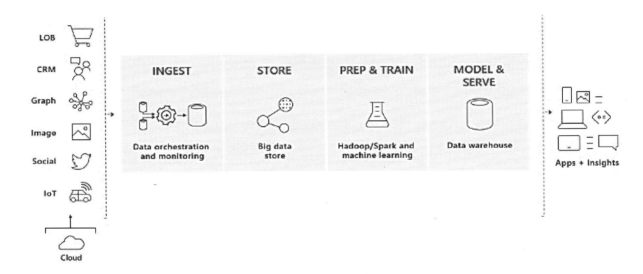

Advantages of Using SQL DW v/s SQL Database

SQL Data Warehouse stores data into relational tables with columnar storage. This format significantly reduces the data storage costs, and improves query performance. Once data is stored in SQL Data Warehouse, you can run analytics at massive scale. Compared to traditional database systems, analysis queries finish in seconds instead of minutes, or hours instead of days.

Azure SQL Data Warehouse Architecture

SQL Data uses a node based scale out architecture to distribute computational processing of Structured data across multiple compute nodes.

It consist of control node and multiple compute nodes. Control node orchestrates the activities of all the compute nodes. SQL Data Warehouse separates compute from storage which enables the user to scale compute independently of the data in your system.

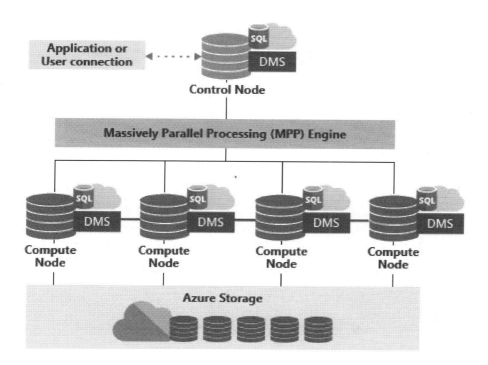

Control Node

The Control node is the brain of the data warehouse. It is the front end that interacts with all applications and connections. Control node orchestrates the activities of compute nodes. When you submit a T-SQL query to SQL Data Warehouse, the Control node transforms it into queries that run against each distribution in parallel. The Control node runs the MPP engine which optimizes queries for parallel processing, and then passes operations to compute nodes to do their work in parallel.

Compute Node

The Compute nodes provide the computational power. Queries passed on by control node are run parallelly across compute nodes. The number of compute nodes range from 1 to 60.

Each Compute node has a node ID that is visible in system views. When compute nodes are added or deleted, SQL Data Warehouse re-maps the distributions to the available Compute nodes.

Compute resources are measured in Data Warehouse Units (DWU).

Storage

User Data after transformation is stored in Azure Storage or Data lake Store. From Storage user Data is loaded in SQL Data Warehouse compute nodes using Polybase SSIS, ADF etc.

Following are the advantages of independent storage and compute:

1. Independently size compute power irrespective of storage needs.
2. Grow or shrink compute power without moving data.
3. Pause compute capacity while leaving data intact, so you only pay for storage.
4. Resume compute capacity during operational hours.

Data Movement Service

Data Movement Service (DMS) is the data transport technology that coordinates data movement between the Compute nodes. Some queries require data movement to ensure the parallel queries return accurate results. When data movement is required, DMS ensures the right data gets to the right location.

Distributions

A distribution is the basic unit of storage and processing for parallel queries that run on distributed data. When SQL Data Warehouse runs a query, the work is divided into 60 smaller queries that run in parallel. Each of the 60 smaller queries runs on one of the data distributions. Each Compute node manages one or more of the 60 distributions. A data warehouse with maximum compute resources has one distribution per Compute node. A data warehouse with minimum compute resources has all the distributions on one compute node.

Data Warehouse Units (DWUs)

A DWU represents measure of compute resources and its performance. Data Warehouse Units (DWUs) are bundled units of CPU, memory, and IO.

To get higher performance, you can increase the number of data warehouse units. As you increase data warehouse units, you are linearly increasing computing resources. By increasing DWU following performance improvement happens:

1. Linearly changes performance of the system for scans, aggregations, and CTAS statements.
2. Increases the number of readers and writers for PolyBase load operations.
3. Increases the maximum number of concurrent queries and concurrency slots.

Azure SQL Data Warehouse performance tiers

Elasticity performance tier has separate Computer and Storage layer.
Performance of Elasticity performance tier is measured in terms of **DWU**.
Compute performance tier introduces NVMe Solid State Disk cache that keeps
the most frequently accessed data close to the CPUs. Performance of Computer
Performance tier is measured in terms of **cDWU**.

DWU range of Elasticity Performance Tier

Service level	Max concurrent queries	Compute nodes	Distributions per Compute node	Max memory/ distribution (MB)	Max memory/ DW (GB)
DW100	4	1	60	400	24
DW200	8	2	30	800	48
DW300	12	3	20	1200	72
DW400	16	4	15	1600	96
DW500	20	5	12	2000	120
DW600	24	6	10	2400	144
DW1000	32	10	6	4000	240
DW1200	32	12	5	4800	288
DW1500	32	15	4	6000	360
DW2000	32	20	3	8000	480
DW3000	32	30	2	12000	720
DW6000	32	60	1	24000	1440

cDWU range of Compute Performance Tier

Service level	Max concurrent queries	Compute nodes	Distributions per Compute node	Max memory/ distribution (MB)	Max memory/ DW (GB)
DW1000c	32	2	30	10	600
DW1500c	32	3	20	15	900
DW2000c	32	4	15	20	1200
DW2500c	32	5	12	25	1500
DW3000c	32	6	10	30	1800
DW5000c	32	10	6	50	3000
DW6000c	32	12	5	60	3600
DW7500c	32	15	4	75	4500
DW10000c	32	20	3	100	6000
DW15000c	32	30	2	150	9000
DW30000c	32	60	1	300	18000

Concurrency slots

Concurrency slots track the resources available for query execution. Queries reserve compute resources by acquiring concurrency slots. Before a query can start executing, it must be able to reserve enough concurrency slots.

Each query will consume one or more concurrency slots. System queries and some trivial queries do not consume any slots.

Design Nugget: Elasticity performance tier scales to 240 concurrency slots. Compute performance tier scales to 1200 concurrency slots.
Design Nugget: A query running with 10 concurrency slots can access 5 times more compute resources than a query running with 2 concurrency slots.

Integrating Structured and Unstructured Data into Azure SQL DW using Azure Data Factory

Azure SQL Data Warehouse does analytics on Structured Data. To use unstructured data you need to transform it into structure dataset and then load into Data Warehouse using Polybase.

Integrating Structured Data with Azure SQL DW

As shown in figure below Data Factory ingest data from Structured data sources such as SQL Server. Azure Data Factory also does Source (SQL Server) and Destination (SQL DW) Table & Schema Mapping. Data Factory will then stage the data in Blob Storage before moving into Azure SQL DW. Azure Data Factory will use Poybase option to load data in Azure SQL DW.

Integrating Non- Structured Data with Azure SQL DW

As shown in figure below Data Factory ingest data from unstructured data sources. Data Factory will then stage the data in Blob Storage or Data Lake store. Unstructured Data is transformed using HDInsight or Data Lake Analytics. Azure Data Factory will use Poybase option to load transformed dataset into Azure SQL DW.

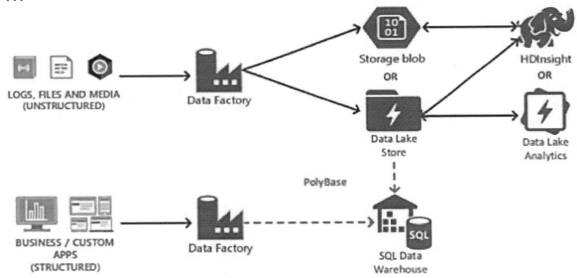

Note: In above we have used Data Factory for ingestion and loading Data in SQL DW. It is not compulsory to use Data Factory. You can use other options.

Azure SQL Data Warehouse Working

Tables

Data is stored in Tables against which queries are performed. Tables are comprised of columns and rows. Columns contain the column name, data type, and any other attributes for the column. Rows contain the records or data for the columns.

Distribution

SQL Data Warehouse divides your data into 60 databases. Each individual database is referred to as a **distribution**. When data is loaded into each table, SQL Data Warehouse has to know how to divide your data across these 60 distributions.

The distribution method is defined at the table level and has following options:

1. **Round robin** distributes data evenly but randomly.
2. **Hash Distributed** distributes data based on hashing values from a single column. **Hash distributed** tables minimize data movement which will in turn optimizes query performance.
3. **Replicated:** Full copy of the table is distributed on each compute node. A replicated table provides the fastest query performance for small tables.

Indexes

Indexes are **special lookup tables** that the database search engine can use to speed up data retrieval. Simply put, an index is a pointer to data in a table. An index in a database is very similar to an index in the back of a book.

SQL Data Warehouse offers following indexing options:

clustered columnstore indexes
clustered indexes
nonclustered indexes.
no index option or heap

- **Clustered columnstore** tables is the default option and offer both the highest level of data compression as well as the best overall query performance.
- Use **cluster index** or non-clustered secondary index Table for queries where a single or very few row lookup is required.
- When you are temporarily landing data on SQL Data Warehouse, using a **heap table** will make the overall process faster. This is because loads to heaps are faster than to index tables and in some cases the subsequent read can be done from cache.

Design Nugget: For small lookup tables, less than 100 million rows, use heap tables. Cluster columnstore tables begin to achieve optimal compression once there is more than 100 million rows.

Partitioning

Partitioning enables you to divide your data into smaller groups of data.

Partitioning is supported on all SQL Data Warehouse Index table types including clustered columnstore, clustered index, and heap. Partitioning is also supported on all distribution types, including both hash and round robin distribution.

Benefits of Partition

1. Improved Data Load Time
2. Improved query Performance

Design Nugget: A minimum of 1 million rows per distribution and partition is needed for optimal compression and performance of clustered columnstore tables.

Loading Data into Azure SQL Data Warehouse

The Best way to load dat into SQL DW is to use Polybase. First transfer the Structured Data to Azure Storage or Azure Data lake Store and then use Polybase to Load Data in parallel to Azure SQL DW.

1. Extract the source data into text files.
2. Land the data into Azure Blob storage or Azure Data Lake Store.
3. Prepare the data for loading.
4. Load the data into SQL Data Warehouse staging tables by using **PolyBase**.
5. Transform the data.
6. Insert the data into production tables.

About Polybase

PolyBase is a technology that accesses data outside of the database via the T-SQL language. With PolyBase, the data loads in parallel from the data source directly to the compute nodes. PolyBase uses T-SQL commands to Load Data. It is the best way to load data into SQL Data Warehouse.

Design Nugget: Azure Blob Storage is used as a staging Platform to Load Data to SQL DW. Data from SQL Server is transferred to Azure Blob Storage and from there Polybase is used to Load Data into Azure SQL DW.

Load from Azure Blob Storage using PolyBase and T-SQL

1. Move your data to Azure blob storage or Azure Data Lake Store and store it in text files.
2. Configure external objects in SQL Data Warehouse to define the location and format of the data
3. Run a T-SQL command to load the data in parallel into a new database table.

Load from SQL Server using bcp

If you have a small amount of data you can use bcp to load directly into Azure SQL Data Warehouse without using Polybase. Summary of loading process:
1. Use the bcp command-line utility to export data from SQL Server to flat files.
2. Use bcp to load data from flat files directly to SQL Data Warehouse.

Load from SQL Server (on-premises or Cloud) using Data Factory

Azure Data Factory is cloud-based data integration service that creates data-driven workflows (Pipelines) in the cloud for orchestrating and automating data movement and data transformation.

Using Pipelines Azure Data Factory (ADF) will ingest Data from SQL Server. Azure Data Factory also does Source (SQL Server) and Destination (SQL DW) Table & Schema Mapping. ADF will then stage the data in Blob Storage before moving into Azure SQL DW. ADF will use Poybase option to load data in Azure SQL DW. In this case you don't need to run T-SQL Commands.

The Biggest advantage of using Azure Data Factory is that it automates ingestion and Loading of data.

Load from SQL Server using SQL Server Integration Services (SSIS)

Use SSIS packages and point SQL Server as the source and SQL Data Warehouse as the destination. Following is the Summary of loading process:

1. Revise your Integration Services package to point to the SQL Server instance for the source and the SQL Data Warehouse for the destination.
2. Migrate your schema to SQL Data Warehouse, if it is not there already.
3. Change the mapping in your packages. Use only the data types that are supported by SQL Data Warehouse.
4. Schedule and run the package.

Load from SQL Server using AZCopy & Polybase

If your data size is < 10 TB, you can export the data from SQL Server to flat files, copy the files to Azure blob storage using AZCopy and then use PolyBase to load the data into SQL Data Warehouse. Following is the Summary of loading process:

1. Use the bcp command-line utility to export data from SQL Server to flat files.
2. Use the AZCopy command-line utility to copy data from flat files to Azure blob storage.
3. Use PolyBase to load into SQL Data Warehouse.

Exercise 16: Create, Connect and Query SQL DW using Sample Database

Step 1 Create Azure SQL DW: In Azure Portal click create a resource>SQL Data Warehouse> Create SQL Data Warehouse blade opens>Select source as **sample** and Enter other information as per your requirement and click create.

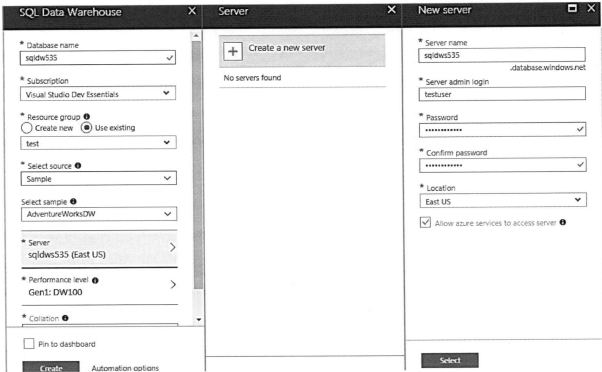

Azure SQL DW Dashboard: Figure below show SQL DW dashboard. Note the Server DNS name and connection strings link in right pane. You can add connection strings in your application to connect to Azure SQL DW.

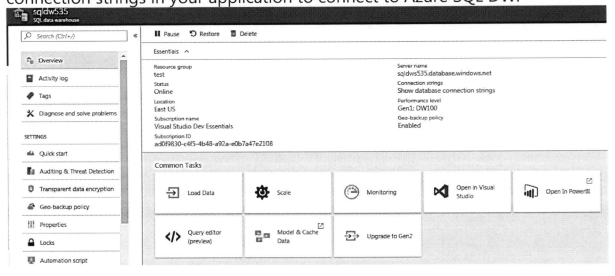

Step 2 Create Azure SQL DW server level firewall rule: Firewall service on newly created Azure SQL DW server prevents external applications and tools from connecting to the server unless a firewall rule is created to open the firewall for specific client IP addresses.

Click the server name (sqldws535.database.windows.net) in right pane> sqldws535 server dashboard opens>Click Firewall and Virtual Networks in left pane> Enter IP address assigned by your ISP in Start IP and End IP Box. Give it a name and click save.

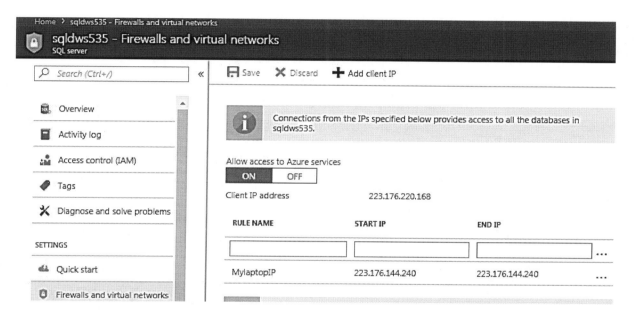

Step 3 Connect to SQL DW using SQL Server Management Studio (SSMS): On the client machine whose IP was entered in step 2, open SSMS and enter Azure SQL database server name, username and password and click connect.

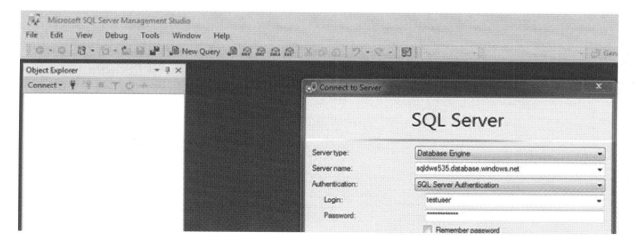

Architecting Microsoft Azure Solutions Study & Lab Guide Part 2: Exam 70-535

SSMS connects to SQL DW Database. Figure below shows sample database AdventureWorks.

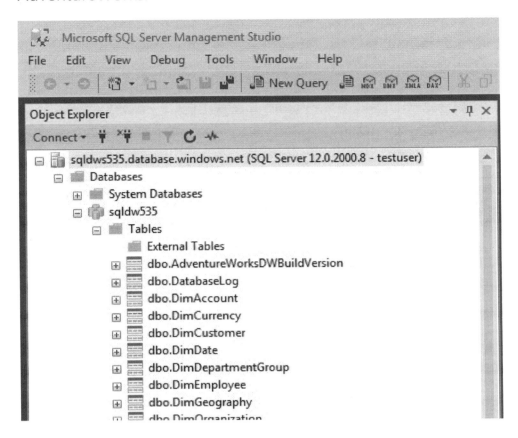

Step 4 Query the sample database: Right Click sqldw535 and select new query>New query window opens in middle pane. Enter and run your query to see the result.

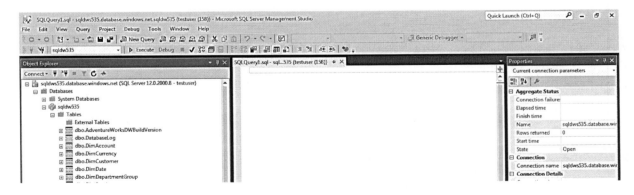

Azure Data lake Analytics

Azure Data lake Analytics is a managed service for Big Data Analytics. Big Data Analytics uses parallel processing model to process huge amount of data (Structure and Unstructured). With Big Data Analytics, queries are split and distributed across parallel compute nodes and processed in parallel.

Azure Data Lake Analytics provisions compute resources to do analytics on terabytes or even exabytes of data stored in a number of supported data sources. Data Lake Analytics supports the following data sources:

1. Data Lake Store
2. Azure Storage

Data Lake Analytics is optimized to work with Azure Data Lake store - providing the highest level of performance, throughput and parallelization (queries are Split in parallel) for your big data workloads.

Features of Azure Data Lake Analytics

Scale instantly and pay per job: With Azure Data Lake Analytics can instantly scale the processing power, measured in Azure Data Lake Analytics Units (AU), from one to thousands for each job. You only pay for the processing which you use per job.

Develop massively parallel programs with U-SQL: With U-SQL you write code once and have it automatically parallelised for the scale you need. Using U-SQL you can process petabytes of data for diverse workload categories such as querying, ETL, analytics, machine learning, machine translation, image processing and sentiment analysis by leveraging existing libraries written in .NET languages, R or Python. (Very Important Concept)

Enterprise-grade security, auditing and SLA: Data Lake Analytics is integrated with Active Directory for user management and permissions and comes with built-in monitoring and auditing. Azure Data Lake Analytics Managed service guarantee a 99.9% enterprise-grade SLA and 24/7 support.
Works with Azure Data Stores: Data Lake Analytics works with Azure Data Lake Store, Azure Storage blobs, Azure SQL Database & Azure Warehouse.

Azure Data lake Analytics Architecture

Azure Data lake is cloud based scalable & distributed compute cluster based on open source Yarn. Yarn is a cluster management technology. It uses **U-SQL software** framework that allows developers to write programs that process massive amounts of unstructured data in parallel across a distributed cluster.

It pairs with Azure Data Lake Store, a cloud-based storage platform designed for Big Data analytics. Data Lake Analytics is optimized to work with Azure Data Lake store

Integrating Non- Structured Data with Azure Data lake Analytics

Azure Data Lake analytics processes unstructured and semi-structured data.

Figure below shows unstructured data being ingested into Data lake store. Azure Data lake Analytics use U-SQL query language to analyse Data.

It also Prepare data for insertion in Azure SQL DW for further analyses and reporting. Azure Data Factory will use Poybase option to load transformed dataset into Azure SQL DW.

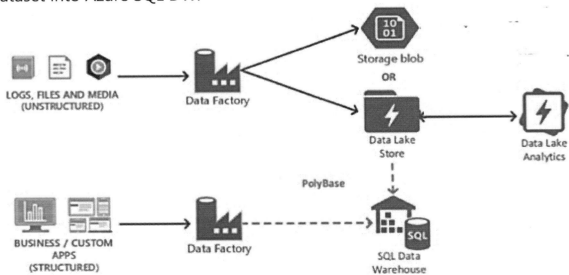

The Biggest advantage of using Azure Data Factory is that it automates ingestion and Loading of data.

What can you do with Data lake Analytics

1. It is Primarily used to process semi-structured and unstructured data such as internet clickstream data, web server logs, social media content, text from customer emails and survey responses, mobile-phone call-detail records and machine data captured by sensors connected to the internet of things.
2. Prepares large amounts of data for insertion into a Data Warehouse for further analyses and reporting.
3. Replacing long-running monthly batch processing with shorter running distributed processes.
4. Using image processing intelligence to quickly process unstructured image data.

Exercise 17: Create Data Lake Analytics Account with associated Data lake Store

Step 1: In Azure Portal Click Create a resource>Analytics> Data Lake Analytics>Create Data lake Analytics account blade opens> Select Data lake Store or create a new Data lake Store and click create.

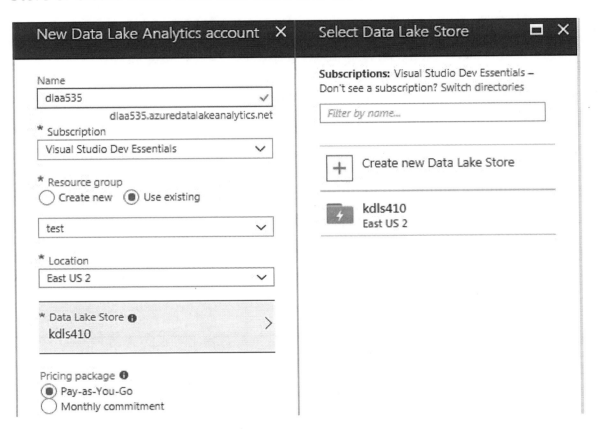

Figure below shows Data lake Analytics Dashboard.

Architecting Microsoft Azure Solutions Study & Lab Guide Part 2: Exam 70-535

Exercise 18: Perform Analytics on Data stored in Data Lake Store using U-SQL Script

In Data lake Analytics Dashboard>Click + New Job>New Job Dashboard opens> Paste your U-SQL Script in the Rectangular Box>Click Submit to see the result of your query.

Exercise 19: Adding Azure Storage as Data Source

In Data lake Analytics Dashboard>Click Data Sources in Left pane>In Right pane click + Add Data Source> Add Data Source Blade opens>Select azure Storage from Drop down box and also select your storage Account from drop down box.

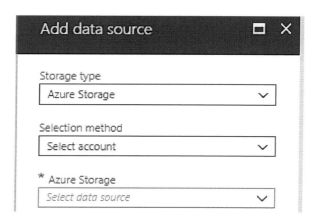

Pricing

You pay for computer power (measured in terms of Analytics Units) used by U-SQL job and only for its duration.

It is available in pay-as-you-go and monthly commitment packages.

Pay as you go model

Usage	Price
Analytics Unit	$2/hour

Monthly commitment

Included Analytics Unit Hours	Price/Month
100	$100
500	$450
1000	$800
5000	$3600
10000	$6500
50000	$29000
100000	$52000
>100000	Contact MS Sales

Azure Analysis Services

Azure Analysis Services creates a managed Analysis Services server instance which performs enterprise-grade BI Data modelling capabilities. It Analysis Structured Data using client tools like Power BI and Excel.

Azure Analysis Services is built on the analytics engine from Microsoft SQL Server Analysis Services.

Azure Analysis Working

With Analysis Services, you combine data from multiple sources, define metrics, and secure your data in a single, trusted semantic data model. Azure Analysis Services then helps you transform complex data into actionable insights using client applications like Power BI, Excel, Reporting Services, third-party, and custom apps.

The figure below shows Azure Analysis Services instances combining and transforming SQL Data from on-premises and cloud. The Data is then being analysed using applications like Power BI and Excel etc.

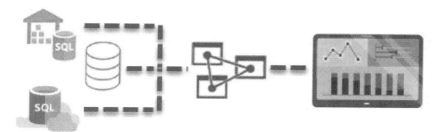

SQL Data   Analysis Service Instance Client Application

Deploying a Tabular Model database

Once you have created Analysis server in your Azure subscription, you can deploy a tabular model database to it. You can use following tools to deploy the tabular model database:

1. SQL Server Data Tools (SSDT)
2. SQL Server Management Studio
3. Azure Portal

Architecting Microsoft Azure Solutions Study & Lab Guide Part 2: Exam 70-535

Data Sources

Azure Analysis Services server supports connecting to data sources in the cloud and on-premises using tools such as SSDT for Visual studio and SSMS.

Data Sources in Cloud: Azure Analysis Services supports following data sources in cloud.

Azure SQL Database
Azure Data Warehouse
Azure Blob Storage
Azure Cosmos DB
Azure Data lake Store
Azure HDInsight HDFS
Azure HDInsight Spark

Data Sources on-premises: Azure Analysis Services supports following data sources on-premises. Connecting to on-premises data sources require an **On-Premises Data Gateway.** Microsoft **On-Premises Data Gateway** connects on-premises data sources to cloud services for consumption. You can benefit from Microsoft cloud services while you keep your business running with the on-premises data.

Access Database	JSON document	SAP HANA
Active Directory	Lines from binary	SAP Business Warehouse
Analysis Services	MySQL Database	SharePoint
Analytics Platform System	OData Feed	SQL Database
Dynamics CRM	ODBC query	Sybase Database
Excel workbook	OLE DB	Teradata Database
Exchange	Oracle Database	
Folder	Postgre SQL Database	

Note: To know more about On-Premises Data Gateway refer to Hybrid Application Chapter.

Azure Analysis Services Tiers and Pricing

Azure Analysis Services is available in developer, basic, and standard tiers. Instance's in each tier come with different QPUs and memory size.

A **Query Processing Unit (QPU)** in Azure Analysis Services is a unit of measure for relative computational performance for query and data processing.

Feature	Developer	Basic	Standard
Perspectives	✓		✓
Multiple partitions	✓		✓
DirectQuery storage mode	✓		✓
Translations	✓	✓	✓
Dax calculations	✓	✓	✓
Row-level security	✓	✓	✓
In-mem storage	✓	✓	✓
Backup and restore	✓	✓	✓

Developer tier

Instance	QPUs	Memory (GB)	Price
Developer	20	3	$0.132/hour

Basic tier

Instance	QPUs	Memory (GB)	Price
B1	40	10	$0.43/hour
B2	80	20	$0.86/hour

Standard tier

Instance	QPUs	Memory (GB)	Price
S0	40	10	$0.81/hour
S1	100	25	$2.03/hour
S2	200	50	$4.06/hour
S4	400	100	$8.11/hour
S8	320	200	$10.38/hour
S9	640	400	$20.76/hour

Exercise 20: Create an Azure Analysis Services server, add a data source, create a model from the data source and query the model database.

For this Exercise we will use SQL DW sample database created in Ex 16

1. In Azure Portal Click + Create a resource> Analytics >Analysis Services>Create Analysis service Blade opens. Enter following as per your req and click create.

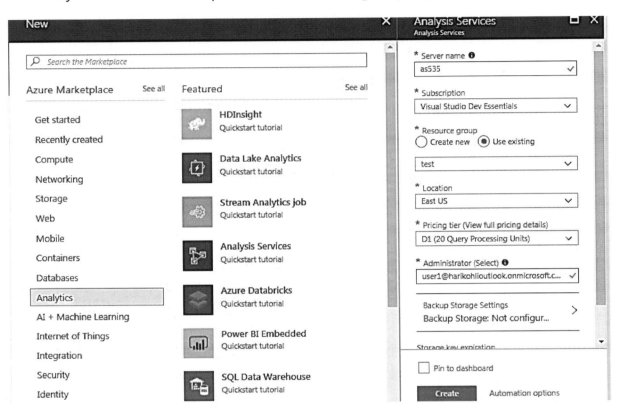

2. Figure below shows Azure Analysis Service dashboard. Note the web designer option in right pane. We will use this option to add SQL DW as data source.

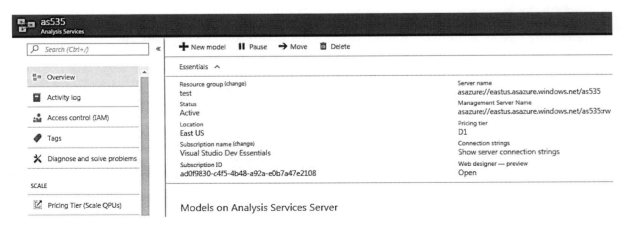

Add SQL DW created in Ex 16 as data source and create a new tabular model from it: In Analysis Service dashboard **click open** under web designer>Web Designer Opens in a browser>Click + ADD in Models>New Model Blade opens> Enter a name and select Azure SQL DW >Connect blade opens>Enter username and password of SQL DW and select the sample database>Click next.

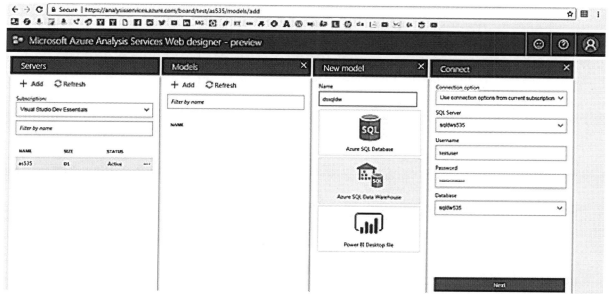

3. In **Tables and views**, select the tables to include in your model, and then click **Create**. Relationships are created automatically between tables

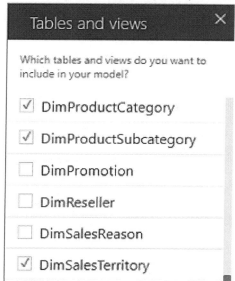

4. Your new model appears in your browser. From here, you can query the model and open data model in Visual studio, Power BI or Excel.

Azure Analysis Services scale-out

In single Analysis server Instance, Analysis Service instance acts as both processing server and query server. In this case if the number of client queries against your server exceeds the Query Processing Units (QPU) for your server's plan, performance can decrease.

With scale-out, you can create a query pool with up to seven additional query replicas (eight total, including your server). You can scale the number of query replicas to meet QPU demands at critical times and you can separate a processing server from the query pool at any time.

Scale-out option is available for servers in the Standard pricing tier only.

Configure scale-out

1. Go to Analysis Server Dashboard>Click scale out in left pane. Configure number of replica as per your requirement.

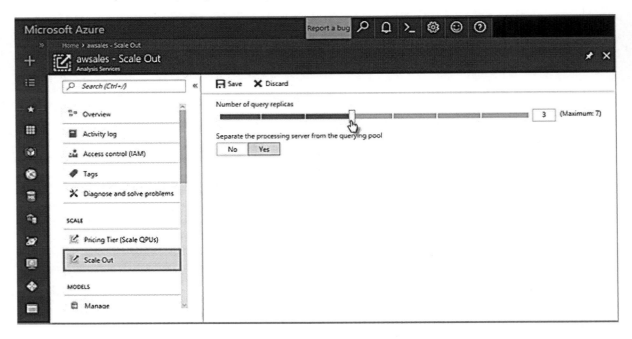

Azure HDInsight

Azure HDInsight provides Big Data as a service using Hadoop components from the Hortonworks Data Platform (HDP). Big Data Processing breaks up large data processing tasks into multiple jobs, and then combine the results to enable massive parallelism.

Big Data Analytics uses parallel processing model to process huge amount of data (Semi-Structure and Unstructured). With Big Data Analytics, queries are split and distributed across parallel compute nodes and processed in parallel.

Azure HDInsight runs distributed processing and analysis of big data sets on clusters of computers. The data to be processed is stored in Azure Blob Storage or Azure Data Lake Store.

Azure HDInsight offers fully managed Apache Hadoop, Spark, HBase, and Storm clusters. You can get up and running quickly on any of these workloads with a few clicks and within a few minutes, without buying hardware or hiring specialized operations teams typically associated with big data infrastructure.

Azure HD Insight Features

Low-cost and scalable: HDInsight enables you to scale workloads up or down. You can reduce costs by creating clusters on demand and paying only for what you use.

Compute & Storage: Decoupled compute and storage provide better performance and flexibility and can independently scale.

Secure and compliant: HDInsight enables you to protect your enterprise data assets with Azure Virtual Network, encryption, and integration with Azure Active Directory. HDInsight also meets the most popular industry and government compliance standards.

Monitoring: Azure HDInsight integrates with Azure Log Analytics to provide a single interface with which you can monitor all your clusters.

Multiple Development Environment: HDInsight provides options for multiple development environment including Visual Studio, Eclipse, and IntelliJ for Scala, Python, R, Java, and .NET.

HDInsight Cluster Architecture

HDInsight Cluster consists of Head Nodes and Workers Nodes. All HDInsight cluster types deploy YARN. **YARN** has two core services – Resource Manager and Node Manager.

The **Resource Manager** grants cluster compute resources to applications like MapReduce jobs. A MapReduce job splits large datasets and organizes the data into key-value pairs for parallel processing across cluster of compute nodes. The **Node Manager** nodes are where the application actually executes in parallel.

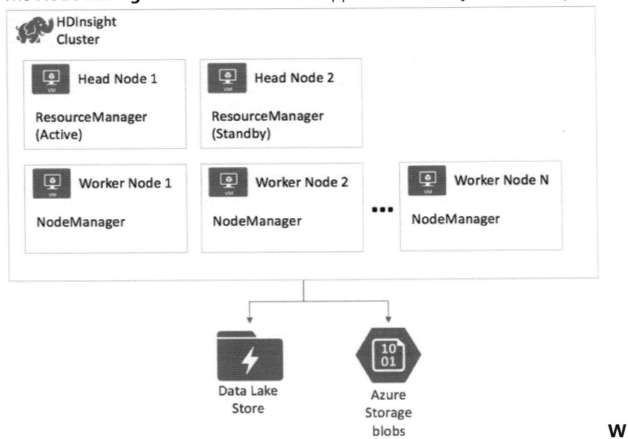

W

orking

When a user submits a MapReduce application to run on the cluster, the application is submitted to the Resource Manager. In turn, the Resource Manager allocates containers on available NodeManager nodes to execute the application in parallel. A container consists of an allocation of CPU cores and RAM memory.

HDInsight Storage Architecture

Hadoop Distributed File System (HDFS) is the standard file system for Hadoop clusters on HDInsight.

Through Hadoop distributed file system (HDFS) interface, you access distributed file system (DFS) that is locally attached to the compute nodes. You can also access data that is stored in Azure Storage or Azure Data lake Store.

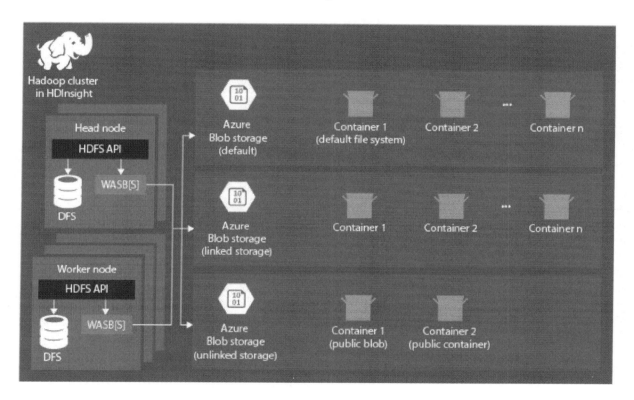

During the HDInsight cluster creation process, you can specify a blob container in Azure Storage as the default file system or Azure Data Lake Store as the default files system.

This advantage of using Blob or Data lake store is that the data is available even after the cluster is deleted.

HDInsight use Cases

Data warehousing: You can use HDInsight to perform interactive queries at petabyte scales over semi-structured or unstructured data in any format. You can also build models connecting them to BI tools.

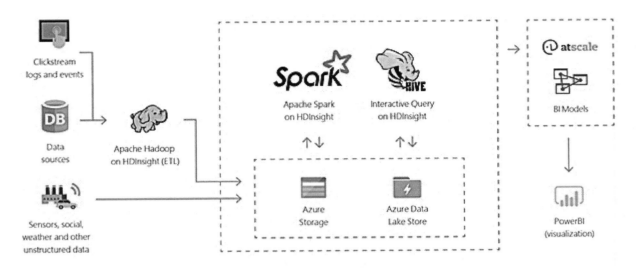

Internet of Things (IoT): You can use HDInsight to process streaming data that's received in real time from a variety of devices.

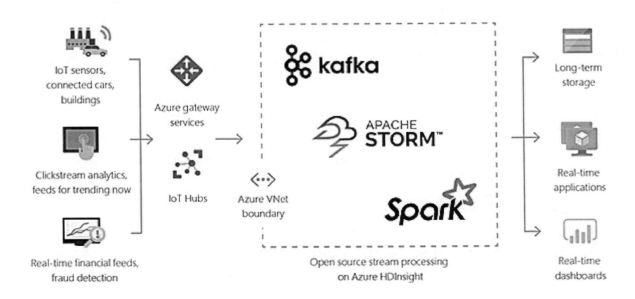

HDInsight use Cases (Continued)

Data science: You can use HDInsight to build applications that extract critical insights from data. You can also use Azure Machine Learning on top of that to predict future trends for your business.

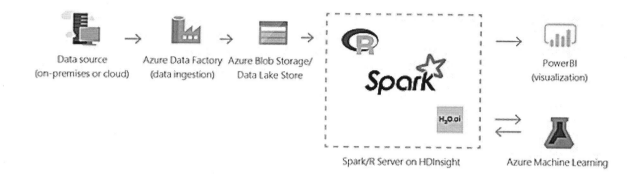

Cluster and Storage Options available with HDInsight

The idea of this exercise is to show you various Cluster and Storage options available during HDInsight Deployment. We are not deploying HDInsight Cluster.

Click +Create a Resource> Click Data + Analytics>Click HDInsight> Create HDInsight Blade opens as shown below.

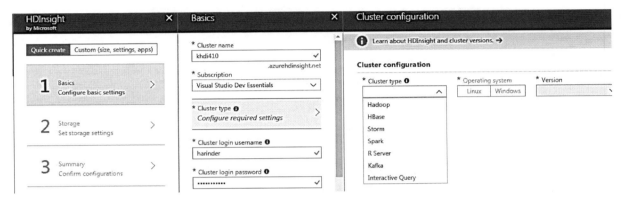

As shown above HDInsight provides 7 Cluster options to choose from: Hadoop, HBase, Storm, Sprak, R Server, Kafka & Interactive Query. During HDInsight deployment you can choose Cluster type depending upon your workload and Analytics requirement.

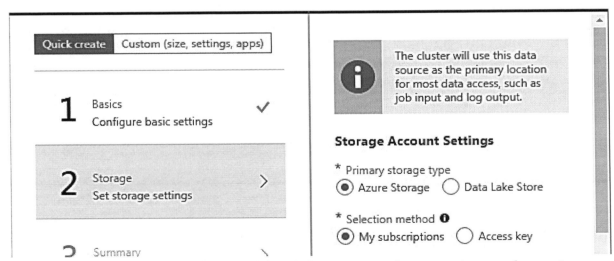

As shown above HDInsight provides 2 Storage options to choose from: Azure Storage and Data Lake Store.

Note 1: You can choose Linux or windows for your HDInsight cluster.

Note 2: MS is retiring windows HDInsight cluster.

Cluster types in HDInsight (7 Types)

Apache Hadoop Cluster

Apache Hadoop cluster process and analyze batch data in parallel using MapReduce.

Apache Hadoop cluster uses Hadoop distributed file system (**HDFS**) for Storage, **YARN** for job scheduling and resource management and **MapReduce** for parallel processing of Big Data Jobs.

Apache Hadoop clusters for HDInsight are deployed with two roles:

Head node (2 nodes)
Data node (at least 1 node)

Storage for Hadoop Cluster

HDFS file system of HDInsight clusters for Hadoop can be associated with either an Azure Storage account or an Azure Data Lake Store.

Components use with Apache Hadoop Cluster : MapReduce, Hive (SQL on Hadoop), Pig, Sqoop and Oozie.

Apache Spark Cluster

Apache Spark cluster uses in-memory processing to boost the performance of big-data analysis applications such as SQL, streaming data and machine learning.

A Spark job can load and cache data into memory and query it repeatedly, much more quickly than disk-based systems. In Spark, data sharing between operations is faster since data is in-memory. In contrast, Hadoop shares data through HDFS, which takes longer to process.

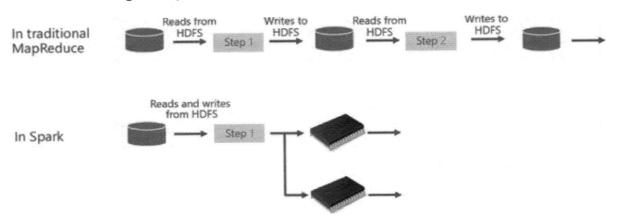

Apache Hadoop clusters for HDInsight are deployed with two roles:

Head node (2 nodes)
Data node (at least 1 node)

Storage for Hadoop Cluster

HDFS file system of HDInsight clusters for Hadoop can be associated with either an Azure Storage account or an Azure Data Lake Store.

Use cases for Spark Cluster
Spark Machine Learning: Apache Spark comes with MLlib, a machine learning library built on top of Spark for creating machine learning applications.
Spark streaming and real-time data analysis: Spark in HDInsight have built in support for ingesting data from Azure Event Hubs for building real-time analytics solutions.
Interactive data analysis and BI: Apache Spark in HDInsight stores data in Azure Storage or Azure Data Lake Store. You can use Microsoft Power BI to build interactive reports from the analyzed data.

Apache HBase Cluster

Apache HBase is an open-source, NoSQL database that is built on Hadoop. It is used for Processing schemaless, NoSQL data. Data is stored in the rows of a table, and data within a row is grouped by column family. HBase is a schemaless database in the sense that neither the columns nor the type of data stored in them need to be defined before using them. The open-source code scales linearly to handle petabytes of data on thousands of nodes.

HBase clusters for HDInsight are deployed with three roles:

1. Head servers (2 nodes)
2. Region servers (at least 1 node)
3. Master/Zookeeper nodes (3 nodes)

Storage for HBase Cluster

HDFS file system of HDInsight clusters for HBase can be associated with either an Azure Storage account or an Azure Data Lake Store. This association ensures that whatever data is uploaded to the cluster storage during analysis is made persistent and the data is available even after the cluster is deleted.

Use Case for HBase

Key Value Store: HBase can be used as a key-value store, and it is suitable for managing message systems.
Sensor data: HBase is useful for capturing data that is collected incrementally from various sources. This includes social analytics, time series, keeping interactive dashboards up-to-date with trends and counters, and managing audit log systems.
Real-time query: Phoenix is a SQL query engine for Apache HBase. It enables querying and managing HBase tables by using SQL.
HBase as a platform: Applications can run on top of HBase by using it as a datastore. Examples include Phoenix, OpenTSDB, Kiji, and Titan. Applications can also integrate with HBase. Examples include Hive, Pig, Solr, Storm, Flume, Impala, Spark, Ganglia, and Drill.

R Server Cluster

R Server clusters provides Terabyte-scale, enterprise grade R analytics with transparent parallelization on top of Spark and Hadoop.

R is the programming language for statistical computing and machine learning. Microsoft R Server is the leading enterprise-class analytics platform for R. Using Microsoft R Server's with HDInsight Cluster allows R processing to occur in parallel, speeding up the analysis of large volumes of data.

R is highly extensible through the use of user-submitted packages for specific functions or specific areas of study.

R Server clusters for HDInsight are deployed with four roles:

Head servers (2 nodes)
Worker (Default is 4 Nodes but you can change to at least 1 node)
Zookeeper (3 nodes)
R Server (1 Node)

Storage for HBase Cluster

HDFS file system of HDInsight clusters for R Server can be associated with either an Azure Storage account or an Azure Data Lake Store.

Use Case for R Server

Machine Learning: R Server includes highly-scalable and distributed set of algorithm such as **microsoftml.** The **microsoftml** module is a collection of Python functions used in machine learning solutions and is used for forecasting (Predictive Analytics) and analysis.

R Server Case Study: Read the case Study how a pharmaceutical company reduced wastage in the supply chain caused by temperature fluctuations https://customers.microsoft.com/en-us/story/merck-co

Apache Storm Cluster

Apache Storm clusters process infinite streams of data in **real-time**. Apache Storm cluster integrates with Event Hub to ingest data in Real time.

Apache Storm clusters for HDInsight are deployed with three roles:

1. Nimbus nodes (2 nodes)
2. Supervisor servers/Worker Nodes (Default is 4 Nodes but you can change to at least 1 node)
3. Zookeeper nodes (3 nodes)

Storage for HBase Cluster

HDFS file system of HDInsight clusters for Storm can be associated with either an Azure Storage account or an Azure Data Lake Store.

Use Cases for Storm

Internet of Things (IoT)
Fraud detection
Social analytics
Extraction, transformation, and loading (ETL)
Network monitoring
Search
Mobile engagement

Apache Kafka Cluster

Apache Kafka cluster is a high throughput, low-latency distributed streaming platform that is used to build real-time streaming data pipelines and applications. Kafka also provides message broker functionality similar to a message queue, where you can publish and subscribe to named data streams.

Kafka is often used with Apache Storm or Spark for real-time stream processing. Kafka introduced a streaming API that allows you to build streaming solutions without requiring Storm or Spark.

Apache Kafka clusters for HDInsight are deployed with three roles :

1. Head (2 x D13 v2),
2. Worker (Default is 4 Nodes but you can change to at least 3 node),
3. Zookeeper (3 x A3)

Kafka Working

Kafka uses consumer groups, partitioning, and replication to offer parallel reading of events with fault tolerance. Kafka stores records in *topics*. Records are produced by *producers*, and consumed by *consumers*. Producers retrieve records from Kafka *brokers*. Each worker node in your HDInsight cluster is a Kafka broker. One partition is created for each consumer, allowing parallel processing of the streaming data. Replication is employed to spread the partitions across nodes, protecting against node (broker) outages.

Use Cases for Kafka

Messaging: Since it supports the publish-subscribe message pattern, Kafka is often used as a message broker.

Activity tracking: Since Kafka provides in-order logging of records, it can be used to track and re-create activities. For example, user actions on a web site or within an application.

Aggregation: Using stream processing, you can aggregate information from different streams to combine and centralize the information into operational data.

Transformation: Using stream processing, you can combine and enrich data from multiple input topics into one or more output topics.

Apache Interactive Query Cluster

Interactive Query (also called Hive LLAP) is an Azure HDInsight cluster type.

Interactive Query or Hive LLAP supports in-memory caching, which makes Hive queries faster and much more interactive.

Low Latency Analytical Processing (LLAP)

LLAP (sometimes known as Live Long and Process) is a new feature in Hive 2.0 that allows in-memory caching of queries. LLAP makes Hive queries up to 26x faster than Hive 1.x in some cases.
HDInsight provides LLAP in the Interactive Query cluster type.

About Hive and HiveQL

Apache Hive is data warehouse software built on Hadoop that allows you to query and manage large datasets in distributed storage by using a SQL-like language called **HiveQL**. Hive is an abstraction on top of MapReduce, and it translates queries into a series of MapReduce jobs.

Interactive Query cluster for HDInsight are deployed with three roles

1. Head (2 x D13 v2),
2. Worker (Default is 4 Nodes but you can change to at least 1 node)
3. Zookeeper (3 x A3)

An Interactive Query cluster is different from a Hadoop cluster. It contains only the Hive service. Note that this feature requires high memory instances.

Components and utilities on Included with HDInsight clusters

Ambari

Apache Ambari provides management and monitoring of a Hadoop cluster by providing an easy to use web UI and REST API.
The Ambari Web UI is available on HDInsight cluster at https://CLUSTERNAME.azurehdidnsight.net.

Figure below shows the status of the cluster.

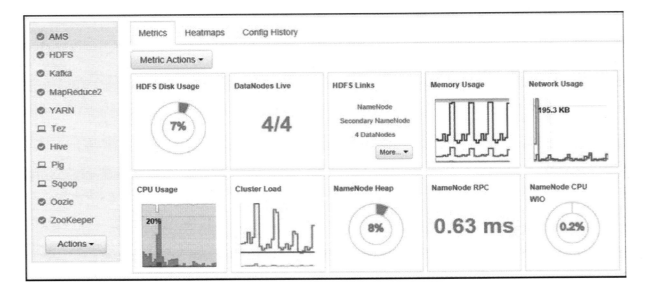

Figure Below shows the Alerts Tab of Ambari Web GUI.

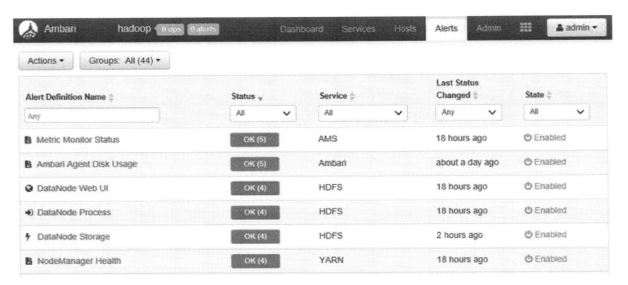

Apache Hive

Apache Hive is data warehouse software built on Hadoop that allows you to query and manage large datasets in distributed storage by using a SQL-like language called HiveQL. Hive is an abstraction on top of MapReduce, and it translates queries into a series of MapReduce jobs.

Hive queries are used with following HDInsight Cluster types:

1. **Interactive Query**: A Hadoop cluster that provides Low Latency Analytical Processing (LLAP) functionality to improve response times for interactive queries.
2. **Hadoop**: A Hadoop cluster that is tuned for batch processing workloads.
3. **Spark**: Apache Spark has built-in functionality for working with Hive.
4. **HBase**: HiveQL can be used to query data stored in HBase.

Pig

Apache Pig allows you to perform complex MapReduce transformations on large datasets by using a simple scripting language called Pig Latin.

Pig allows you to define processing as a series of transformations that the data flows through to produce the desired output. The Pig Latin language allows you to describe the data flow from raw input, through one or more transformations, to produce the desired output.

MapReduce

MapReduce is software framework for Hadoop for writing applications to batch process big data sets in parallel. A MapReduce job splits large datasets and organizes the data into key-value pairs for processing. MapReduce jobs run on YARN.

MapReduce is the legacy software framework and is being replaced by MapReduce 2.0, or MRv2.

Oozie

Apache Oozie is a workflow coordination system that manages Hadoop jobs. It is integrated with the Hadoop stack and supports Hadoop jobs for MapReduce, Pig, Hive, and Sqoop. It can also be used to schedule jobs specific to a system, like Java programs or shell scripts.

Phoenix

Apache Phoenix is a relational database layer over HBase. Phoenix includes a JDBC driver that allows you to query and manage SQL tables directly. Phoenix translates queries and other statements into native NoSQL API calls - instead of using MapReduce - thus enabling faster applications on top of NoSQL stores.

Sqoop

Apache Sqoop is a tool that transfers bulk data between Hadoop and relational databases such as SQL, or other structured data stores.

Apache Tez

Apache Tez is a framework that allows data intensive applications, such as Hive, to run much more efficiently at scale. Tez is enabled by default for Linux-based HDInsight clusters.

ZooKeeper

Apache ZooKeeper coordinates processes in large distributed systems using a shared hierarchical namespace of data registers (znodes). Znodes contain small amounts of meta information needed to coordinate processes: status, location, configuration.

Exercise 21: Create and Query HDInsight Hadoop Cluster

1. Click +Create a Resource> Click Analytics>Click HDInsight> Create HDInsight Blade opens as shown below>Select Hadoop Cluster>Click select>Click Next.

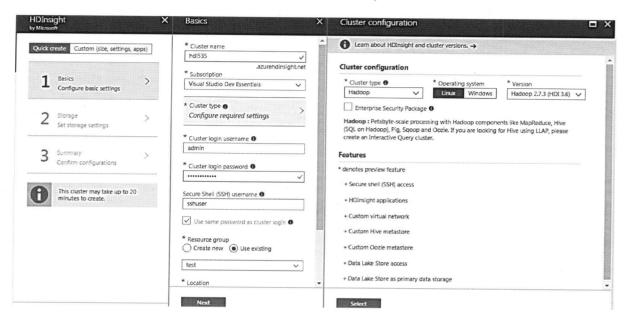

In Storage Setting>Select sa535 Storage Account>click next>In summary click create.

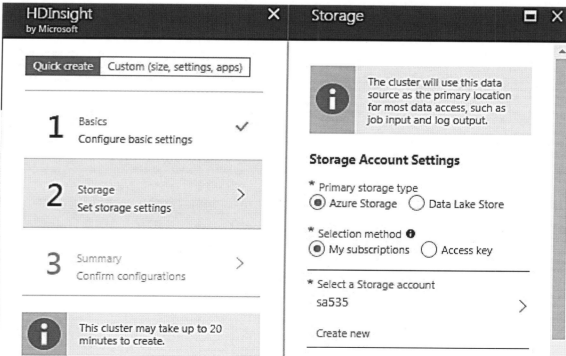

Sa535 Storage Account was created in Storage Account Chapter.

2. Figure below shows Azure HDInsight dashboard. Note Ambari Views link in Right pane.

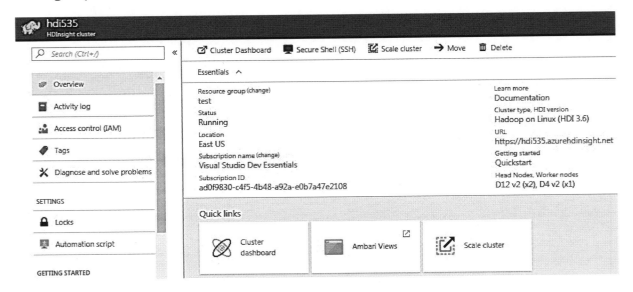

3. **Go to Ambari Dashboard**: Click Ambari Views in Right pane>A new browser windows opens with Ambari Dashboard.

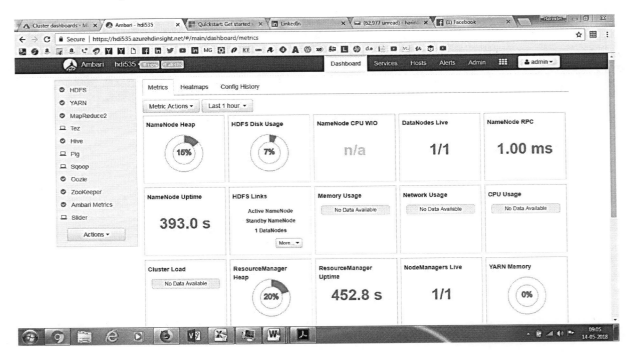

4. **Run Hive query**: Click tab on adjacent to Admin Tab>Select Hive 2.0>Hive dashboard opens with query Tab>Enter your query here and execute it to see the results

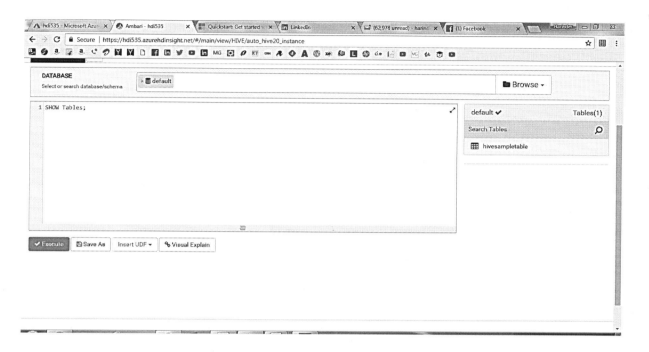

Chapter 7 Azure Data Services

This Chapter covers following

- Azure Data lake Store
- Data Catalog
- Azure Data Factory

This Chapter Covers following Lab Exercises

- Create Data Lake Store account and upload Data
- Create Hadoop Cluster with Data Lake as Primary Storage
- Create Data lake Analytics Cluster with Data Lake as Primary Storage

Chapter Topology

In this chapter we will add Data Lake Store to the topology.

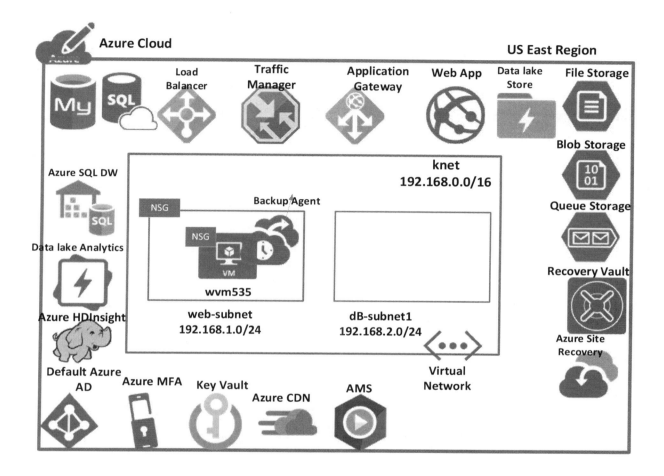

Azure Data lake Store

Azure Data Lake Store is an enterprise-wide hyper-scale storage repository for storing data of any size and type and performing analytics on the stored data.

Data Lake Store can scale throughput to support any size of analytic workload. You get massive throughput to run analytic jobs with thousands of concurrent executors which efficiently read and write hundreds of terabytes of data.

What can be done with Azure Data lake Store

1. It **stores data** by ingesting data from various sources including on-premises computer, Azure Blob Storage, Streamed Data, Relational Data and Web Server Data, Data associated with Azure HDInsight clusters
2. **Run analysis** on data stored in Data lake Store using big data applications. Currently, you can only use Azure HDInsight and Azure Data Lake Analytics to run data analysis jobs on the data stored in Data Lake Store.
3. Processed data can be **downloaded** and/or **exported** to SQL Data Warehouse using Polybase and Data Factory or to on-premises SQL Server or to other repositories.

The Figure below shows various sources from which data can be ingested in Data lake Store and Processing of Stored Data by applications.

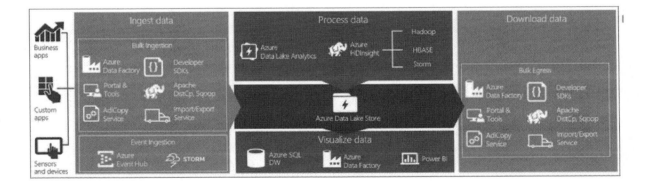

Stored Data can be downloaded or moved to other repository or computer to be analysed by applications such DW, Hive etc

Features of Data Lake Store

Built for Hadoop: The Azure Data Lake store is an Apache Hadoop file system (HDFS) compatible and works with the Hadoop ecosystem. Your existing HDInsight applications or services that use the WebHDFS API can easily integrate with Data Lake Store. Data Lake Store also exposes a WebHDFS-compatible REST interface for applications.

Unlimited storage: Azure Data Lake Store provides unlimited storage and is suitable for storing a variety of data for analytics. Data is stored durably by making multiple copies and there is no limit on the duration of time for which the data can be stored in the data lake.

Performance-tuned for big data analytics: Azure Data Lake Store is built for running large scale analytic systems that require massive throughput to query and analyze large amounts of data. The data lake spreads parts of a file over a number of individual storage servers. This improves the read throughput when reading the file in parallel for performing data analytics.

All types of Data: Azure Data Lake Store store any data in their native format, without requiring any prior transformations. Data Lake Store does not require a schema to be defined before the data is loaded, leaving it up to the individual analytic framework to interpret the data and define a schema at the time of the analysis. Being able to store files of arbitrary sizes and formats makes it possible for Data Lake Store to handle structured, semi-structured, and unstructured data.

Azure Data Lake, Stores data in folders and files.

Comparing Data lake Store and Azure Blob Storage

Features	Azure Data Lake Store	Azure Blob Storage
Storage Structure	Data Lake Store account contains folders, which in turn contains data stored as files.	Storage account has containers, which in turn has data in the form of blobs.
Storage	Optimized storage for big data analytics workloads.	General purpose object store for a wide variety of storage scenarios
Use Cases	Batch, interactive, streaming analytics and machine learning data such as log files, IoT data, click streams, large datasets	Any type of text or binary data, such as application back end, backup data, media storage for streaming and general purpose data.
File System	Hierarchical file system	Object store with flat namespace
Authentication	Based on Azure Active Directory Identities	Based on shared secrets - Account Access Keys and Shared Access Signature Keys.
Authentication Protocol	OAuth 2.0. Calls must contain a valid JWT (JSON Web Token) issued by Azure Active Directory	Hash-based Message Authentication Code (HMAC)
Analytics Workload Performance	Optimized performance for parallel analytics workloads. High Throughput and IOPS.	Not optimized for analytics workloads
Size limits	No limits on account sizes, file sizes or number of files	Limits are there.
Geo-redundancy	Locally-redundant (multiple copies of data in one Azure region)	Locally redundant (LRS), globally redundant (GRS), read-access globally redundant (RA-GRS).

Step by Step Using Azure Data Lake Store for big data processing

Big Data Processing involves four stages: Ingest data into Data Lake Store, Processing the data, Download data from Data Lake Store, Visualize data in Data Lake Store.

Ingest data into Data Lake Store: You can ingest data in Data Lake store from various sources using different tools.

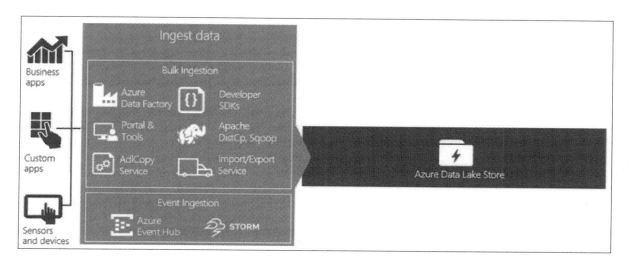

Process data stored in Data Lake Store: Once the data is available in Data Lake Store you can run analysis on that data using the supported big data applications. Currently, you can use Azure HDInsight and Azure Data Lake Analytics to run data analysis jobs on the data stored in Data Lake Store.

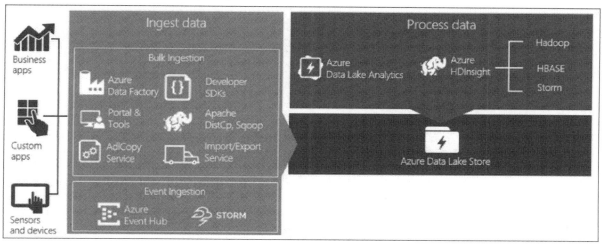

Download or move data from Data Lake Store

You can download or move processed data from Azure Data Lake Store to other destination for Processing.

You can move data to other repositories to interface with your existing data processing pipelines. For example, you might want to move data from Data Lake Store to Azure SQL Database or on-premises SQL Server for further analysis

You can download data to your local computer for processing in IDE environments while building application prototypes.

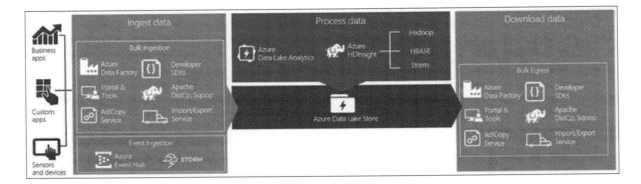

Visualize data in Data Lake Store

You can create visual representations of data stored in Data Lake Store using mix of Azure services. For example you can use Azure Data Factory to move data from Data Lake Store to Azure SQL Data Warehouse and then integrate Power BI with Azure SQL Data Warehouse to create visual representation of the data.

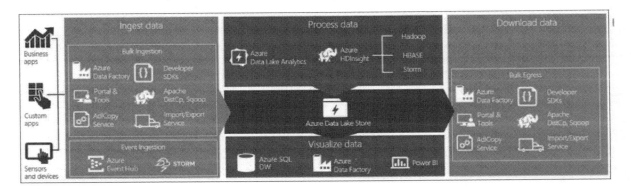

Architecting Microsoft Azure Solutions Study & Lab Guide Part 2: Exam 70-535

Integrating Data Lake Store with other Azure Services

Azure Data Lake Store can be used in conjunction with following Azure services to enable a wider range of scenarios:

Data Lake Store with Azure HDInsight

You can provision an Azure HDInsight cluster that uses Data Lake Store as the HDFS-compliant storage. Hadoop and Storm clusters can use Data Lake Store only as an additional storage. HBase clusters can use Data Lake Store as the default storage, or additional storage, or both.

Data Lake Store with Azure Data Lake Analytics

Azure Data Lake Analytics provisions resources and lets you do analytics on terabytes or even exabytes of data stored in a number of supported data sources. Data Lake Store is one of the supported Data source on which Azure Data Lake Analytics can perform Analytics.

Data Lake Analytics is specially optimized to work with Azure Data Lake Store - providing the highest level of performance, throughput, and parallelization for you big data workloads.

Data Lake Store with Azure Data Factory

Azure Data Factory can be used to orchestrate the ingestion of data from Azure tables, Azure SQL Database, Azure SQL DataWarehouse, Azure Storage Blobs, and on-premises databases to Azure Data Lake Store.

Data Lake Store with Azure Storage Blobs

You can copy data from Azure Blob Storage to Data lake store for analytics using command line tool AdlCopy.

Data Lake Store with Azure SQL Database

You can use Apache Sqoop to import and export data between Azure SQL Database and Data Lake Store. The Data can be used for Analytics.

Use Data Lake Store with Azure Stream Analytics

You can store output of Azure Stream Analytics Data in Data lake Store. Stored Data can be further analysed or Visualised with Power BI.

Data Lake Store with Power BI

You can use Power BI to import data from a Data Lake Store account to analyze and visualize the data.

Use Data Lake Store with Data Catalog

You can register data from Data Lake Store into the Azure Data Catalog to make the data discoverable throughout the organization.

Data Lake Store with SQL Server Integration Services (SSIS)

You can Load Data in Sql Server or SQl Database using the Azure Data Lake Store connection manager in SSIS to connect an SSIS package with Azure Data Lake Store.

Data Lake Store with SQL Data Warehouse

You can use PolyBase to load data from Azure Data Lake Store into SQL Data Warehouse.

Data Lake Store with Azure Event Hubs

You can use Azure Data Lake Store to archive and capture data received by Azure Event Hubs. You can then perform Analytics on Data using Data lake Analytics.

Exercise 22: Create Data Lake Store account and upload Data

Click + Create a Resource> Data + Analytics> Data lake Store> Create Data lake Store Blade opens>Fill as per requirement and click create.

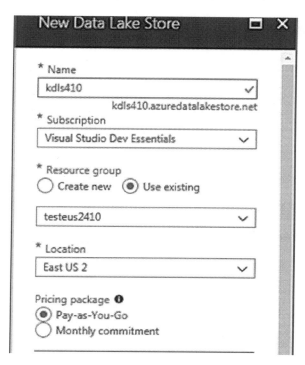

Figure below shows Data lake Store Account Dashboard

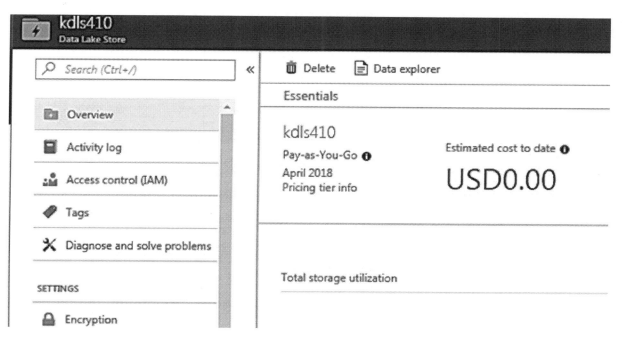

Create folders in Azure Data Lake Store account

Click Data Explorer in Dashboard

In Data lake Explorer click New Folder> Enter a Name>Click OK.

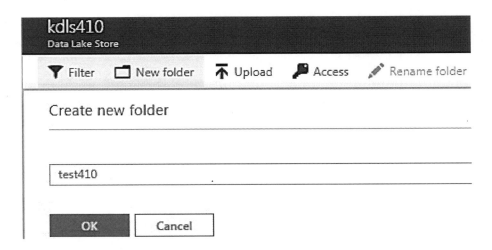

Upload data to Azure Data Lake Store account

In Data Explore Blade click upload> In upload Files blade click Folder icon in right and select your file to upload>Click Add Selected Files.

Exercise 23: Create Hadoop Cluster with Data Lake as Primary Storage

Click + Create a Resource> Data + Analytics> HDInsight> Create HDInsight Blade opens>Configure Basic Settings and click next.

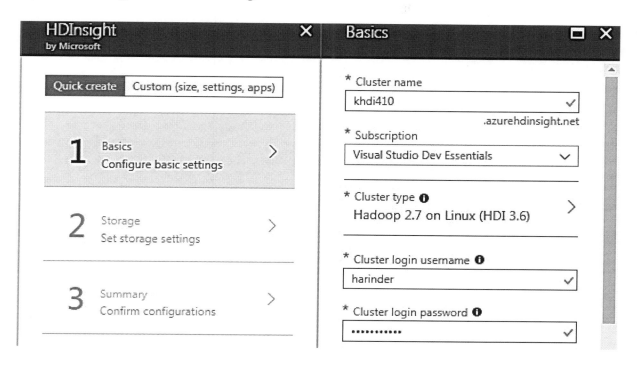

In Storage Settings> Select Data lake Store Account as Primary Storage type.

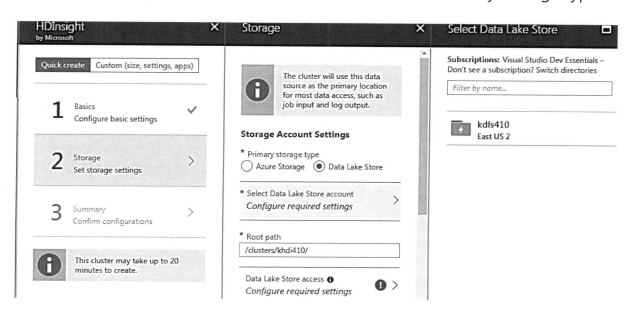

Using HDInsight you can perform Analytics on Data in Data lake Store.

Architecting Microsoft Azure Solutions Study & Lab Guide Part 2: Exam 70-535

Exercise 24: Create Data lake Analytics Cluster with Data Lake as Primary Storage

Click + Create a Resource> Data + Analytics> Click See All in top right>Select Data Lake Analytics> Click Create> Create Data Lake Analytics Blade opens>Select Data lake Store Account as your Primary Storage.

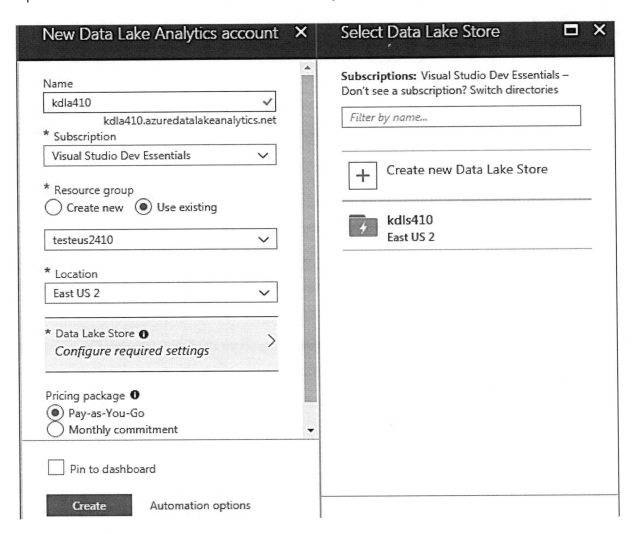

Using Data lake Analytics you can perform Analytics on Data in Data lake Store.

Azure Data lake Pricing

Azure Data lake Pricing depends upon following 2 components:

1. Storage used. Storage is available in pay-as-you-go and monthly commitment packages.
2. Transaction done against stored Data

Storage Pricing (Pay as You go model)

Usage	Price/Month
First 100 TB	$0.039 per GB
Next 100 TB to 1,000 TB	$0.038 per GB
Next 1,000 TB to 5,000 TB	$0.037 per GB
Over 5,000 TB	Contact MS Sales

Transaction prices

Usage	Price
Write operations (per 10,000)	$0.05
Read operations (per 10,000)	$0.004
Delete operations	Free

Data Catalog

Before we go into details of Data Catalog, let's discuss why we need it in first place. In 21st century information economy, Data is a critical asset for any organization. Data can be used by Decision Makers, Sales and Marketing team, R&D team & Production planning team to get a competitive advantage, predict consumer behaviour, Sales outcome or getting better product quickly in the market place etc.

In organisation Data is usually lying in disparate places.

Microsoft Azure Data Catalog is a fully managed cloud service that serves as a system of registration and system of discovery for enterprise data sources.

Azure Data Catalog is an enterprise-wide information metadata catalog. With Data Catalog, you register, discover, annotate (enrich) and connect to data assets.

Data Catalogue does not stores or imports Data. The data remains in its existing location, but a copy of its metadata is added to Data Catalog.

Data Catalog is designed to manage disparate information assets. Data Catalog makes it easy to find data assets, understand them, and connect to them with tools of their choice.

Data Catalog includes a crowdsourcing model of metadata and annotations. It is a single, central place for all of an organization's users to contribute their knowledge and Data Sources.

Design Nugget: You can have only one data catalog per organization (Microsoft Azure Active Directory domain).

Advantages

1. Data Catalog helps organizations get more value from their existing investments.
2. It reduces the time to gain insights from available data and increases the value to organizations.

Data Catalog Working in Brief

Data is discovered by registering data source with Data Catalog. The data remains in its existing location, but a copy of its metadata is added to Data Catalog, along with a reference to the data-source location. The metadata is also indexed to make each data source easily discoverable via search and understandable to the users who discover it.

After a data source has been registered, Data Assets are discovered. Discovery in Azure Data Catalog uses two primary mechanisms: searching and filtering. By using a combination of searching and filtering, you can quickly navigate the data sources that have been registered with Azure Data Catalog to discover the data assets you need.

After a data source has been registered, its metadata can then be enriched, either by the user who registered it or by other users in the enterprise. Any user can annotate a data source by providing descriptions, tags, or other metadata, such as documentation and processes for requesting data source access.

Organisational users can quickly find data that matches their needs, understand the data to evaluate its fitness for the purpose, and consume the data by opening the data source in their tool and application of their choice.

At the same time, users can contribute to the catalog by tagging, documenting, and annotating data sources that have already been registered. They can also register new data sources, which can then be discovered, understood, and consumed by the community of catalog users.

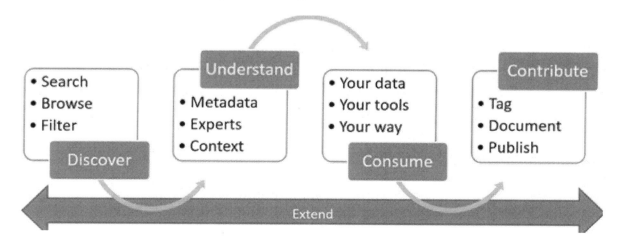

Data Sources

The following table shows all data sources that are supported by the Data Catalog.

You can publish metadata by using a public API or a click-once registration tool, or by manually entering information directly to the Azure Data Catalog web portal.

Azure Data Lake Store directory
Azure Data Lake Store file
Azure Blob storage
Azure Storage directory
Azure Storage table
HDFS directory
HDFS file
Hive table
Hive view
MySQL table
MySQL view
Oracle Database table
Oracle Database view
Azure SQL Data Warehouse table
SQL Data Warehouse view
SQL Server Analysis Services dimension
SQL Server Analysis Services KPI
SQL Server Analysis Services measure
SQL Server Analysis Services table
SQL Server Reporting Services report
SQL Server table
SQL Server view
Teradata table
Teradata view

Salesforce object
SharePoint list
Azure Cosmos DB collection
Generic ODBC table
Generic ODBC view
Cassandra table
Cassandra view
Sybase table
Sybase view
MongoDB table
MongoDB view
HTTP endpoint
HTTP file
OData entity set
OData function
PostgreSQL table
PostgreSQL view
SAP HANA view
FTP Directory
FTP File
HTTP report
SAP HANA view
DB2 table
DB2 view

Step By Step creating and working with Data Catalog

1. **Provision Data Catalog**: In this step Data Catalog is provisioned.
2. **Register data assets**: In this procedure, you register data assets with the data catalog. Registration is the process of extracting key structural metadata such as names, types, and locations from the data source and copying that metadata to the catalog.
3. **Discover data assets**: In this step you use the Azure Data Catalog portal to discover data assets that were registered in the previous step.
4. **Annotate data assets**: In step you provide annotations (information such as descriptions, tags, documentation, or experts) for the data assets.
5. **Connect to data assets**: In this step you open data assets in integrated client tools (such as Excel and SQL Server Data Tools) and a non-integrated tool (SQL Server Management Studio).
6. **Manage data assets**: In this step you set up security for your data assets. Data Catalog does not give users access to the data itself. The owner of the data source controls data access.
7. **Remove data assets**: In this step you learn how to remove data assets from the data catalog. This step is optional.

Provision Data Catalog & Register a Data Source

1. Go Data Catalog home page @ https://azure.microsoft.com/en-us/services/data-catalog/>Click get Started.

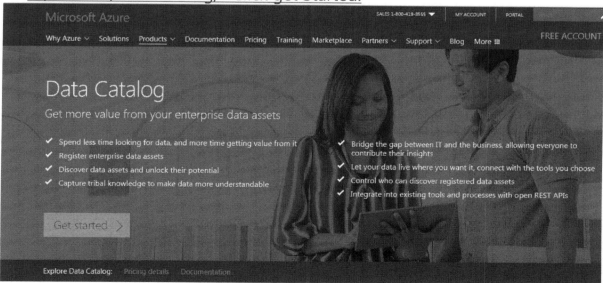

How to Start with Azure Data Catalog

Register Organisation's Central high-value data sources: Every organisation has company wide Data sources which are managed centrally by respective verticals. Central IT can start Data Catalog by registering and annotating common enterprise data sources.

Register team-based data sources: Different teams have useful, line-of-business data sources. Get started with Azure Data Catalog by identifying and registering key data sources used by many different teams, and capture the team's tribal knowledge in Azure Data Catalog annotations.

Self-service business intelligence - Teams spend much time combining data from multiple sources. Register and annotate data sources in a central location to eliminate a manual data source discovery process.

Data Catalog Editions and Pricing

Free - Supports unlimited users and 5,000 registered data assets; registered data assets are discoverable by all users.

Standard - Supports unlimited users and 100,000 registered data assets; includes asset-level authorization restricting visibility as needed.

Features & Pricing	Free	Standard
Max number of Users	Unlimited	Unlimited
Max number of Catalog Objects or Registered Data Assets	5000	100000
Azure AD Authorization	NA	Yes
Price	Free	$1 per/user/month

Azure Data Factory

Azure Data Factory is a Managed Azure Service which provides Data Orchestration as a service. Azure Data Factory helps you create, schedule, monitor and manage data pipelines. A data pipeline consists of activities which can **move data** between on-premises and cloud data stores and **transform data** to produce trusted information.

Azure Data Factory ingests data from Multiple Data sources (on-premises or cloud). It then processes, transforms and moves Data to different compute and storage services (HDInsight, Spark, Azure Data Lake Analytics and Azure Machine Learning) using Data Pipeline. The Data is then published to be consumed by end users and applications.

The figure below shows various stages of Data as it is moved through Azure Data Factory Managed Data Pipeline.

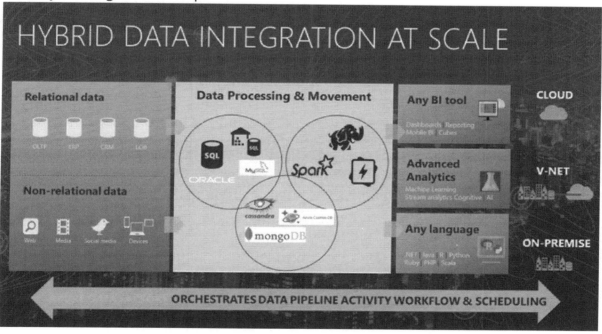

The benefit of Data Factory is that it **automates the ingestion of Data** (on-premises and Cloud) using built in connectors and the **loading of Data** to various Azure Services (HDInsight Hadoop, Azure Data Lake Analytics and Azure Machine Learning) using managed Data Pipelines.

Data Factory Working

The pipelines (data-driven workflows) in Azure Data Factory typically perform the following four steps as shown in the figure below.

Connect & Collect: Enterprises have data of various types - structured, unstructured, and semi-structured. Data is located in disparate sources - on-premises and in the cloud.

Without Data Factory, enterprises must build write custom services to integrate these data sources and processing.

Using Built in connectors in Data Factory, Data from on-premises and cloud is ingested into Data Factory pipeline to be moved to a centralization data store in the cloud for further analysis. For example, you can collect data in Azure Data Lake Store and transform the data later by using an Azure Data Lake Analytics compute service.

Transform and enrich: After data is present in a centralized data store in the cloud, process or transform the collected data by using compute services such as HDInsight Hadoop, Spark, Data Lake Analytics, and Machine Learning.

Publish: After the raw data has been refined into a business-ready consumable form, load the data into Azure Data Warehouse, Azure SQL Database, Azure CosmosDB, or whichever analytics engine your business users can point to from their business intelligence tools.

Monitor: After you have successfully built and deployed your data integration pipeline, providing business value from refined data, monitor the scheduled activities and pipelines for success and failure rates. Azure Data Factory has built-in support for pipeline monitoring via Azure Monitor, API, PowerShell, Microsoft Operations Management Suite, and health panels on the Azure portal.

Data Factory Components

Pipeline: A pipeline is a logical grouping of activities that performs a unit of work. Together, the activities in a pipeline perform a task. Advantage of pipeline is that the pipeline allows you to manage the activities as a set instead of managing each one individually.

Activity: Activities represent a processing step in a pipeline. The activities in a pipeline define actions to perform on your data. Data Factory supports three types of activities: data movement activities, data transformation activities, and control activities.

Dataset: **Dataset** simply points or references the data you want to use in your activities as inputs and outputs. An input dataset represents the input for an activity in the pipeline and an output dataset represents the output for the activity.

Linked Service: A linked service links a data store or a compute resource to the data factory. Linked services are much like connection strings, which define the connection information needed for Data Factory to connect to external resources. Linked services are used for two following purposes in Data Factory:
* To represent a **data store** that includes an on-premises SQL Server database, Oracle database, file share, or Azure blob storage account etc.
* To represent a **compute resource** that can host the execution of an activity.

The following diagram shows the relationships among pipeline, activity, dataset, and linked service in Data Factory:

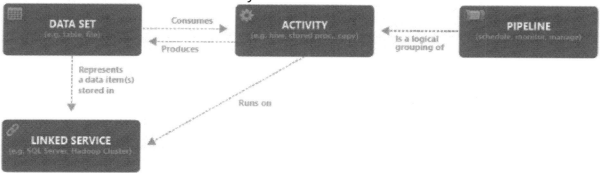

Design Nugget: Before you create a dataset, you must create a **linked service to** link your data store to the data factory.

Architecting Microsoft Azure Solutions Study & Lab Guide Part 2: Exam 70-535

Activity Types

Data Movement Activity: It is a Copy Activity in Data Factory to copy data from a source data store to a sink data store. Data from any source can be written to any sink. Following is the **partial list** of data stores supported by Data Factory.

Category	Data Store	Source Data store	Sink Data Store
Azure	Azure Blob Storage	✓	✓
Azure	Azure Cosmos DB	✓	✓
Azure	Azure Data Lake Store	✓	✓
Azure	Azure Database for MySQL	✓	
Azure	Azure SQL Database	✓	✓
Azure	Azure SQL Data Warehouse	✓	✓
Database	Amazon Redshift	✓	
Database	DB2	✓	
Database	MariaDB	✓	
Database	SAP HANA	✓	✓
Database	SQL Server	✓	✓
Database	Oracle	✓	✓

Data transformation activities: Data Transformation Activity in Data Factory is used to transform Data ingested. For example, you may use a copy activity to copy data from an on-premises SQL Server to an Azure Blob Storage. Then, use a Hive activity that runs a Hive script on an Azure HDInsight cluster to **process/transform data** from the blob storage to produce output data. Following is the partial list of Data Transformation Activities.

Data transformation activity	Compute environment
Hive	HDInsight
Pig	HDInsight
MapReduce	HDInsight
Stored Procedure	Azure SQL, Azure SQL DW, SQL Server
U-SQL	Azure Data Lake Analytics

Control activities: Control Activities are control plane activities on pipelines.

Control activity	Description
Execute Pipeline Activity	Allows a Data Factory pipeline to invoke another pipeline.
Lookup Activity	

Ingesting & Transforming Unstructured and Structured Data using Azure Data Factory (ADF)

Figure below shows Azure Data Factory ingesting Structured and Unstructured Data.

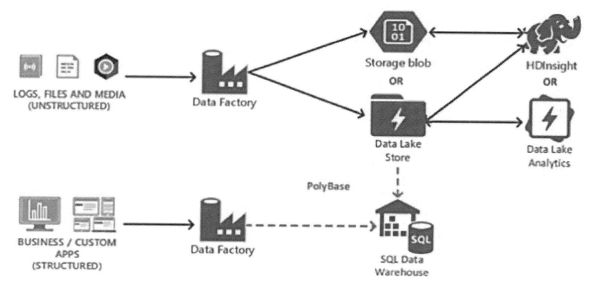

Loading and Transforming Unstructured Data: Using Built-in connectors Azure Data Factory copies data from source Data store to sink Data store which is in this case is Blob Storage or Data lake Store as shown in figure above. You can now use Data Transformation activity such as Hive activity or MapReduce or U-SQL activity to perform analytics on the data using HDInsight or Data lake Analytics Cluster.

Loading and Transforming structured Data: Using Built-in connectors Azure Data Factory copies data from source Data store to sink Data store which is in this case is a staging Blob storage. Data factory will use Polybase to load data from staging Data store to Azure SQL Data Warehouse. You can now use Data Transformation activity such as query activities to perform analytics on the data using SQL Data Warehouse compute cluster.

The Biggest advantage of using Azure Data Factory is that it automates ingestion and Loading of data. Without Data Factory ingestion and movement of Data between various Azure services would be a manual process and would require specialised skills.

Chapter 8 Azure IOT Solutions

This Chapter covers following

- Azure Stream Analytics
- Azure IOT Hub
- Azure IOT Hub Device Provisioning Service (DPS)
- Azure Event Hubs
- Azure IoT Edge
- Azure Time Series Insight
-

This Chapter Covers following Case Studies

- Real Time Prediction of breakdown of Industrial Machinery using Stream Analytics and Machine Learning
- Visualize real-time IoT Device Data using Power BI
- Visualize real-time IoT Device Data using Azure Web App

This Chapter Covers following Lab Exercises

- Deploy Stream Analytics Job to Process Real Time Data
- Deploying IOT Hub
- Add & Connect IoT Device to IoT Hub
- Sending output of IOT Hub to Stream Analytics
- IOT Hub Device Provisioning Service Setup
- Link the IoT Hub with Device Provisioning service
- Create Event Hub Namespace
- Create Event Hub
- Configure Event Producers to Send Events to Event Hub
- Send Output of Event Hub to Stream Analytics
- Deploying IoT Edge in 5 Steps
- Create Time Series Insight Environment

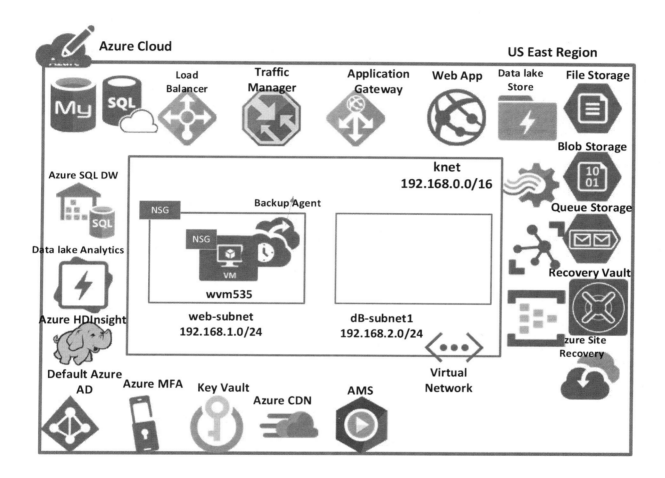

Chapter Topology

In this chapter we will add Azure Stream Analytics, IoT Hub, Event Hub, IOT Edge and Time Series Analytics to the topology.
Please Note IOT edge and Time Series Analytics are not shown in the diagram.

Note: In further chapter we will not be showing Chapter Topology as there is no space left in the Diagram.

Azure Stream Analytics

Azure Stream Analytics is Managed stream processing service which performs real time analytics on streaming data. Azure Stream Analytics is an event-processing engine in the cloud that provides insights from data generated by devices, sensors, cloud infrastructure services, and applications in **real-time**.

With out-of-the-box integration for Azure IoT Hub and Azure Event Hubs, Azure Stream Analytics can simultaneously ingest and process millions of real-time events per second and can deliver actionable insights or alerts using power rich visual dashboards, and kick off actions to other services.
Azure Stream Analytics can also connect with Azure Blob service to ingest historical data.

Azure Stream Analytics transforms incoming data, triggers an alert when a specific error or condition appears in the stream and can displays this real-time data in your dashboard using Power BI.

Figure below show Stream Analytics Service processing input streaming data from IOT devices and applications via integration with Event Hubs and IOT Hub.

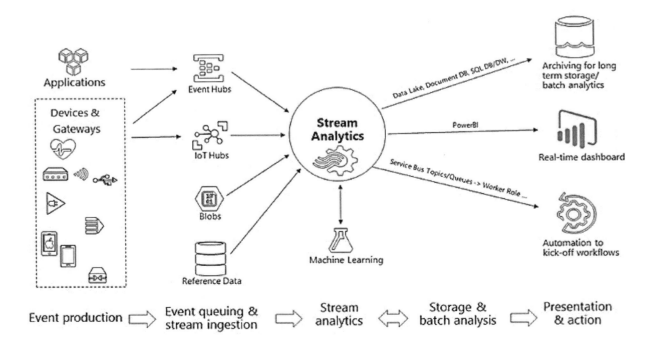

Stream Analytics Service Output

Stream Analytics results can be written from Stream Analytics to Azure Storage Blobs or Tables, Azure SQL DB, Azure Data Lake Stores, DocumentDB, Event Hubs, Azure Service Bus Topics or Queues. Stream Analytics output can be send to Power BI where it can graphically visualize Streaming Data. Output of Stream analytics can be further processed by workflows, used in batch analytics via Azure HDInsight or processed again as a series of events.

Advantages of Stream Analytics

1. Stream Analytics enables real-time insights on data as business events occur. It also stores this information in a repository for historical analysis at a later time.
2. Stream analytics have Pre-built adaptors to connect to various Azure Services like SQL Database, Blob Storage, Data lake Store, Azure Machine Learning, Event Hub, IoT Hub, Cosmos DB, Power BI etc obviating the need to write software code.
3. Stream Analytics processes data at a high throughput with predictable results and no data loss.
4. There is no hardware or other up-front costs. There is no time-consuming installation or setup activities. You can set up and run Stream analytics in minutes.

Stream Analytics Use Cases

1. Personalized, real-time stock-trading analysis and alerts offered by financial services companies.
2. Real-time fraud detection.
3. Data and identity protection services.
4. Reliable ingestion and analysis of data generated by sensors and actuators embedded in physical objects (Internet of Things, or IoT)
5. Web clickstream analytics
6. Customer relationship management (CRM) applications issuing alerts when customer experience within a time frame is degraded.

Exercise 25: Deploy Stream Analytics Job to Process Real Time Data

1. Prerequisite: One of the source (Event Hub or IOT Hub etc) for Real Time data ingestion is already configured. This will be shown in Exercise 26 where will send output of IoT Hub to Stream Analytics Job.
2. In Azure Portal Click +Create a resource> Analytics> Stream Analytics Job> New Stream Analytics Job Blade opens>Fill as per req and click create.

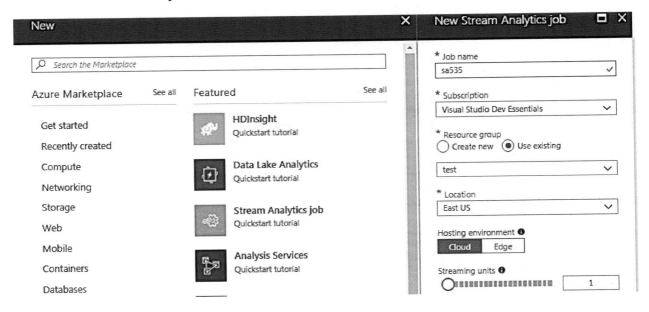

3. Figure below shows Stream Analytics Dashboard.

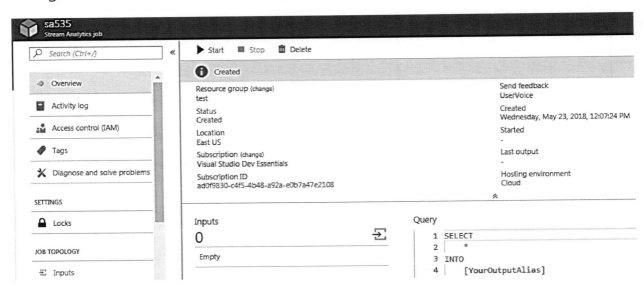

4. **Configure input for the stream analytics job** >Click input in left pane in Stream Analytics Dashboard>Click + Add Stream Input. You can see below you have 3 options to input Data: Event Hub, IOT Hub and Blob Storage.

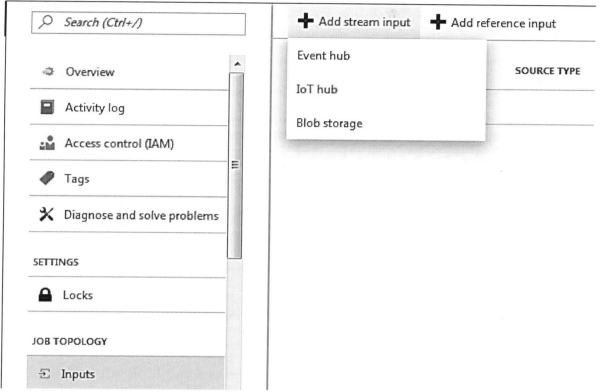

Lets say we selected IOT Hub. Select The IoT Hub from the drop down box. In Exercise 28 we will add IOT Hub to Stream Analytics and query IOT Device Data.

5. **Quering the IoT Device Data in Stream Analytics**: Click query in left pane of Stream analytics Job Dashboard.

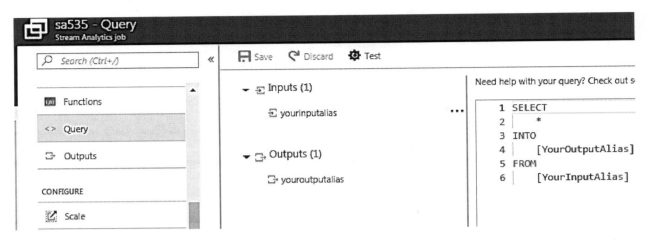

6. **Configure output for the stream analytics job** >Click outputs in left pane in Stream Analytics Dashboard>Click + Add. You can see below you have multiple options to output Stream Analytics Data.

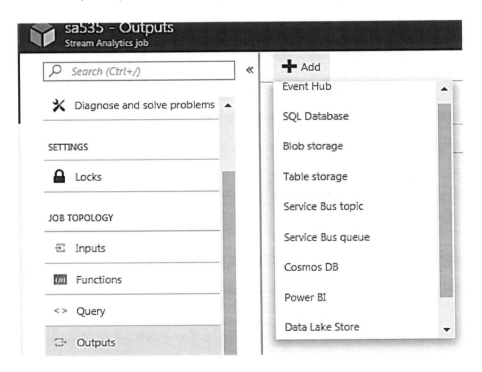

Real Time Analytics with Stream Analytics

Stream Analytics enables real-time insights on data as business events occur. It also stores this information in a repository for historical analysis at a later time.

Figure below shows real time data being ingested into Stream Analytics through IoT Hub. Using continuous query you can get results in real time as business event occurs.

You can also do Analytics on historical data from Blob Storage.

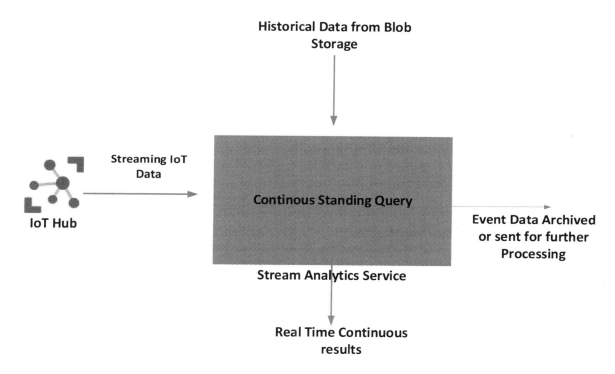

The advantage of Real Time Analytics is that you can take corrective actions in real time as business event occurs.

Case Study 4: Real Time Prediction of breakdown of Industrial Machinery using Stream Analytics and Machine Learning

Machine learning is a technique of data science that helps computers **learn from existing data** in order to **forecast future behaviors, outcomes, and trends.**

Azure Machine Learning is a fully managed cloud based predictive analytic service. Azure Machine Learning can make use of streaming data to enable real-time prediction.

Combining the real-time analytic capabilities of Azure Stream Analytics with the real-time predictive analytics capabilities of Azure Machine Learning can help businesses rapidly deploy data solutions to support complex information challenges.

Figure below shows Machine health Sensor Data from Industrial Machinery being ingested into Event Hub.

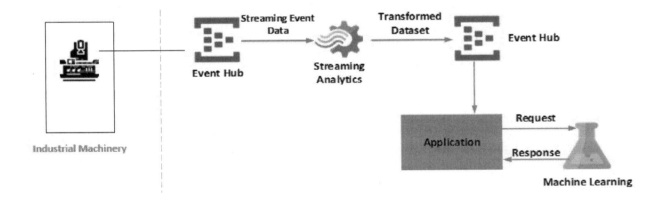

Solution Working

Event Sensor will send maintenance data from Industrial machines in real-time to Event Hub. Azure Streaming Analytics will analyze and transform the Sensor data in real-time. This transformed and filtered data will be consumed by application through event hub. Machine learning will analyze this data in real time to predict the breakdown of the Machine.

Azure Stream Analytics Scalability & Pricing

Azure Stream Analytics is priced by the number of streaming units required to process the data into the service.

A Standard Streaming Unit is a blend of compute, memory and throughput. Required Streaming units can be selected through the Stream Analytics Dashboard in Azure portal or Stream Analytics management APIs as shown below.

Streaming Units can be used to scale out a job in order to achieve higher throughput. Depending on the complexity of the query and the throughput required, more streaming units may be necessary to achieve your application's performance requirements.

Stream Analytics can handle up to 1 GB of incoming data per second.

Streaming units are billed hourly, based on the maximum number of units selected during this hour.

Usage	Price
Streaming Unit	$0.11/hour

Azure IOT Hubs

Azure IOT Hub is the ingestion platform for million of IOT devices. Azure IOT Hub is a fully managed service that enables reliable and secure **bidirectional** communications between IOT devices and IoT Hub.

IOT devices can use standard or custom protocols including HTTP, Advanced Message Queuing Protocol (AMQP) and MQ Telemetry Transport (MQTT) to connect with IOT Hub.

Azure IOH Hub Features

Bi-directional communication: IOT Hub securely connect your Internet of Things (IOT) assets and provides Bi-directional Communication between IoT Hub and IoT devices.

Scale: Azure IoT Hub scales to millions of simultaneously connected devices and millions of events per second.

Per-device authentication: You can provision each device with its own security key to enable it to connect to IoT Hub. The IoT Hub identity registry stores device identities and keys. Enables secure communications and access control using per-device security keys or X.509 certificates.

Device Twins: Manage your IOT devices at scale with device management using Device Twins. Device twins are JSON documents that store device state information like metadata, configurations, and conditions. IoT Hub maintains a device twin for each device that you connect to IoT Hub.

Integrate IoT Hub events into your business applications using Event Grid: IoT Hub integrates with Azure Event Grid. Use this integration to configure other Azure services or third-party applications to listen for IoT Hub events. Azure Event Grid enables you to react quickly to critical events in a reliable, scalable, and secure manner.

Edge Intelligence: Take advantage of edge intelligence with the IoT Edge. IoT Edge analyzes IoT device data at the edge instead of in the cloud. IoT edge device perform computing & Analytics locally before the data is sent to the cloud.

Device provisioning: The IoT Hub Device Provisioning Service enables zero-touch, just-in-time device provisioning to the right IoT hub without requiring human intervention, enabling you to provision millions of devices.

Azure IOT Hub Architecture

The following diagram shows a typical IoT solution architecture. In this architecture, IoT devices collect data that they send to IoT Hub. The IoT Hub makes the data available for processing by other back-end services from where data is delivered to other line-of-business applications or to human operators through a dashboard or other presentation device.

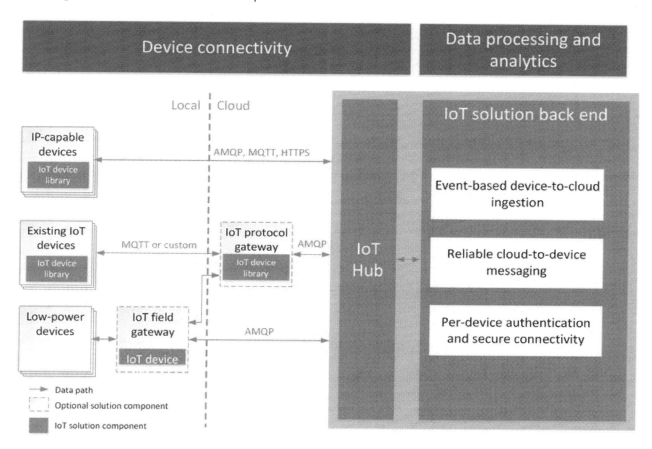

IOT Devices

IP Capable IoT Devices connect directly with IoT Hub using AMQP, HTTP or MQTT Protocol.

IP Devices using custom protocol connect to IoT Hub through Protocol Gateway. Non IP capable IoT Devices or low powered IoT Devices connect to IoT hub using Field Gateway.

Azure IOT Gateways

Gateway act as intermediary between your device and IOT Hub. A gateway in an IOT solution is typically either a **protocol gateway** that is deployed in the cloud or a **field gateway** that is deployed locally with your devices.

Protocol Gateway

A protocol gateway performs protocol translation, for example Custom Protocol to AMQP and is deployed in Cloud. It can also be deployed in field.

Field Gateway

Field Gateway connects group of Low power and non IP capable IOT devices to IoT Hub. This helps in reducing cost of IoT devices. Low power IoT Devices which have no connection to Electricity outlet can operate on batteries for long time.

A field gateway can also run analytics on the edge, make time-sensitive decisions to reduce latency, provide device management services, enforce security and privacy constraints and can also perform protocol translation.

Figure below shows IoT devices connecting to IoT Hub through IoT Field Gateway..

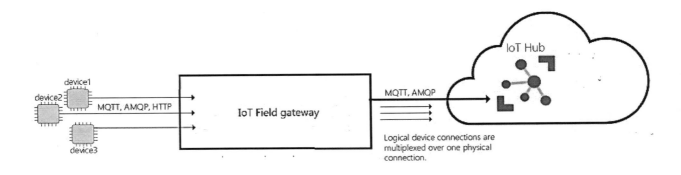

IoT Hub as Part of Real Time Streaming Solution

Figure below shows IoT Hub placement in real time streaming solution. This is one of the solution. You can have other solutions involving IoT Hub. For Example Stream Analytics can be replaced by HDInsight Kafka Cluster. Another option is Time series Insight environment.

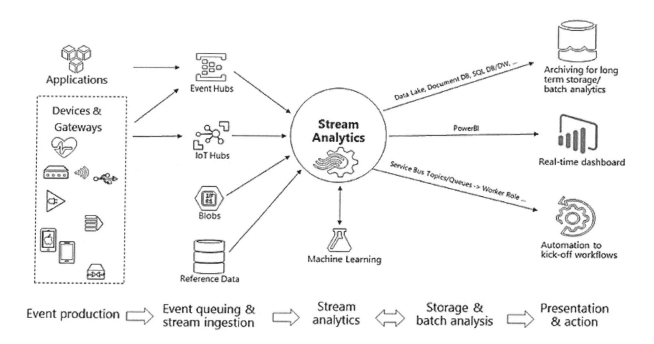

IoT Hub acts as ingestion platform for events from IoT devices. IoT Hub also does device management of IoT devices.

IoT Hub will ingest real time data into Azure Stream Analytics Platform. You can query IoT data in Stream Analytics. You can Output IoT data from SA to User Dashboard using Power BI.

IoT data from SA can go to Azure Storage for Archiving or to Application.

For Example Smart Electricity Meters installed in homes can sent data to IoT Hub. IoT Hub will then ingest IoT devices data in SA in real time. Electricity Billing application will pick IoT Data from SA for generating Electricity Bills, Troubleshooting and Diagnostics.

Exercise 26: Deploying IOT Hub

1. Login to Azure Portal @ https://portal.azure.com
2. Click +Create a Resource> Internet of Things> IoT Hub> Create IoT Hub Blade opens>Fill as per requirement and click create.

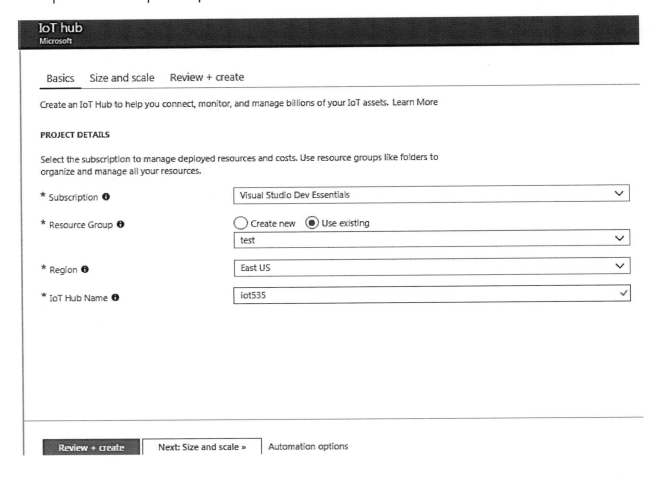

Following Properties are shown in Size and scale. We selected Free tier and all default values.

IOT Hub Units define how many messages IoT Hub can process per day. For Example each unit of the S1 edition allows up to 400,000 messages per day across all connected devices. If you have a requirement 600,000 messages per day from all IOT devices then you can use 2 IoT hub units of S1 edition.

Device to Cloud partition: Number of Partitions relates the device-to-cloud messages to the number of simultaneous readers of these messages.

Exercise 27: Add & Connect IoT Device to IoT Hub in 2 steps using identity Registry

Every IoT hub has an identity registry that stores information about the devices permitted to connect to the IoT hub. Before a device can connect to an IoT hub, there must be an entry for that device in the IoT hub's identity registry. A device must also authenticate with the IoT hub based on credentials stored in the identity registry.

Adding IoT Device is a 2 step process. First create IoT device-id and also copy device-id connection string. Second add IoT device-id connection string to IoT device in the field.

1. Go to IoT Hub Dashboard>click IoT devices in left pane>In right pane Click + Add> Add Device blade opens> enter req information and click save.

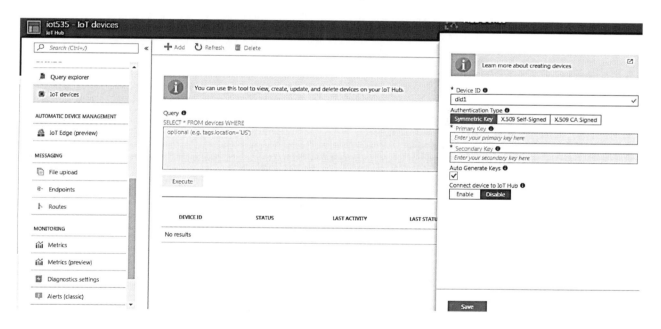

The above option provides creating per IOT device identity.

You can also perform bulk exports of device identity to IoT Hub's identity registry.

2. After the device is created click the device ID in the IoT Devices pane and copy Primary Connection string.

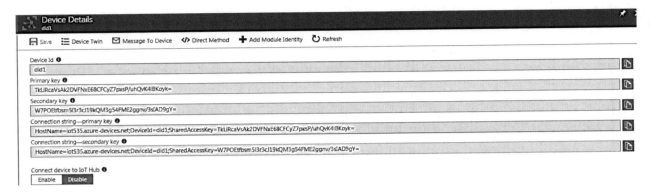

3. Add the connection string to IOT Device in the field.

Note: 3 options in top Pane for Managing IoT Devices. Device Twin, Message to Device and Direct Method.

Exercise 28: Sending output of IOT Hub to Stream Analytics

1. Go to Stream Analytics Job Dashboard created in Exercise 25>Click input in left pane> In Right Pane click +Add Stream Input and select IOt Hub> New input blade opens>Enter as per your req and click save.

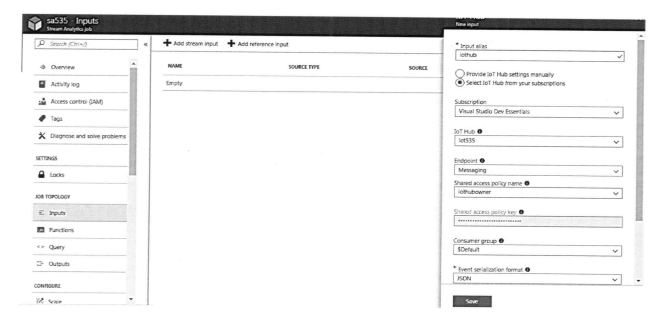

2. **Query the IoT Device data received from IoT Hub**: Click Query in left pane> In right pane you can enter your query to do real time analytics on IoT device data.

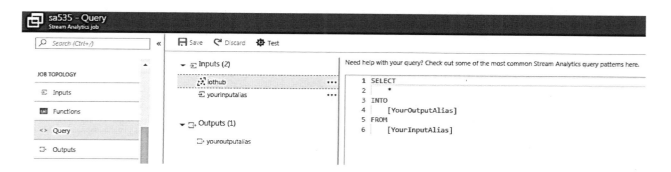

IoT Device Management

IoT device Management can be done from IoT Hub Dashboard using Device Twin, Message to Device and Direct Method option.

Direct Method

With direct method you can initiate device management actions on IoT devices such as reboot, factory reset, and firmware update from the cloud. Direct methods follow a request-response pattern and are meant for communications that require immediate confirmation of their result. For example, interactive control of the device such as turning on a fan.

Device Twins

Device twins are JSON documents that store device state information including metadata, configurations, and conditions. Azure IoT Hub maintains a device twin for each device that connect to IoT Hub. Device Twins perform following Device Management action on IoT devices:

1. Store device-specific metadata in the cloud. For example, the deployment location of a vending machine.
2. Report current IoT device state information such as available capabilities and conditions from your device app. For example whether a device is connected to IoT hub over cellular or WiFi.
3. Query your device metadata, configuration, or state.

You can do Iot device management from IoT Devices pane in IoT Hub dashboard.

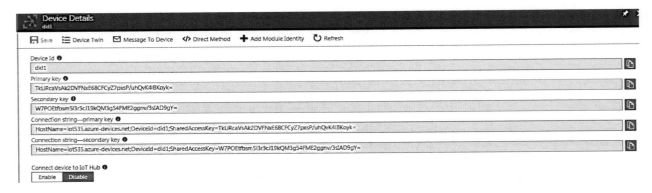

IoT Hub Endpoints

IoT hub exposes a set of built-in endpoints your solution back end can use to communicate with your devices.

By default, IoT Hub routes all messages which do not match any other routes to the built-in endpoint.

IOT Hub Custom Endpoints: Custom Endpoints link existing Azure services in your subscription to your IoT hub. IoT Hub currently supports the following Azure services as Custom endpoints:

Azure Storage containers
Event Hubs
Service Bus Queues
Service Bus Topics.

IOT Hub can route IOT device messages and Data to Custom Endpoints.

To Add Custom Endpoint: Click Endpoints in left Pane> In right pane click +Add > Custom Endpoint Blade> Choose your endpoint and click ok.

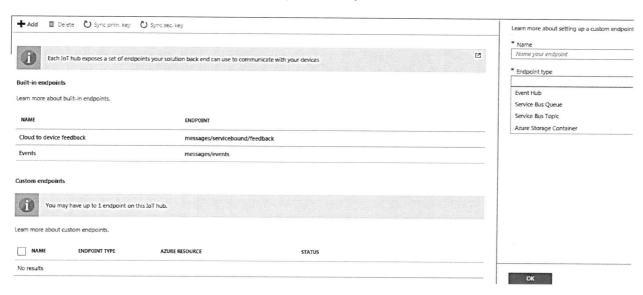

Consumer Groups in IoT Hub

Consumer Groups are used by applications such as Stream Analytics and Web App to pull data independently from Azure IoT Hub. Every IoT hub is created with a default consumer group.

To Add Consumer group: Click Endpoints in left Pane> In right pane click Events>Under Consumer groups enter a name and click save.

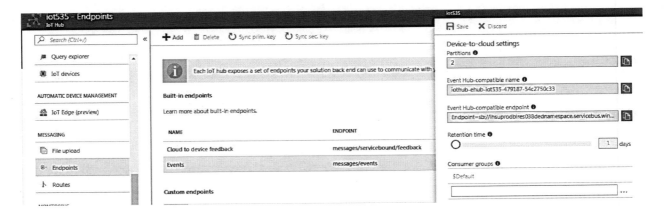

Case Study 5: Visualize real-time IoT Device Data using Power BI

Power BI is a Business Intelligence tool from Microsoft. Power BI give graphical view of the data.

Figure below shows Architecture of the setup.

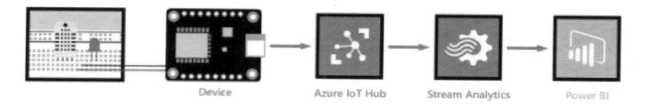

Device   Azure IoT Hub   Stream Analytics   Power BI

Brief Working of the Setup

IoT devices in the field will inject data generated by devices into IoT Hub. In IoT Hub create consumer Groups or use default consumer group. Consumer groups are used by applications to pull data from Azure IoT Hub.

Create Stream Analytic Job and add Iot Hub as input to Stream Analytics Job. Stream Analytics will read data from IoT Hub using consumer groups. Consumer Groups are added in IoT Hub and are used by applications like Stream Analytics to pull data from Azure IoT Hub.
Add Power BI as output to Stream Analytics job and specify Power BI workspace name and Dataset name.
Run the Stream Analytics Job.

Sign in to your Power BI account. Go to the group workspace that you set when you created the output for the Stream Analytics job. Visualize your IoT Data graphically in Power BI.

Case Study 6: Visualize real-time IoT Device Data using Azure Web App

Web Apps is a fully managed compute platform that is optimized for hosting websites and web applications. Web Apps is a managed VM with pre-installed web server and an option to choose application framework (You can choose from Dot Net, PHP, Node.js, Python & Java).

Figure below shows Architecture of the setup.

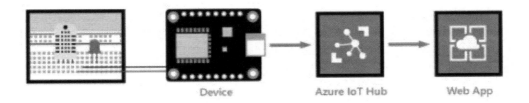

Device   Azure IoT Hub   Web App

Brief Working of the Setup

IoT devices in the field will inject data generated by devices into IoT Hub. In IoT Hub add consumer Groups or use default consumer group. Consumer groups are used by applications to pull data from Azure IoT Hub.

Create Web App. In Web App Dashboard click Application settings and in Right pane under App settings add following Key Value Pairs:

Key	Value
Azure.IoT.IoTHub.ConnectionString	From IoT Device Pane
Azure.IoT.IoTHub.ConsumerGroup	The name of the consumer group that you add to your IoT hub

Upload IoT Data Monitoring Application to Web App. Web Application will read real time data from IoT Hub using consumer group. Web application will process the data and will show the result in the Web Browser.

IOT Hub Tiers & Pricing

IOT Hub comes in Free, Basic and Standard Tier.

Feature	Basic	Standard
Device-to-cloud telemetry	✓	✓
Per-device identity	✓	✓
Message Routing, Event Grid Integration	✓	✓
HTTP, AMQP, MQTT Protocols	✓	✓
File upload from devices	✓	✓
Device Provisioning Service (DPS) support	✓	✓
Monitoring and diagnostics		✓
Cloud-to-device messaging		✓
Device Management, Device Twin		✓
IoT Edge		✓

Free Tier

Edition	Messages/Day/Hub Unit	Message Size	Pricing
F1	8,000	0.5 KB	Free

Basic Tier

Edition	Messages/Day/ Hub Unit	Message Size	Pricing
B1	4,00,000	4 KB	$10
B2	60,00,000	4 KB	$50
B3	3000,00,000	4 KB	$500

Standard Tier

Edition	Messages/Day/ Hub Unit	Message Size	Pricing
S1	4,00,000	4 KB	$25
S2	60,00,000	4 KB	$250
S3	3000,00,000	4 KB	$2500

The Free edition is suitable for gaining familiarity and testing out the capabilities.
S1 & B1 edition is for IoT solutions that generate relatively small amounts of data.
S2 & B2 edition is suitable for IoT solutions that generate large amounts of data.
S3 & B3 is suitable for IoT solutions that generate very large amounts of data.

Scaling IOT Hub Tiers

IOT Hub Units define how many messages per day can be processed by IoT Hub. Maximum number of messages an IoT Hub can process per day is determined by the **tier** selected and number of IoT Hub units. Table Below shows Max number of Hub Units available with Standard tier.

Edition	Messages/Day/IOT Hub Unit	Max IoT Hub Units
S1	4,00,000	200
S2	60,00,000	200
S3	3000,00,000	10

For Example each unit of the S1 edition allows up to 400,000 messages per day across all connected devices. If you have a requirement 600,000 messages per day from all IOT devices then you can use 2 IoT Hub units of S1 edition.

Scaling IOT Hub Units: In IoT Hub Dashboard click Pricing and Scaling in left Pane> Increase the Hub unit as per your requirement> Click Save. You can also change the pricing tier here if required.

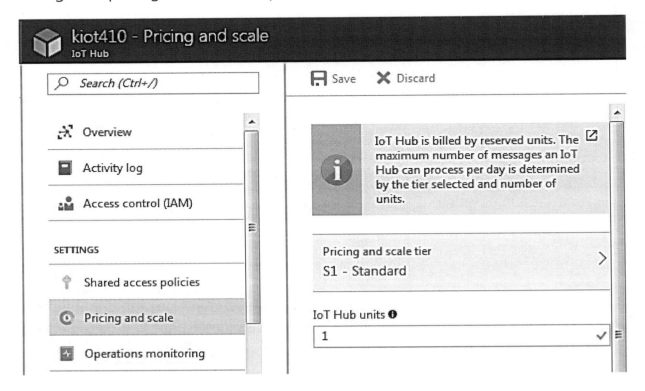

IOT Hub Device Provisioning Service (DPS)

The IoT Hub Device Provisioning Service is a helper service for IoT Hub that enables zero-touch and just-in-time provisioning of millions of IoT devices in a secure and scalable manner.

Device Provisioning Service reduces the time to deploy IoT devices and lowers the risk of manual error by automating provisioning steps.

Features of Device Provisioning Service

1. It enables Zero-touch provisioning without hardcoding IoT Hub connection information at the factory (initial setup).
2. Connecting devices to their owner's IoT solution based on sales transaction data (multitenancy).
3. Connecting a device to the IoT hub with the lowest latency (geo-sharding).
4. Re-provisioning based on a change in the device.

Working of Device Provisioning Service

Figure below shows DPS working. **Only first step is manual and rest are automated.**

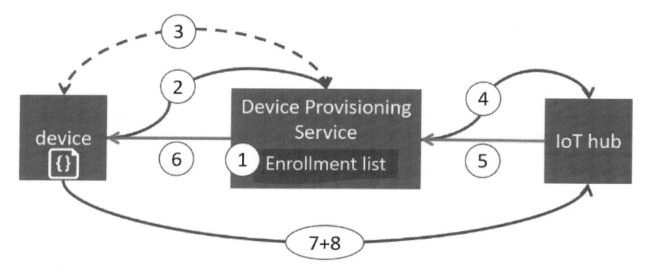

1. Device manufacturer adds the device registration information to the enrollment list in the Azure portal. (Manual Step in Factory).

2. Device contacts the provisioning service endpoint set at the factory. The device passes the provisioning service its identifying information to prove its identity.
3. The provisioning service validates the identity of the device by validating the registration ID and key against the enrollment list entry using either a nonce challenge (Trusted Platform Module) or standard X.509 verification (X.509).
4. The provisioning service registers the device with an IoT hub and populates the device's desired twin state.
5. The IoT hub returns device ID information to the provisioning service.
6. The provisioning service returns the IoT hub connection information to the device. The device can now start sending data directly to the IoT hub.
7. The device connects to IoT hub.
8. The device gets the desired state from its **device twin** in IoT hub.

Exercise 29: IOT Hub Device Provisioning Service Setup

Click +Create a Resource> Internet of Things> IoT Hub Device Provisioning Service> Create IoT Hub DPS Blade opens>Fill as per requirement and click create.

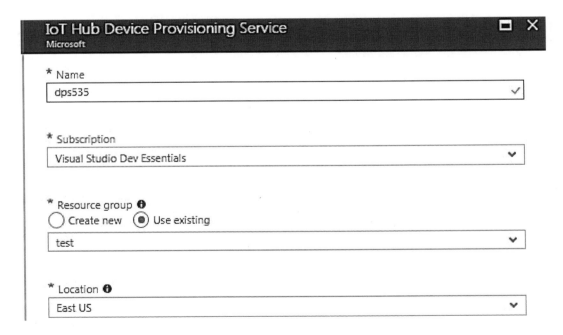

Exercise 30: Link the IoT Hub with Device Provisioning service

In DPS dashboard click Linked to IOT Hubs> + Add> Add link to Iot Hub blade opens>Select your IoT Hub created in Exercise 26 and Access Policy from drop down box and click save.

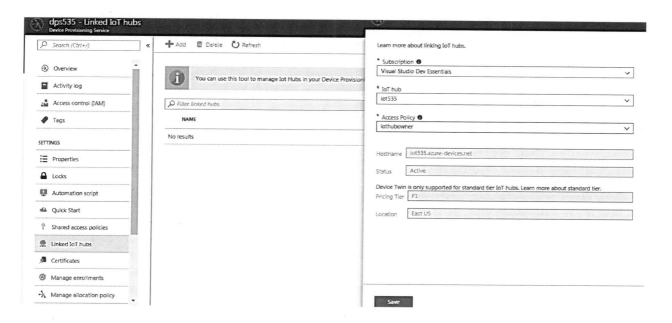

IOT Hub Device Provisioning Service (DPS) Pricing

Tier	Pricing
S1	$0.10 per 1,000 operations

Azure Event Hubs

Azure Event Hubs is a managed service capable of ingesting millions of events per second from connected devices, Applications, Websites & Real Time Streaming Events.

Event Hubs is the intermediate ingestion point of events between the data sources and the event processing engine. Data is collected into an Event Hub and then transformed using Services such as Stream Analytics or Machine Learning. Figure below shows placement of Event Hub in Real Time Analytic Solutions.

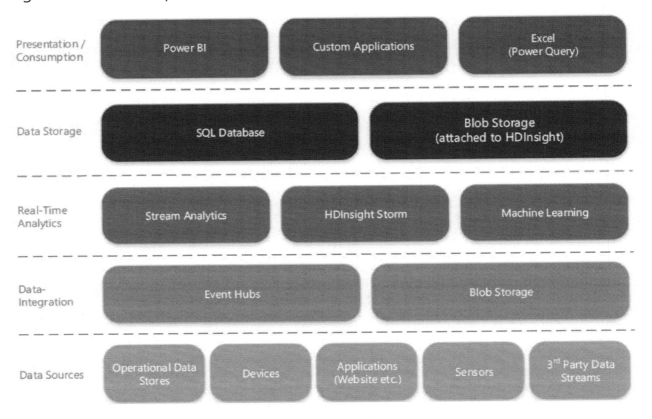

Input to Event Hub: Recall that in IoT Hub, Device identity has to be created in IoT Hub before a device can sent data to the IoT Hub. But in Event Hub, Event producers send Event Data after authenticating to Event Hub using Shared Access Signatures.

Input sources can be IOT Devices, Sensors, Applications, Websites, Real time Twitter Streams or 3rd Party Streams (Streams are sent to a Web Application. In Web Application, Connection string and authentication of Event Hub is specified. Web Application then sends real-time stream to Event Hub).

Output of Event Hub can be sent to Azure Stream Analytics for Analytics in Real time, Azure Storage for Archiving, Data lake store for Batch Analytics or to the Supported Application. The figure below shows output of Event Hub being ingested into Stream Analytics Service. <u>Azure Services like Stream Analytics have built in adaptor to connect to Event Hub.</u>

As shown in the figure above Event Hub also supports Stream Analytics as input Data source.

Events are persisted in Event Hub for a period of time which can be configured through Event Hub dashboard.

Event Hub Use Case

1. Telemetry data collected from industrial machines, connected vehicles, or other devices.
2. Traffic information from web farms.
3. In-game event capture in console games.
4. Behavior tracking in mobile apps.

Event Hub Anti Use Case

1. Does not support Bi-Directional Communication with devices. You cannot send messages back to devices to update properties or invoke an action.
2. Cannot implement Device-level identity helps to secure your system.
3. No support for Edge computing as in the case of IOT Hub using IoT edge.

Event Hub Architecture

Event Hubs is a managed service that sits between event publishers and event consumers to decouple the production of an event stream from the consumption of those events.

Event Hub uses Publish/Subscribe model. Event Producers publish event to event Hubs. Event are stored in Event Hub. Subscribers can register for specific events.

Figure below shows the Architecture of Event Hub Solution.

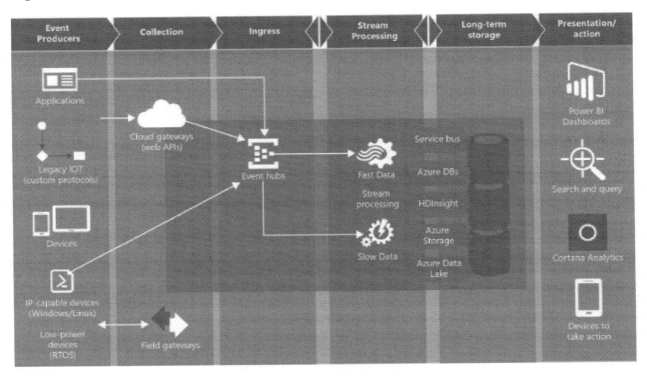

Event Hubs Solution components and features

Event producers/publishers is an entity that sends data to an event hub. Event producers can be IOT devices, IOT Gateways and Applications. Event publishers publish events using HTTPS or AMQP 1.0.

SAS tokens: Event producers use a Shared Access Signature (SAS) token to identify themselves to an event hub.

Partition: A partition is an ordered sequence of events that is held in an event hub. The number of partitions is specified at creation of Event Hub and must be between 2 and 32. You cannot change this afterwards.

Partition enables each consumer to only read a specific subset or partition of the event stream

Partitions help in scaling Event hub Processing, Availability and Parallelization. The number of partitions in an event hub directly relates to the number of concurrent readers you expect to have. There can be at most 5 concurrent readers on a partition per consumer group; however **it is recommended that there is only one active receiver on a partition per consumer group**.

A single partition has a maximum scale of one throughput unit.

Figure below shows Event Hub configured with 4 Partitions. Partitions are independent and contain their own sequence of data, they often grow at different rates.

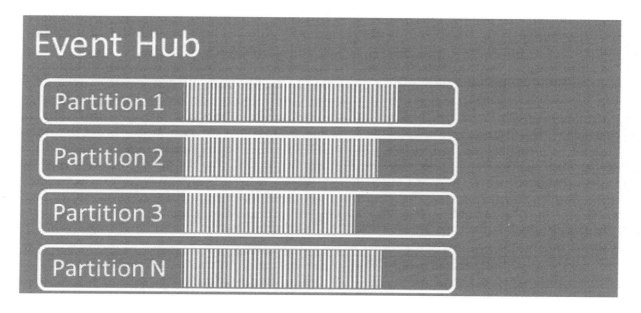

Partition Key maps incoming event data into specific partitions. The partition key is a sender-supplied value passed into an event hub. If you don't specify a partition key when publishing an event, a round-robin assignment is used. The event publisher is only aware of its partition key, not the partition to which the events are published. This decoupling of key and partition insulates the sender from needing to know too much about the downstream processing.

Event consumers is an entity that reads event data from an event hub. Event Consumers can be Azure Stream Analytics, Azure Machine learning service, Blob storage & Data lake store etc. Event consumers must subscribe for specific events they want to use. Event consumers connect via AMQP 1.0. Many of the Event consumers like Azure Stream Analytics have built in adaptor to connect to Azure Event Hubs.

Consumer groups: The publish/subscribe mechanism of Event Hubs is enabled through consumer groups. Consumer groups enable multiple consuming applications to each have a separate view of the event stream, and to read the stream independently at their own pace and with their own offsets. **You can only access partitions through a consumer group.** There can be at most 5 concurrent readers on a partition per consumer group; however it is recommended that there is only one active receiver on a partition per consumer group. You can create up to 20 consumer groups for a Standard tier event hub.

In a stream processing architecture, each downstream application equates to a consumer group. If you want to write event data to long-term storage, then that storage writer application is a consumer group.

The figure below shows the Event Hubs stream processing architecture.

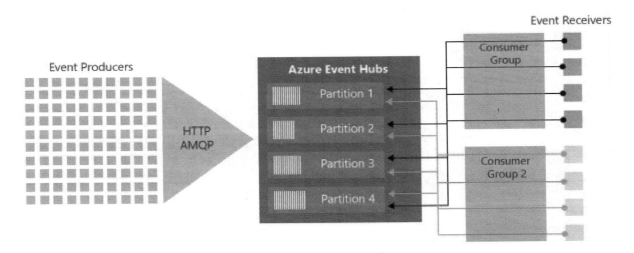

Azure IoT Hub and Azure Event Hubs Comparison

Both Azure IoT Hub and Azure Event Hubs are cloud services that can ingest large amounts of data and process or store that data for business insights.

IoT Hub was developed with the specific capabilities needed to support at-scale internet of things (IOT) scenarios.

Event Hubs is designed for event ingestion at a massive scale, both in the context of inter-datacenter and intra-datacenter scenarios (Ingestion from Azure Services) but doesn't provide the rich IoT-specific capabilities that are available with IoT Hub.

Some of the important differentiator's between IoT Hub and Event ingestion services are as follows:

1. IoT Hub includes features that enrich the relationship between your devices and your backend systems.
2. IoT Hub Bi-directional communication capabilities mean that while you receive data from devices you can also send messages back to devices to update properties or invoke an action.
3. IoT Hub Device-level identity helps secure your system.

Table below shows comparison between IOT Hub and Event Hubs.

	IoT Hub Standard tier	IoT Hub Basic tier	Event Hubs
Device-to-cloud messaging	✓	✓	✓
Protocols: HTTPS, AMQP, AMQP over websockets	✓	✓	✓
Protocols: MQTT, MQTT over websockets	✓	✓	
Per-device identity	✓	✓	
File upload from devices	✓	✓	
Device Provisioning Service	✓	✓	
Cloud-to-device messaging	✓		
Device twin and device management	✓		
IoT Edge	✓		

Architecting Microsoft Azure Solutions Study & Lab Guide Part 2: Exam 70-535

Azure Event Hub Capacity

The capacity of Event Hubs is controlled by throughput units. A single throughput unit includes the following capacity:

Ingress Events (events sent into an event hub): Up to 1 MB per second or 1000 events per second (whichever comes first).
Egress Events (events consumed from an event hub): Up to 2 MB per second.
Storage: Up to 84 GB of event storage.

Number of throughput units is selected during Event Namespace creation. By enabling Auto-inflate feature, you can automatically increase the number throughput units as your usage increases.

Figure below shows throughput unit options that can be selected during Event Namespace creation.

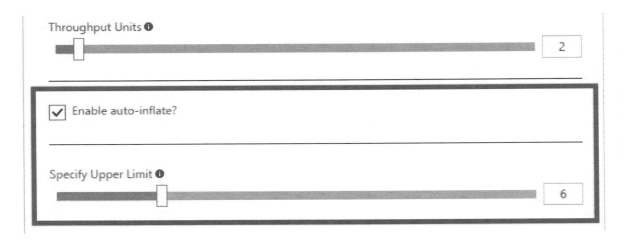

Throughput units are billed per hour and are pre-purchased. Up to 20 throughput units can be purchased for an Event Hubs namespace and are shared across all Event Hubs in the namespace.

Design Nugget: A single partition has a maximum scale of one throughput unit. The number of throughput units should be less than or equal to the number of partitions in an event hub.
Design Nugget: As you increase the number of throughput units in your namespace, you may want additional partitions to allow concurrent readers to achieve their own maximum throughput.

Azure Event Hub Tiers & Pricing

Azure Event Hub comes in 3 tiers: Basic, Standard & Dedicated. The Dedicated tier is not available to deploy from Azure Portal. Customers need to contact billing support to get Dedicated Cluster.

The Standard tier of Azure Event Hubs provides features beyond what is available in the Basic tier. The following features are available only in Standard & Dedicated Tier:

1. Longer event retention
2. Additional brokered connections, with an overage charge for more than the number included
3. More than a single Consumer Group
4. Capture

	Basic	Standard	Dedicated
Ingress events	$0.028 per million events	$0.028 per million events	Included
Throughput unit (1 MB/s ingress, 2 MB/s egress)	$0.015/hour	$0.03/hour	Included
Message size	256 KB	256 KB	1 MB
Publisher policies		Yes	Yes
Consumer groups	1 Default Group	20	20
Message replay	Yes	Yes	Yes
Maximum throughput units	20	20	
Brokered connections	100 Included	1000 Included	25K Included
Additional brokered connections		Yes	Yes
Message retention	1 day included	1 day included (See Note 1)	Up to 7 days included
Capture		$0.10/hour	Included

Note 1: In the standard tier, Messages can be retained up to seven days, but message retention over one day will result in overage charges.

Exercise 31: Create Event Hub Namespace

1. Click + New> Internet of Things>Event Hubs>Create Event Hubs Namespace blade opens> Enter information as per your Requirement and click create.

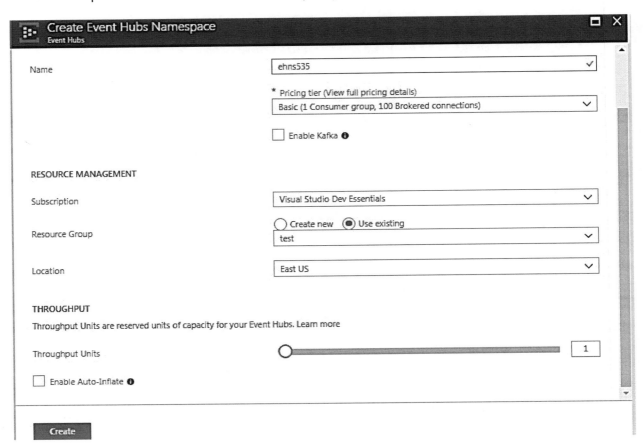

Figure below shows Event Hub Name space Dashboard.

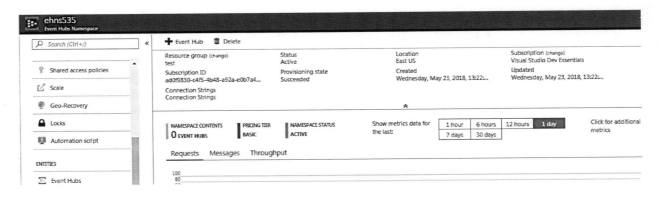

Note 1: By enabling Auto-Inflate feature throughput-units will automatically increase based on usage to a specified upper limit.

Exercise 32: Create Event Hub

1. In Event Namespace Dashboard Click Event Hubs in left pane>Click +Event Hub>Create Event Hub Blade open> Enter information as per your requirement and click create.

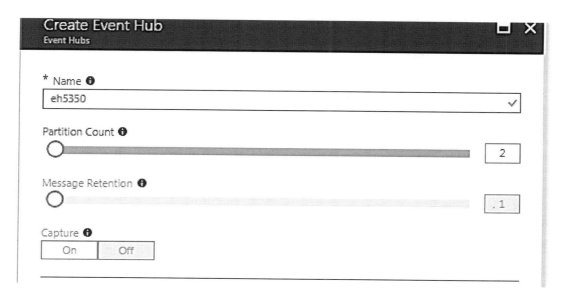

2. Figure below shows Dashboard of newly created Event Hub. From here we can create consumer groups. Through consumer groups Event consumers will read event data from event Hubs. A default consumer group is created with Event Hub.

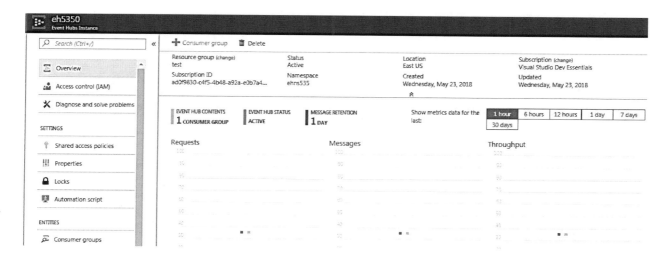

Exercise 33: Configure Event Producers to Send Events to Event Hub

Copy Connection string-Primary Key from Event Hub Namespace Dashboard. Connection string will be used by Event Producers to connect and authenticate to Event Hub and sending events to Event Hub.

1. In Event Namespace Dashboard>Click shared Access Policies>Click the Policy in right pane> Root policy opens in Extreme Right pane. Copy Connection String-Primary Key.

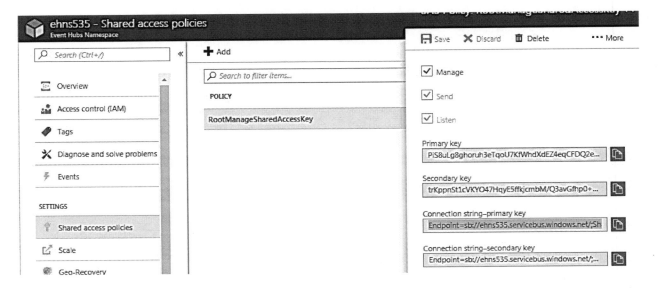

2. In Event Producers add Connection string-Primary Key from Event Hub Namespace and Event Hub Path Name.

Exercise 34: Send Output of Event Hub to Stream Analytics

1. Go to Stream Analytics Job Dashboard created in Exercise 25>Click input in left pane> In Right Pane click +Add Stream Input and select Event Hub> New input blade opens>Enter as per your req and click save.

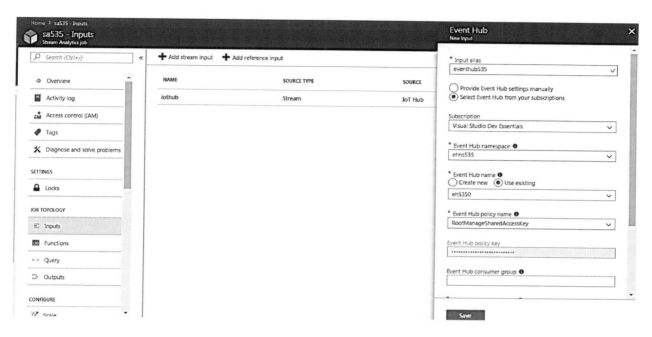

2. **Query the Event Hub data**: Click Query in left pane> In right pane you can enter your query to do real time analytics on data ingested in Event Hub.

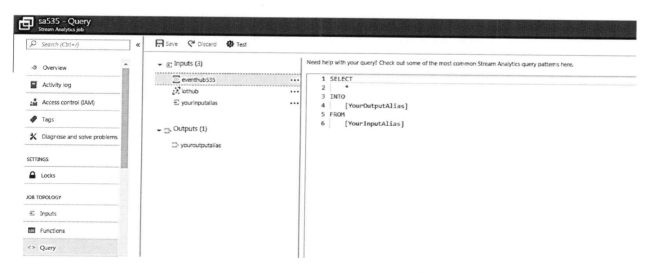

Event Hub Capture

Event Hub Capture enables you to automatically capture the streaming data in Event Hubs and save it to your choice of either a Blob storage account, or an Azure Data Lake Service account. You can enable Capture from the Azure portal.

Enabling Event Hub Capture: In Event Hub Dashboard click capture in left pane> In right pane select on to enable Event capture.

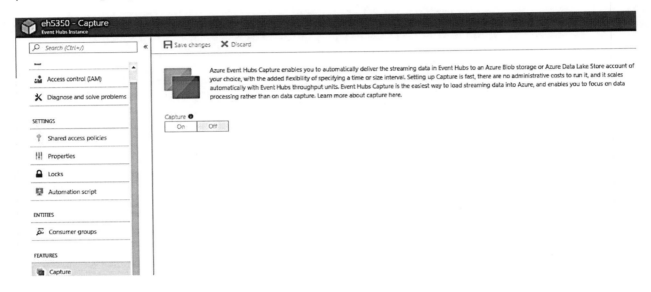

Note: Capture is greyed out in above figure as we have deployed Basic Tier. Capture Feature is supported in Standard Tier onwards.

Azure IoT Edge

Azure IoT Edge is a Managed Internet of Things (IoT) service that builds on top of IoT Hub.

Azure IoT Edge deploys cloud services such as Artificial Intelligence, Azure Machine Learning, Azure Functions and Azure Stream Analytics to IoT devices, allowing you to process data and run analytics locally on your edge devices instead of in the cloud. You can also deploy custom code which can run complex business logic on edge devices.

Azure IoT Hub is required for the secure management of devices and services deployed to the edge via Azure IoT Edge. Each IoT Hub supports upto 1000 IoT edge devices.

Azure IoT Edge is designed to run on both Windows and Linux hardware. IoT Edge is typically deployed on Gateway Class IOT device with sufficient memory and other resources.

IoT Devices in the field will connect to IoT Gateway which will be running Azure IOT Edge runtime and Modules as shown in the figure below.

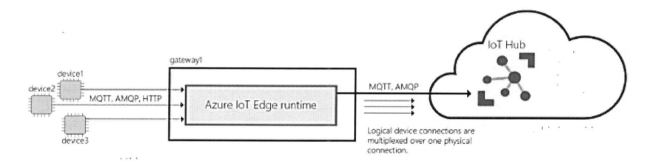

IoT Edge analyzes IoT device data at the edge instead of in the cloud. IoT edge device perform computing & Analytics locally before the data is sent to the cloud.

By moving parts of your workload to the edge, your devices can spend less time sending messages to the cloud and react more quickly to changes in status.

Azure IoT Edge components

Azure IoT Edge is made up of three components: The IoT Edge runtime, IoT Edge modules and Cloud based interface.

IoT Edge runtime: The IoT Edge runtime runs on each IoT Edge device and performs communication operations and management of the modules deployed to each device. IoT edge runtime consist of 2 modules: IoT Edge Hub and the IoT Edge agent.

IoT Edge Hub: IoT Edge hub is responsible for communication. It acts as a local proxy for IoT Hub by exposing the same protocol endpoints as IoT Hub.

IoT Edge agent: IoT Edge agent manages deploying and monitoring the modules. It is responsible for instantiating modules, ensuring that they continue to run, and reporting the status of the modules back to IoT Hub.

IoT Edge Modules: IoT Edge modules are docker containers that run Azure services, 3rd party services, or your own code. They are deployed to IoT Edge devices and execute locally on those devices.

Azure services running on the edge as containers can be Azure Machine learning, Azure Functions or Azure Stream Analytics.

3rd Party services can be image recognition and Artificial Intelligence etc.

You can also deploy your own containers using custom code. Azure IoT Edge supports both Linux and Windows. It supports Java, .NET Core 2.0, Node.js, C, and Python.

The figure below shows Docker Containers Modules and Azure IoT Edge runtime installed and running on IoT Edge device.

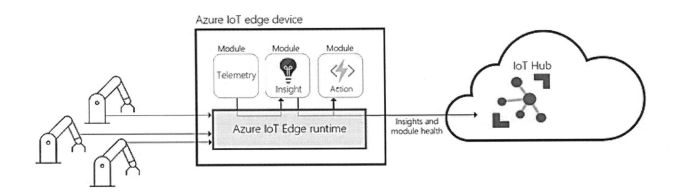

IoT Edge cloud interface: Azure cloud-based interface which enables you to remotely monitor and manage IoT Edge devices. IoT Edge cloud interface provide control plane for the deployment and Management of Modules in Azure IoT edge device.

The figure below shows Deployment of Container modules to IoT edge devices from cloud.

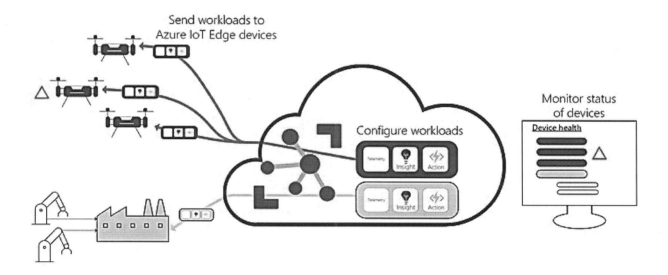

Design Nugget: Azure IoT Edge can run either Windows containers or Linux containers.
Design Nugget: You have the option to deploy modules to your IoT Edge devices from the cloud apart from local deployment.

Exercise 35: Deploying IoT Edge in 5 Steps

Step 1 Use IoT Hub Created in Exercise 26.

Step 2 Register an IoT Edge device: Log on to Azure Portal and go to IoT Hub Dashboard>click IoT Edge in left Pane>Click add IoT edge device>Add device blade open>Give a device id and click save to add the IoT device.

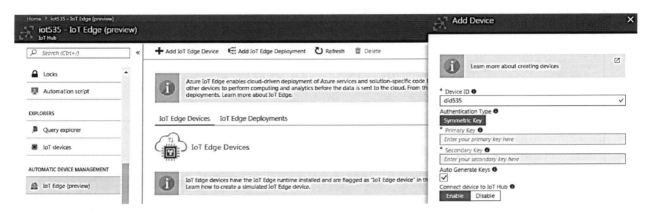

Step 3 Connect IOT Edge device to IOT Hub: In IOT Hub Dashboard Select your edge device> Copy the Primary Connection String. In Field add Primary Connection string to IoT Edge Device

Step 4a Deploy module to IoT Edge in field from the cloud: Log on to Azure Portal and go to IoT Hub Dashboard> click IoT Edge in left Pane>Select IoT Edge device you created in step 2 in Right Pane> Device detail Blade opens.

Step 4b Click Set Modules> Click + Add> You can select from IoT Edge Module, Azure Stream Analytics Module or Azure Machine Learning Module.

Step 5 Connect IOT devices to IOT Edge in the field: You can do analytics on IoT device data locally on IoT edge device.

Azure Time Series Insight

Azure Time Series Insights is a fully managed storage, analytics and visualization service for managing IoT-scale time-series data in the cloud.

It provides massively scalable time-series data storage and enables you to explore and analyze billions of IoT or connected events streaming in from all over the world in seconds.

Time Series Insights is built for storing, visualizing, and querying large amounts of time series data, such as that generated by IoT devices.

Figure below shows Data from Event & IoT Hub being stored in Time series insight Managed storage (SSD). TSI explorer being used to visualize the data.

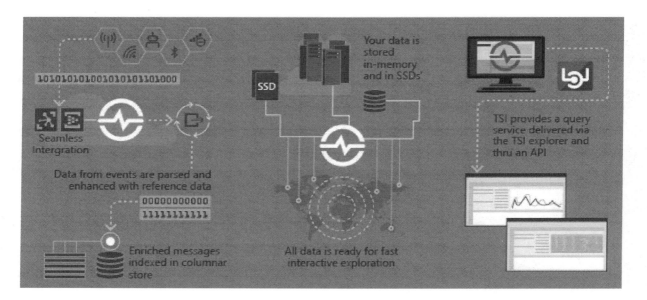

Time Series Insights Features

1. Time Series Insights is fully integrated with cloud gateways like Azure IoT Hub and Azure Event Hubs.
2. Time Series Insights manages the storage of data. TSI stores data in memory and SSD's for up to 400 days.
3. Time Series Insights provides out-of-the-box visualization via the TSI explorer.
4. Time Series Insights provides a query service, both in the TSI explorer and by using APIs.

Use Cases

Use Time Series Insights to store and manage terabytes of time-series data, explore and visualize billions of events simultaneously, conduct root-cause analysis, and to compare multiple sites and assets.

Storing and Managing Time-Series Data

Time Series Insights has a database designed for time series data. TSI provides scalable and fully managed storage which can store upto 3 TB of Data per month for S2 SKU with 10 units.

Real-time data exploration

Time Series Insights provides an explorer that visualizes all data streaming into an environment. The data is useful for validating whether a device is emitting data as expected and monitoring an IoT asset for health, productivity, and overall effectiveness.

Root-cause analysis and anomaly detection

Time Series Insights has tools like patterns and perspective views to conduct and save multi-step root-cause analysis. Further, Time Series Insights works in conjunction with alerting services like Azure Stream Analytics, so alerts and detected anomalies can be viewed in near real-time in the Time Series Insights explorer.

Global view of multi-site time-series data

You can connect multiple event sources to a Time Series Insights environment. This means that data streaming in from multiple, disparate locations can be viewed together in near real-time.

Applications

Time Series Insights exposes REST Query APIs, enabling you to build applications that use time series data.

Exercise 36: Create Time Series Insight Environment

1. Click +Create a resource> Click Internet of Things> Click Time Series Insights>Time Series Insight Environment blade opens>Fill the details as per your requirements and click create.

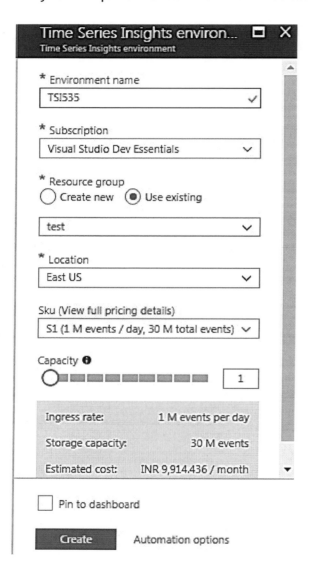

1. **Add an Event Source (Event Hub or IOT Hub)**: Go to Time Series Insight Dashboard and Click Event Sources.

2. Click + **Add**. Fill Details as per your req. **select Event Hub from drop down box.**

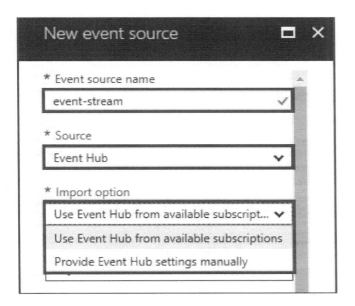

Visualising Data with Azure Time Series Insights explorer

Time Series Insights explorer is used to create visualizations of your data. It gives you a global view of your data, which lets you quickly validate your IoT solution and avoid costly downtime to mission-critical devices. You can discover hidden trends, spot anomalies, and conduct root-cause analyses in near real time.

Time Series Insights explorer is accessed through Web Browser.

Pre-Requistities for using Time Series Insights explorer

1. Create a Time Series Insights environment.
2. Add an event source to ingest data and store it.

Explore and query data with Time Series Insights explorer

1. Log on to explorer @ https://insights.timeseries.azure.com/
2. Select your Time Series Insights environment. Dashboard opens

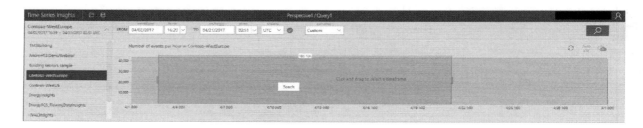

3. Select the time span of the data you want to query by using from and to configuration in top window.

Time Series Insight tiers and Pricing

Time Series Insight comes in S1 and S2 SKU.

Using Azure portal you can increase or decrease capacity within a given pricing SKU. Changing the pricing tier SKU is not allowed.

S1 SKU ingress rates and capacities

S1 SKU Capacity in units	Ingress Rate/Day	Maximum Storage Capacity/Month
1	1 GB (1 million events)	30 GB (30 million events) per month
2	2 GB (2 million events)	60 GB (60 million events) per month
10	10 GB (10 million events)	300 GB (300 million events) per month

S2 SKU ingress rates and capacities

S2 SKU Capacity in units	Ingress Rate/Day	Maximum Storage Capacity/Month
1	10 GB (10 million events)	300 GB (300 million events) per month
2	20 GB (20 million events)	600 GB (600 million events) per month
10	100 GB (100 million events)	3 TB (3 billion events) per month

Note: you can choose any units between 1 & 10.

The data is retained in Time Series Insights based on the selected retention days. Retention is configurable in the Azure portal. The longest allowable retention period is a rolling year of 12 months + 1 month, which is defined as 400 days.

Design Nugget: If your daily maximum ingress rate exceeds the defined maximum then in that case data retention period is decreased.
Design Nugget: An environment can be scaled up to 10 times by adding upto 10 units

Pricing

	S1	S2
Price (per unit/month)	$150.00	$1350.00

Chapter 9 Azure Messaging Solutions

This Chapter covers following

- Azure Service Bus
- Azure Service Bus Queues
- Azure Service Bus Topics
- Azure Service Bus Relay
- Azure Event Grid

This Chapter Covers following Lab Exercises

- Implementing Service Bus Name Space
- Implementing Service Bus Queues
- Implementing Service Topics
- Implementing Relay Namespace
- Implementing Relay Hybrid Connection
- Creating Event Subscription when Event Publisher is Azure Service
- Creating Event Subscription when Event Publisher is Custom Topic

Azure Service Bus

Service Bus provides Messaging as a Service (MaaS). Azure Service Bus is a messaging infrastructure that sits between applications allowing them to exchange messages.

Service Bus Messaging entities provide temporary decoupling between applications by storing or passing message generated by one application for another application.

Service Bus Messaging Entities

Service Bus supports two distinct messaging patterns: *Service Bus Messaging and Azure Relay*.

The messaging entities that form the core of the brokered messaging capabilities in Service Bus are **Queues, Topics/Subscriptions & Relays.** Queues and Topics use Service Bus Messaging Pattern. All three entities store and forward messages in different ways.

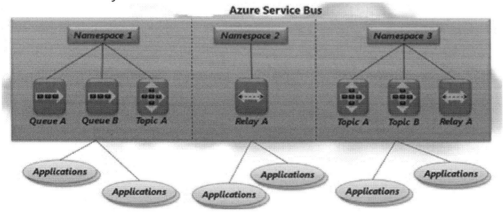

Queues: *Queues* allow one-directional asynchronous communication. Queues stores sent messages until they are received. Each message is received by a single recipient.

Topics: *Topics* provide one-directional asynchronous communication using *subscriptions. A* single topic can have multiple Receivers.

Relays: *Relays* provide Synchronous bi-directional communication between applications. Relay does not store messages. Azure Relay service connects application within corporate network to application outside the corporate network without having to open a firewall connection or configure VPN.

Service Bus Queues

Service Bus Queues acts as an intermediary that stores sent messages until they are received. Each message is received by a single recipient.

Service Bus Queues, allow one-directional asynchronous communication.

Service Bus Queues entities provide temporary decoupling between applications. Service Bus Queues store sent messages until they are received or deleted.

Service Bus queues are similar to Queue Storage but offer additional capabilities such as **advanced middleware capabilities (dead lettering, auto-forwarding, sessions, duplicate detection, etc.).**

The figure below shows Service bus queue storing the message by the sender. The queue then passes the message to the receiver when it is ready to receive it.

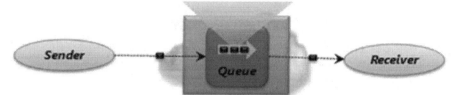

A key benefit of using queues is to achieve "temporal decoupling" of application components. In other words, the producers (senders) and consumers (receivers) do not have to be sending and receiving messages at the same time, because messages are stored durably in the queue. Furthermore, the producer does not have to wait for a reply from the consumer in order to continue to process and send messages.

A related benefit is "load leveling. Load leveling enables producers and consumers to send and receive messages at different rates. In many applications, the system load varies over time; however, the processing time required for each unit of work is typically constant. Intermediating between message producers and consumers with a queue means that the **consuming application only has to be provisioned to be able to handle average load instead of peak load.**

Service Bus Queues offer First In, First Out (FIFO) message delivery to one or more competing consumers. Each message is received and processed by only one message consumer.

Service Bus queues Capabilities

Following capabilities can be enabled during Service Bus Queue creation.

Duplicate Detection: Duplicate Detection configures queue to keep a history of all messages sent to the queue for a configurable amount of time. During that interval queue will not accept any duplicate messages.

Dead Lettering: Dead Lettering involves holding messages that cannot be successfully delivered to any receiver in a separate Queue.after they have expired. Messages do not expire in Dead Letter Queue.

Sessions: Sessions guarantee first-in first-out delivery of messages.

Partitioning: With partitioning queue is partitioned across multiple message brokers and message stores. This increases the throughput of the queue.

Service Bus Topics

Topics provide one-directional communication between sender and multiple receivers using *subscriptions*. **Topic Store messages from producer similar to queues.** A single topic can have multiple subscriptions.

The difference between Topic and queues is that topics enable each receiving application to create its own *subscription* by defining a *filter*. A subscriber will then see only the messages that match that filter.

The figure below shows message from sender going to multiple receivers through Service Bus topics. The sender Message is stored in topics. The Figure below shows sender, topic messaging broker and three subscribers.

- Subscriber 1 receives only messages that contain the property *Seller="Ava"*.
- Subscriber 2 receives messages that contain the property *Seller="Ruby"* and/or contain an *Amount* property whose value is greater than 100,000. Perhaps Ruby is the sales manager, so she wants to see both her own sales and all big sales regardless of who makes them.
- Subscriber 3 has set its filter to *True*, which means that it receives all messages. For example, this application might be responsible for maintaining an audit trail and therefore it needs to see all the messages.

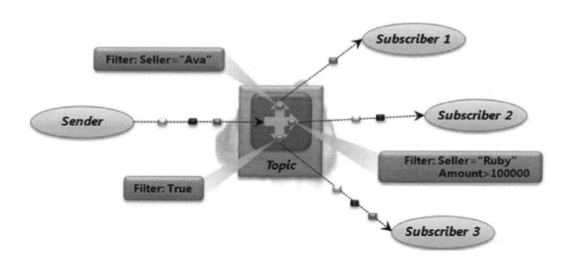

Service Bus Architecture (Queues and Topics)

Service Bus is organized by *scale units*. A scale unit is a unit of deployment and contains all components required run the service. A Service Bus namespace is mapped to a scale unit. The scale unit handles all types of Service Bus entities (queues, topics, subscriptions).

Figure below shows Service Bus Architecture.

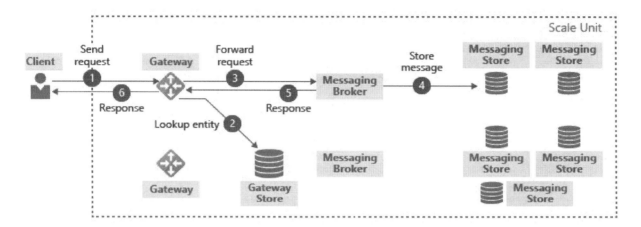

Service Bus scale unit components

A set of gateway nodes. Gateway nodes authenticate incoming requests. Each gateway node has a public IP address.

A set of messaging broker nodes. Messaging broker nodes process requests concerning messaging entities.

One gateway store. The gateway store holds the data for every entity that is defined in this scale unit. The gateway store is implemented on top of a SQL Database instance.

Multiple messaging stores. Messaging stores hold the messages of all queues, topics and subscriptions that are defined in this scale unit. It also contains all subscription data. Unless partitioning messaging entities is enabled, a queue or topic is mapped to one messaging store. Subscriptions are stored in the same messaging store as their parent topic. Except for Service Bus Premium Messaging, the messaging stores are implemented on top of SQL Database instances.

Exercise 37: Implementing Service Bus Namespace

A namespace is a scoping container for all messaging components. Multiple queues and topics can reside within a single namespace, and namespaces often serve as application containers.

1. In Azure Portal click + Create a resource> Integration> Service Bus> create namespace blade opens>Enter information as per your req.

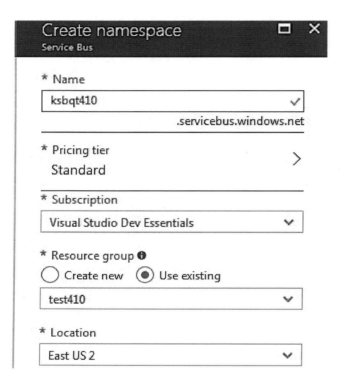

2. **Copy Primary Connection string**: Connection string will be used by applications to connect and authenticate to Service Bus.
   Click Shared Access Policies in left pane>Click Root Policy>Copy Primary Connection String in Extreme right pane.

Architecting Microsoft Azure Solutions Study & Lab Guide Part 2: Exam 70-535

Exercise 38: Implementing Queues

1. **Creating queues**: Click Queues in Service Bus namespace dashboard (created in Previous Exercise) >+Queue>create queue blade opens> Enter information as per your requirement and click create.

Note the 4 options in create Queue blade: Duplicate detection, Dead lettering, Sessions and Partitioning.

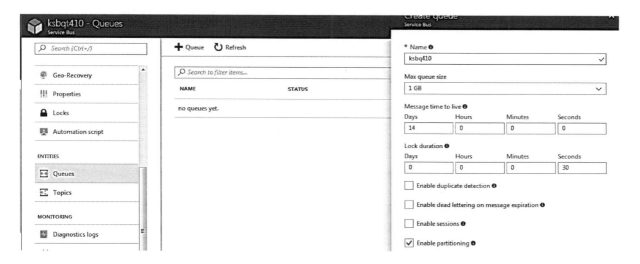

2. In both sender application and Receiver application add the Primary Connection of the Service Bus Namespace and name of the Queue. Configure your application to use Service Bus.

Exercise 39: Implementing Topics & Subscriptions

1. **Creating Topics**: Click topics in Service Bus namespace dashboard > +Topic>create Topic blade opens> Enter information as per your requirement.

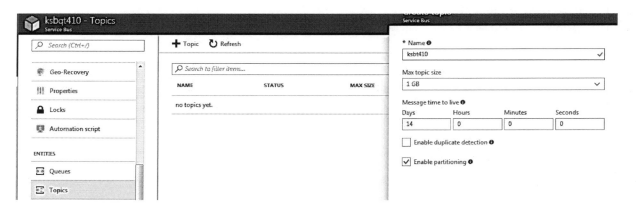

2. **Create Subscription**: Click the newly created Topic in Namespace Dashboard> topic dashboard opens>Click Subscription in left pane> Create Subscription blade opens> Enter information as per your req and click create.

3. In sender application add the Primary Connection string of the Service Bus Namespace and the name of Topic created. Configure your application to use Service Bus.

4. In Receiver application add the Primary Connection string of the Service Bus Namespace and the name of Subscription created. Configure your application to use Service Bus.

Azure Service Bus Relay

Azure Service Bus Relay managed cloud service connects application within corporate network to application or clients outside the corporate network without having to open a firewall connection or configure VPN on corporate network.

Azure Relay provides Synchronous bi-directional communication between applications. Azure Relay does not store messages.

The figure below shows Azure Relay Service providing Synchronous bi-directional communication between applications.

Relay supports a variety of different transport protocols and web services standards.

Service Bus Relay Working

In the relayed data transfer pattern, an on-premises service connects to the relay service through an outbound port and creates a bi-directional socket for communication tied to a particular rendezvous address. The client can then communicate with the on-premises service by sending traffic to the relay service targeting the rendezvous address. The relay service will then "relay" data to the on-premises service through a bi-directional socket dedicated to each client. The client does not need a direct connection to the on-premises service, and the on-premises service does not need any inbound ports open on the firewall.

The client that waits for and accepts connections is the listener. The client that initiates a new connection towards a listener via the Relay service is called the sender.

Service Bus Relay Example

An airline reservation system running in on-premises datacenter is to be be accessed from check-in kiosks, mobile devices, and other computers. Using Azure Relay, clients can connect to Corporate Application without configuring any VPN or configuring Firewall rules.

Azure Relay Connection Types

Azure Relay provides following 2 option for connecting Application and client through Azure Relay Service.

Hybrid Connection: Hybrid Connections uses standard based HTTP and WebSockets Protocols. The Azure Relay Hybrid Connections can be implemented on any platform and in any language that has a basic WebSocket capability, which explicitly includes the WebSocket API in common web browsers.

WCF Relays: WCF Relay is the legacy relay offering based on Windows Communication Foundation (WCF). WCF Relay works for the full .NET Framework (NETFX) and for WCF. You initiate the connection between your on-premises service and the relay service using a suite of WCF relay bindings.

Table below shows difference between WCF and Hybrid Connections.

	WCF Relay	Hybrid Connections
WCF	✓	
.NET Framework	✓	✓
.NET Core		✓
JavaScript/NodeJS		✓
Standards-Based Open Protocol		✓
Multiple RPC Programming Models		✓

Exercise 40: Implementing Relay Namespace & Connections

1. In Azure Portal click + Create a resource> Enterprise Integration> Click See all in top right> Select Relay Tile>click create> create namespace Relay blade opens>Enter information as per your req and click create.

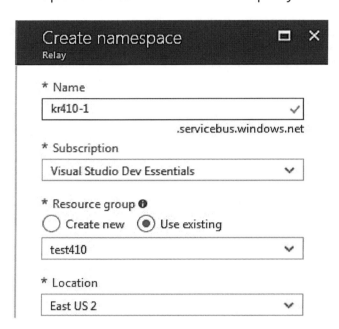

2. **Copy Connection string-Primary Key**: Connection string-Primary Key will be used by applications to connect and authenticate to Relay Service.
Click Shared Access Policies in left pane>Click Root Policy>Copy Primary connection String in Extreme right pane.

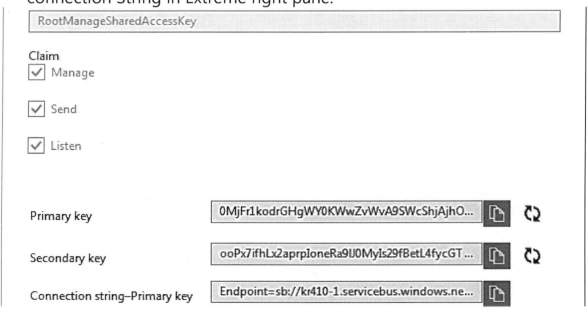

3. **Create Hybrid Connection**: Click Hybrid Connection in left pane> + Hybrid Connection> Create Hybrid Connection Blade opens> enter information as per your requirement and click ok.

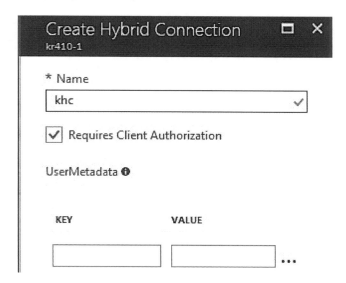

4. **Copy URL of Hybrid Connection**: Click created Hybrid connection in Relay Namespace>Hybrid connection dashboard opens> Copy the URL.

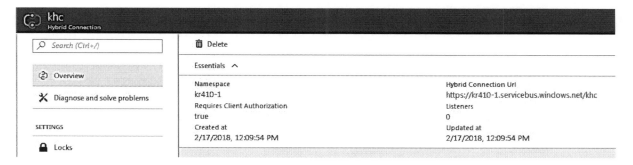

5. In both sender application and Receiver application or client add the Connection string-Primary Key copied in step 2 and each other endpoint address. Configure your application to use Azure Relay.

Comparing Queues, Topics and Relays

Features	Queues	Topics	Relays
Communication	Asynchronous	Asynchronous	Synchronous
Message Storing	Yes	Yes	No
Receivers	Single	Multiple	Single

Service Bus Tiers

Service Bus comes in Basic, standard, and premium tiers. Service Bus premium runs in dedicated resources to provide higher throughput and more consistent performance.

	Basic	Standard	Premium
Queues	☐	☐	☐
Scheduled messages	☐	☐	☐
Topics	X	☐	☐
Transactions	X	☐	☐
De-duplication	X	☐	☐
Sessions	X	☐	☐
ForwardTo/SendVia	X	☐	☐
Message Size	256 KB	256 KB	1 MB
Brokered connections included	100	1000	1000 per MU
Brokered connections (overage allowed)	X	Billable	1000 per MU
Resource isolation	X	X	☐

Azure Notification Hubs

Azure Notification Hubs provides a scalable, cross-platform push notification infrastructure that enables you to either broadcast push notifications to millions of users at once, or tailor notifications to individual users.

Azure Notification Hubs provides push notification to iOS, Android, Windows, or Kindle devices, working with APNs (Apple Push Notification service), GCM (Google Cloud Messaging), WNS (Windows Push Notification Service), MPNS (Microsoft Push Notification Service), and more.

Azure Notification Hubs plugs into any back end—Microsoft .NET, PHP, Java, Node.js—whether it's located on-premises or in the cloud.

Challenges with Push Notification without using Notification Hub

Push notifications is a form of app-to-user communication where users of mobile apps are notified of desired information in a pop-up or dialog box.
Push notifications are delivered through platform-specific infrastructures called *Platform Notification Systems* (PNSes).

To send a notification to all customers across the iOS, Android, and Windows versions of an app, the developer must work with Multiple Platform Notification Services such as APNS (Apple Push Notification Service), FCM (Firebase Cloud Messaging), and WNS (Windows Notification Service) etc.
Setting up and working with Multiple Platform-specific infrastructures is one of biggest operational and Administrative overhead.

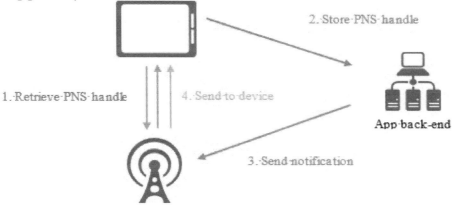

How Notification Hubs overcome conventional Push Notification Challenges

Notification Hubs multi-platform notification infrastructure reduces push-related codes and simplifies your backend.

With Notification Hubs, devices are merely responsible for registering their PNS handles with a hub, while the backend sends messages to users or interest groups, as shown in the following figure:

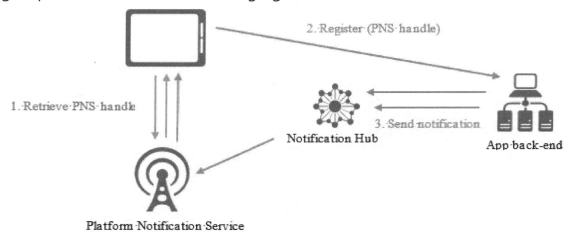

Advantages of Notification Hubs

Cross platforms: Support for all major push platforms including iOS, Android, Windows, and Kindle and Baidu. Provides common interface to push to all platforms in platform-specific or platform-independent formats with no platform-specific work.

Cross backends: Cloud or on-premises using .NET, Node.js, Java, etc.

Rich set of delivery patterns: *Broadcast to one or multiple platforms, Push to device, Push to user, Push to segment with dynamic tags, Localized push, Silent push, Scheduled push, Direct Push and Personalized push.*

Rich telemetry: General push, device, error, and operation telemetry is available in the Azure portal and Per Message Telemetry tracks each push.

Scalability: Send messages to millions of devices.

Azure Notification Hubs Tiers & Pricing

Notification Hubs is offered in three tiers—free, basic, and standard. Base charge and quotas are applied at the namespace level. Pushes exceeding included amounts are aggregated at the subscription level for each tier.

	Free	**Basic**	**Standard**
Base charge per namespace	Free	$10/month	$200/month
Included pushes per subscription per tier	1 million	10 million	10 million
Additional pushes 10–100 million	NA	$10	$10
Additional pushes over 100 million	NA	$1	$2.50
Namespaces per tier	100	100	Unlimited
Hubs per namespace	100	100	100
Active devices per namespace	500	200,000	10,000,000
X-plat push to individual devices	✓	✓	✓
Push variables	✓	✓	✓
Telemetry	Limited	Limited	Rich
Queryable audience (registration queries)	✓	✓	✓
Scheduled push			✓
Bulk import			✓
Multi-tenancy			✓
SLA	None	Covered	Covered

Azure Event Grid

Event Grid is a fully managed event routing service that provides reliable message delivery at massive scale. Event Grid is broker between Event Publishers and Event Subscribers. Event Grid will store events for a maximum of 24 hours. At the end of this time, events will be deleted.

Event Grid uses a publish-subscribe model. Publishers emit events. Event Grid stores event. Subscribers decide which events they want to handle.

Event Grid enables you to create subscriptions to events raised by Azure services or third-party resources.

Event Grid has built-in support for events coming from Azure services, like storage blobs and resource groups. Event Grid also has custom support for application and third-party events, using custom topics and custom webhooks.

Architecture

The figure below shows events produced by event publishers being delivered to Event handlers through Event Grid.

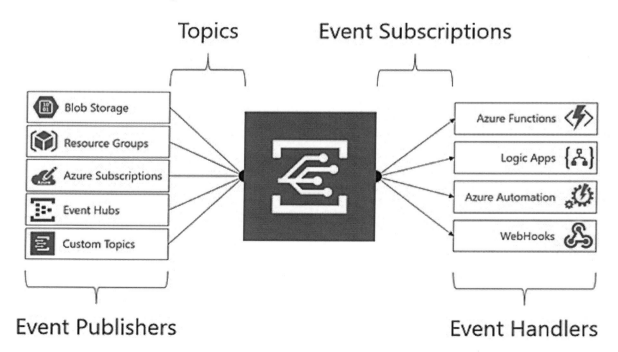

Components involved in Event Grid working

Event Grid connects data sources and event handlers. Event grid has following five components:

Events: What happened. Generated by Event Publishers.

Event publishers: Event publishers generate events to Event Grid. Event publishers can be Azure service or custom services which generate events. Currently, the following Azure services have built-in publisher support for event grid:

Resource Groups (management operations)
Azure Subscriptions (management operations)
Event Hubs
IoT Hub
Storage Blob
Storage General-purpose v2 (GPv2)
Custom Topics
Additional Azure Event Publishers will be added by MS on Regular basis.

Topics: The endpoint where publishers send events.

Event subscriptions: The endpoint to route events to Event Handler or to multiple handlers. Subscriptions are also used by handlers to intelligently filter incoming events.

Event handlers: Azure app or service reacting to the event. Currently, the following Azure services have built-in handler support for Event Grid:

Azure Functions
Logic Apps
Azure Automation
WebHooks
Microsoft Flow

Design Nugget: You create topic only when using Custom Event Publishers. If Event Publishers are Azure Services than you select a topic.

Features of Event Grid

Simple to setup: Aim events from your Azure resource to any event handler or endpoint without adding any code.

Built-in Events: Get up and running quickly with resource-defined built-in events.

Custom Events: Event Grid route, filter, and reliably deliver custom events in your app.

Advanced filtering: Filter on event type or event publish path to ensure event handlers only receive relevant events.

Fan-out - Subscribe multiple endpoints to the same event to send copies of the event to as many places as needed.

High throughput - Build high-volume workloads on Event Grid with support for millions of events per second.

Advantages of Event Grid

1. You don't have to write code to subscribe to events. Many Event Handlers such as Azure Functions, Logic Apps, Webhooks & Azure Automation have built in support for Event Grid.

2. Eliminate polling—and the associated cost and latency. With Event Grid, apps can listen for and react to events from virtually all Azure services, as well as custom sources. These events are delivered through push semantics, simplifying your code and reducing your resource consumption.

3. Many Azure services such as Blob Storage, Event Hub etc can generate events to Event Grid without writing any code.

Event Grid use cases

Serverless Architectures

Event Grid can automatically trigger a serverless function whenever Event handler generates a specific Event to Event Grid.

For example, use Event Grid to instantly trigger a serverless function to run image analysis each time a new photo is added to a blob storage container.

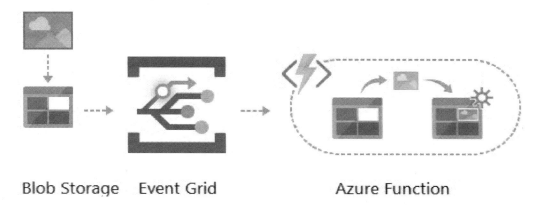

Blob Storage   Event Grid   Azure Function

Automatic Policy Enforcement on Azure Resources

With Event Grid you can automatically enforce required compliance on specific Azure resources using Azure Automation.

For example, Event Grid can notify Azure Automation when a virtual machine is created, or a SQL Database is spun up. These events can be used to automatically check that service configurations are compliant according to organization policies and tag the non-compliant Azure Resources.

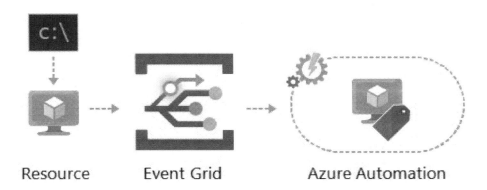

Resource   Event Grid   Azure Automation

Demonstration Exercise 41: Creating Event Subscription when Event Publisher is Azure Service

1. Event Grid is enabled through Event Handler (Azure Function, Logic Apps, Azure Automation etc) Dashboard (For this exercise we will use Azure Function App which is already created).> In Right Pane you can see Add Event Grid Subscription box.

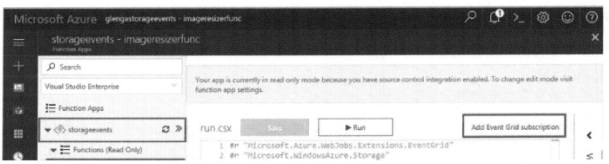

2. Click Add Event Grid Subscription>Create Event Subscription Blade opens

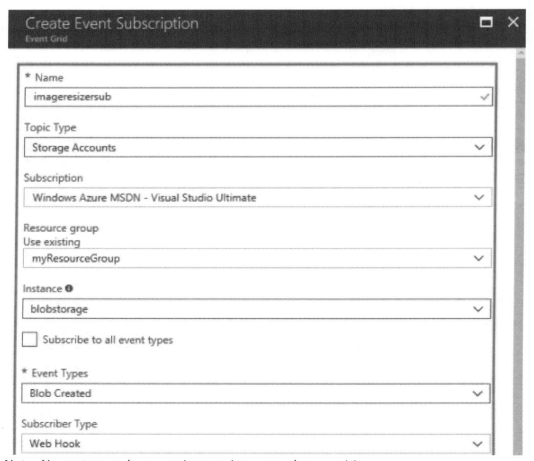

Note: No custom code was written to integrate these entities.

Architecting Microsoft Azure Solutions Study & Lab Guide Part 2: Exam 70-535

Demonstration Exercise 42: Creating Event Subscription when Event Publisher is Custom Topic

1. **Create a Custom Topic**: In Azure Portal click create a resource>In search box type Event Grid> In search results click Event Grid Topics>Event Grid Topic Blade opens>Click create>Create Topic Blade opens>Enter as per your requirement and click create.

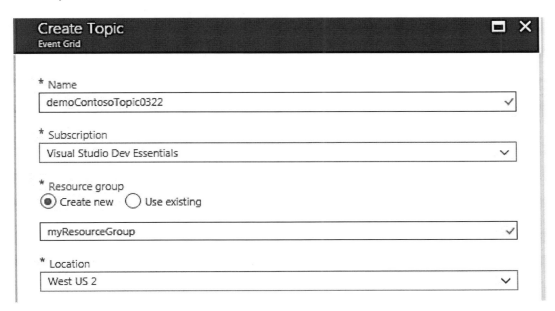

2. **Go to Event Handler Dashboard** (For this exercise we will use Azure Function App which is already created)> In Right Pane you can see Add Event Grid Subscription box.

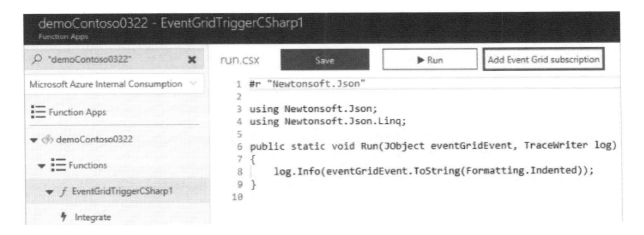

3. Click Add Event Grid Subscription Box in Event Handler Dashboard> Create Event Subscription Blade opens> Select Information from drop down boxes and click create.

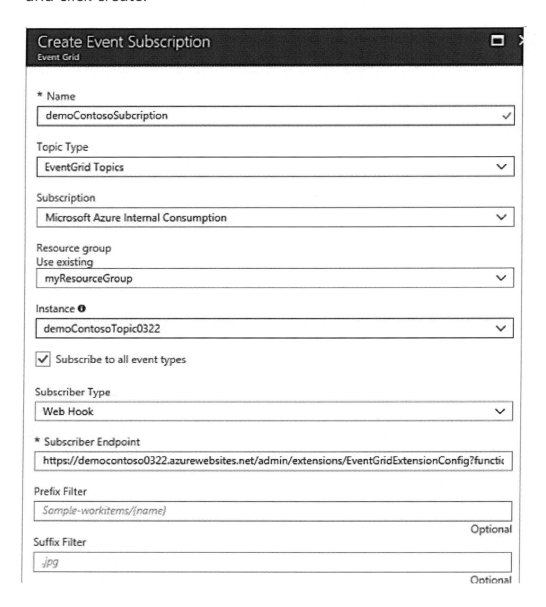

Here select the Topic Type, Custom Event Publisher Instance which is demoContosoTopic0322, Event Type and Subscriber type. **Important point here is that no custom code was written to integrate these entities.**

Event Grid Pricing

Event Grid pricing is based on operations performed. Operations include all ingress events, advanced match, delivery attempt, and management calls. Pricing includes a monthly free grant of 100,000 operations.

Price per million operations	$0.30
Free usage per month	100,000 operations

Chapter 10 Azure Serverless Computing

This Chapter covers following

- Azure Functions
- Azure Logic Apps
- Azure API Management

This Chapter Covers following Lab Exercises

- Publishing Hello World using http triggered Functions
- Create Logic App workflow (Delete Old Azure Blobs)
- Step by Step Implementing API Management

Azure Functions

Azure Functions is a serverless compute service that enables you to run compute code on-demand in response to a variety of events, without having to explicitly provision compute infrastructure.

Events can be occurring in Azure or 3rd party service as well as on-premises systems. Azure Functions makes it easy to connect to data sources for generating, processing and reacting to events.

Azure Function Features

Serverless: No worry about the infrastructure and provisioning of servers.
Choice of language: Write functions using C#, F#, Node.js, Python, PHP, batch, bash, or any executable using easy-to-use web-based interface.
Pay-per-use pricing model: Pay only for the time spent running your code.
Accelerate development: Write your code in the Functions editor in the portal or set up continuous integration and deploy your code through GitHub, Visual Studio Team Services etc.
Simplified integration: Easily leverage Azure services and external services such as Box, Dropbox, Microsoft OneDrive, SendGrid etc to get input into or output from Functions without writing any code.
Integrated security - Protect HTTP-triggered functions with OAuth providers such as Azure Active Directory, Facebook, Google, Twitter and Microsoft Account.

Common scenarios for Azure Functions

Real-time stream processing: Internet of Things (IoT) devices send messages to Azure Stream Analytics, which then calls an Azure Function to transform the message. This function processes the data and creates a new record in an Azure SQL database.

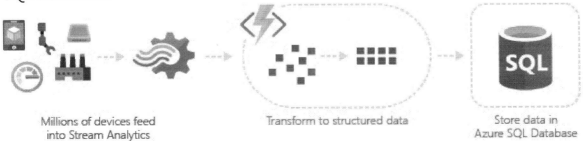

Millions of devices feed into Stream Analytics   Transform to structured data   Store data in Azure SQL Database

Azure service event processing: Azure Functions supports triggering an event based on an activity in an Azure service. For example, execute serverless code that reads newly discovered test log files in an Azure Blob storage container, and transform this into a row in an Azure SQL Database table.

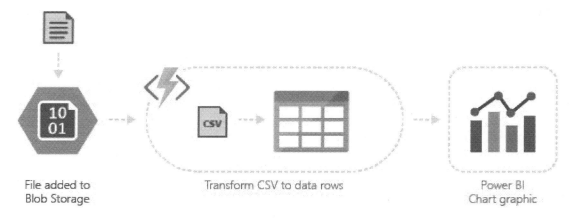

File added to   Transform CSV to data rows   Power BI
Blob Storage   Chart graphic

SaaS event processing: Azure Functions supports triggers based on activity in a SaaS service. For example, a file saved in OneDrive, triggers a function that uses the Microsoft Graph API to modify the spreadsheet, and creates additional charts and calculated data.

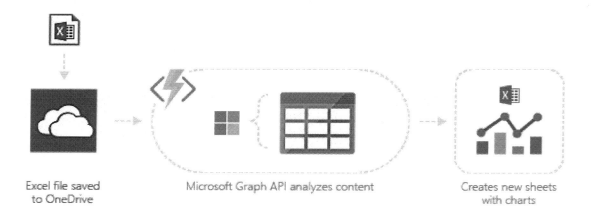

Excel file saved   Microsoft Graph API analyzes content   Creates new sheets
to OneDrive   with charts

Serverless mobile back ends: A mobile back end can be a set of HTTP APIs that are called from a mobile client using the WebHook URL. For example, a mobile application can capture an image, and then call an Azure Function to get an access token for uploading to blob storage. A second Azure Function is triggered by the blob upload and resizes the image to be mobile-friendly.

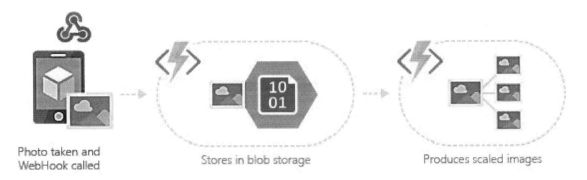

Photo taken and
WebHook called

Stores in blob storage

Produces scaled images

Pre-Built Triggers built in Function

Azure Functions integrates with various Azure and 3rd-party services. These services can trigger your function and start execution, or they can serve as input and output for your code. The following service integrations are supported by Azure Functions:

Azure Cosmos DB
Azure Event Hubs
Azure Event Grid
Azure Mobile Apps (tables)
Azure Notification Hubs
Azure Service Bus (queues and topics)
Azure Storage (blob, queues, and tables)
GitHub (webhooks)
On-premises (using Service Bus)
Twilio (SMS messages)

Exercise 46: Publishing Hello World using http triggered Functions

1. In Azure Portal Click the + **Create a resource** >**Compute > Function App**> Create Function App Blade opens> Enter the following and click create. It will take around 45-60 seconds to complete the deployment operation.

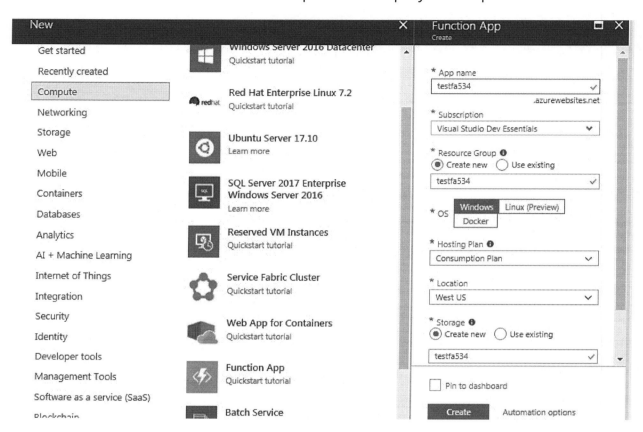

2. Figure below shows Function App Dashboard. Expand the function App.

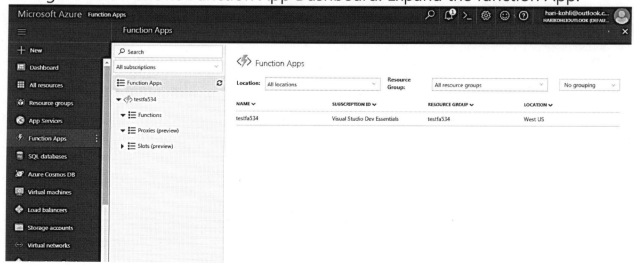

Architecting Microsoft Azure Solutions Study & Lab Guide Part 2: Exam 70-535

3. In the Function App testfa534 Dashboard>Click + next to Function> select WebHook + API, Choose C # for your function, and click Create this function.

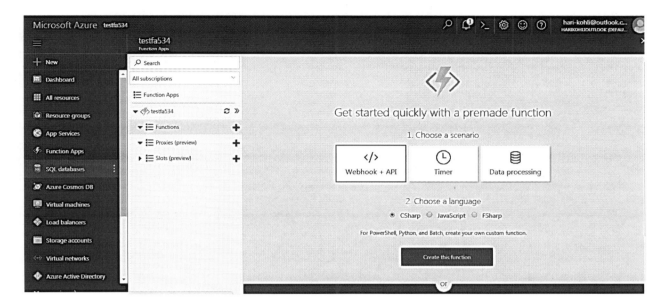

4. A function is created in C# language using the template for an HTTP triggered function.

5. In your new function, click <u></> Get function URL</u> (Top Right), select default (Function key), and then click Copy.

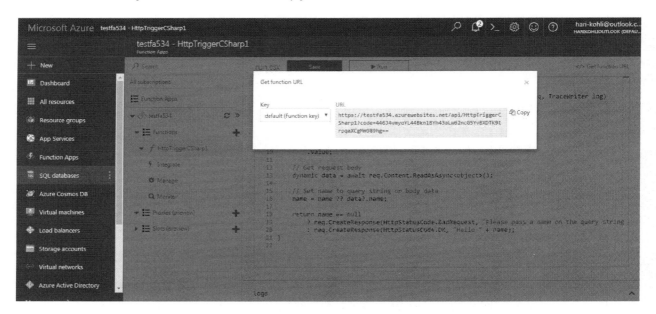

6. Test the Function by sending an http request. Open a Browser and paste the copied function URL. Add to the URL **&name=world**

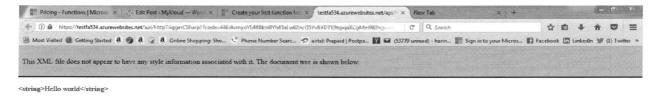

You can see from above how Hello World was executed without creating Virtual Machine Infrastructure in Azure Cloud.

Architecting Microsoft Azure Solutions Study & Lab Guide Part 2: Exam 70-535

Azure Functions pricing

Azure Functions has two kinds of pricing plans.

Consumption Plan: Azure Functions consumption is billed monthly and is sum of resource consumption per second and executions. Consumption plan pricing includes a monthly free grant of 1 million requests and 400,000 GB-s of resource consumption per month.

Resource consumption in gigabyte-seconds (GB-s): Computed as a combination of memory size and execution time for all functions within a function app.

Executions: Counted each time a function is executed in response to an event trigger.

App Service plan: Run your functions just like your web, mobile, and API apps. If you are already using App Service for your other applications, you can run your functions on the same plan at no additional cost. Refer to Web App Chapter for App Service Plan.

You only pay for the resources and execution when the code runs. You don't pay for the idle time.

Consumption Plan

Meter	Price	Free Grant Per Month
Resource Consumption	$0.000016/GB-s	400,000 GB-s
Executions	$0.20 per million executions	1 million executions

Note – Cost of Storage is separate. A storage account is created by default with each Functions app. The storage account is not included in the free grant. Standard **storage rates** and **networking rates** charged separately as applicable.

Azure Functions scale and hosting

When you're using a Consumption plan, instances of the Azure Functions host are dynamically added and removed based on the number of incoming events. This plan scales automatically, and you are charged for compute resources only when your functions are running. On a Consumption plan, a function can run for a maximum of 10 minutes.

The default timeout for functions on a Consumption plan is 5 minutes. The value can be increased to 10 minutes for the Function App by changing the property functionTimeout in the host.json project file.

When you use the Consumption hosting plan, function code files are stored on Azure Files shares on the function's main storage account. When you delete the main storage account of the function app, the function code files are deleted and cannot be recovered.

In the Consumption plan, the scale controller automatically scales CPU and memory resources by adding additional instances of the Functions host, based on the number of events that its functions are triggered on. Each instance of the Functions host is limited to 1.5 GB of memory. An instance of the host is the Function App, meaning all functions within a funciton app share resources within an instance and scale at the same time.

Azure Functions uses scale controller to monitor the rate of events and determine whether to scale out or scale in. The scale controller uses heuristics for each trigger type. For example, when you're using an Azure Queue storage trigger, it scales based on the queue length and the age of the oldest queue message.

The unit of scale is the function app. When the function app is scaled out, additional resources are allocated to run multiple instances of the Azure Functions host. Conversely, as compute demand is reduced, the scale controller removes function host instances. The number of instances is eventually scaled down to zero when no functions are running within a function app.

Figure below shows Function scalability based on incoming events.

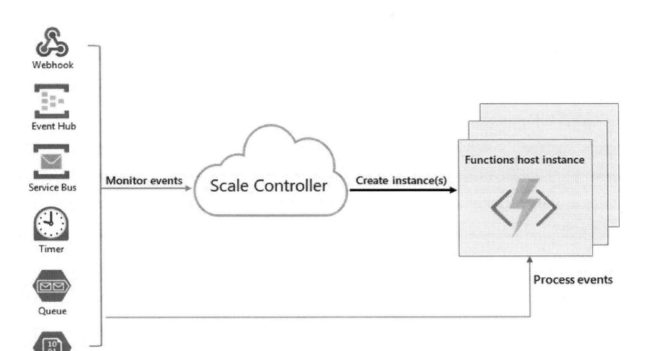

Understanding scaling behaviors

Scaling can vary on a number of factors, and scale differently based on the trigger and language selected. However there are a few aspects of scaling that exist in the system today:

- A single function app will only scale to a maximum of 200 instances. A single instance may process more than one message or request at a time though, so there isn't a set limit on number of concurrent executions.
- New instances will only be allocated at most once every 10 seconds.

Logic Apps

Azure Logic Apps automates business process execution and workflow using an easy-to-use visual designer without writing a single line of code.

Connect your business-critical apps and services with Azure Logic Apps, automating your workflows without writing a single line of code.

Logic Apps uses connectors and triggers which are used to start logic app workflows. Every logic app workflow starts with a <u>trigger</u>. The trigger fires when a specific event happens or when new data meets the condition that you set. Each time the trigger fires, the Logic Apps engine creates a logic app instance that starts and runs your workflow. You can add action to be taken by Logic App instance when the trigger fires.

Connectors

Logic Apps connectors are used to connect Logic App instance to Applications and Data sources in Azure, on-premises and other clouds.

You configure triggers on connectors to start the Logic App workflow. You also define action to be taken by Logic App instance.

The connectors are available as either **built-in actions** or **managed connectors**.

Built-in actions: The Logic Apps engine itself provides built-in actions for communicating to endpoints and performing tasks. For example, you can use these actions for calling HTTP endpoints, Azure Functions and Azure API etc.

Use logic apps to communicate with any endpoint over HTTP.

Azure Functions
Create functions that run custom snippets of C# or node.js, and then use these functions in your logic apps.

Request
Provides a callable HTTPS URL typically used as a webhook in other applications. When the logic app receives a request to this URL, the logic app starts.

Schedule
Start logic apps based on simple or complex recurrence schedules. For example, create schedules from as simple as recur every day to recur hourly on the last Friday of every month between 9:00 am and 5:00 pm.

Architecting Microsoft Azure Solutions Study & Lab Guide Part 2: Exam 70-535

Managed Connectors: Provide access to APIs for various services by creating API connections that the Logic Apps service hosts and manages. **There are 4 types of Managed Connectors.**

Standard Connector: Standard Connectors provide access to cloud based Applications. Example of Standard connectors include, Power BI, OneDrive, Event Hubs, Azure Blob Storage, Twitter, Sharepoint online etc.

Azure Blob Storage	If you want to automate any tasks with your storage account, then you should look at this connector. Supports CRUD (create, read, update, delete) operations.	**Dynamics 365 CRM Online**	One of the most-asked for connectors. It has triggers and actions to help automate workflows with leads, and more.
Event Hubs	Consume and publish events on an Event Hub. For example, you can get output from your logic app using Event Hubs, and then send the output to a real-time analytics provider.	**FTP**	If your FTP server is accessible from the internet, then you can automate workflows to work with files and folders. SFTP is also available with the SFTP connector.
Office 365 Outlook	Lots of triggers, and a lot more actions to use Office 365 email and events within your workflows. This connector includes an *approval email* action to approve vacation requests, expense reports, and so on. Office 365 users are also available with the Office 365 Users connector.	**Salesforce**	Easily sign in with your Salesforce account to get access to objects, such as Leads, and more.
Service Bus	The most popular connector within logic apps, it includes triggers and actions to do asynchronous messaging and publish/subscribe with queues, subscriptions, and topics.	**SharePoint Online**	If you do anything with SharePoint, and could benefit from automation, we recommend looking at this connector. Can be used with an on-premises SharePoint, and SharePoint Online.

On-premises connectors: Connect to server applications on-premises using the on-premises data gateway. On-premises connectors include SharePoint Server, SQL Server, Oracle DB, file shares etc.

DB2

Oracle DB

SharePoint
Server

File
System

SQL
Server

BizTalk
Server

Integration account connectors: These connectors process business-to-business messages with AS2 / X12 / EDIFACT, and encode and decode flat files. If you work with BizTalk Server, then these connectors are a good fit to expand your BizTalk workflows into Azure. BizTalk Server also has a <u>Logic Apps adapter</u> that includes receiving from a logic app, and sending to a logic app.

AS2
decoding

AS2
encoding

EDIFACT
decoding

EDIFACT
encoding

Integration account connectors are available only when you purchase an integration account.

Enterprise connectors: Includes MQ and SAP.

MQ

SAP

Exercise 47: Create Logic App workflow (Delete Old Azure Blobs)

Creating Logic App instance is a 2 step process: Create logic app and then add a connector to configure trigger and define an action.

1. Log on to Azure portal>Click +Create a resource>Click Enterprise Integration>click Logic App>create logic app blade opens> Fill as per your requirement and click create.

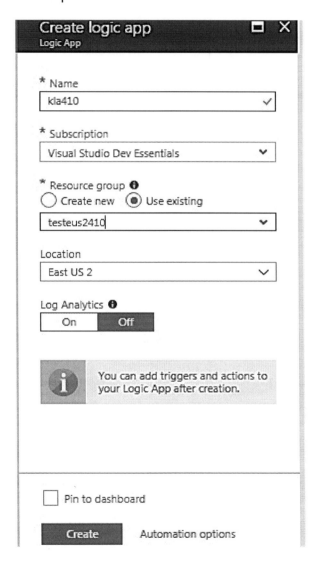

2. Figure below shows Logic app dashboard with Logic app designer selected in left pane. You add connector either by choosing Blank logic app or a pre-configured logic app template. Blank logic app gives you the option of choosing and searching from many pre-defined connectors and triggers.

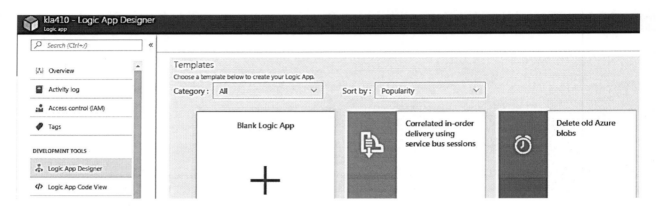

3. Lets select a Delete old Azure blobs>Delete Old Azure Blobs template opens>Click use this template>Click create>Select your storage account and click create.

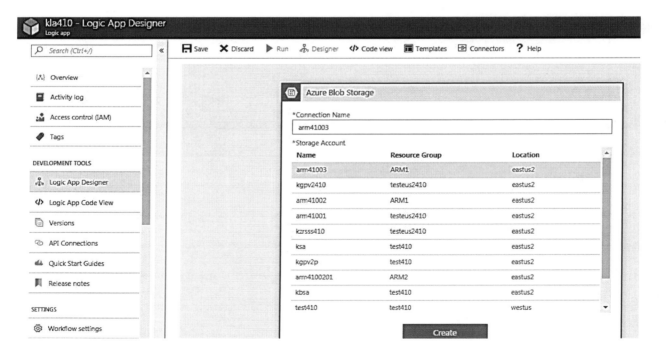

Note: Delete Old Azure Blob Template scans a storage account once a Second/Minute/Hour/day/Week/Month and delete all blobs older than defined value.

4. Click continue to connect Logic App to Storage account.

5. Connects to storage accounts. Select a schedule>Container/folder>Select Delete Blob connector>Click save.

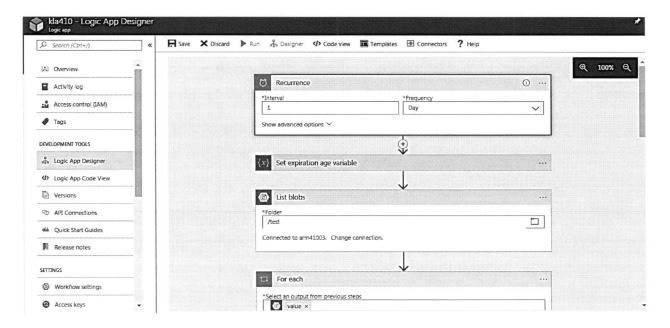

Logic Apps pricing

Every time a Logic App definition runs the triggers, action and connector executions are metered.

	PRICE PER EXECUTION
Actions	$0.000025
Standard Connector	$0.000125
Enterprise Connector	$0.001

API Management (APIM)

API Management (APIM) is a gateway service that sits between apps that consume your service and your API implementation.

Azure API Management publishes APIs of Application Platform to external partners, employees and developers securely and at scale.

It includes a developer portal for documentation, Self-service sign up, API key management and Developer only console to explore API.

It also includes Publisher portal to configure gateway service and too see analytics about your published API.

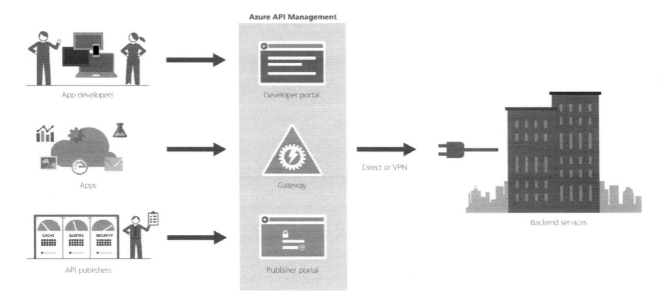

API Management adds following features to API implementation:

Access control
Rate limiting
Monitoring
Event logging,
Caching

How API Management is implemented

Import API of Backend Application: Import API of Backend Application platform into API Management Instance. The APIM API becomes a facade for the backend API. At the time you import the backend API, both the source API and the APIM API are identical. APIM enables you to customize the facade according to your needs without touching the backend API.

Publish APIM API: By Publishing APIM API developers can subscribe to the product and begin to use the product.
APIM API Products can be **open** or **protected**. Protected products must be subscribed to before they can be used, while open products can be used without a subscription.

Why do we need API Management (APIM)

API Management (APIM) helps organizations publish APIs of Application platform to external partners and internal developers to unlock the potential of their data and services.

API Management helps organization bring revenue by monetizing their application platform as well as drive adoption of their application platform.

Common scenarios of API Management

Enabling ISV partner ecosystems to onboard through the developer portal and building an API facade to decouple from internal implementations that are not ripe for partner consumption.

Running an internal API program by offering a centralized location for the organization to communicate about the availability and latest changes to APIs, gating access based on organizational accounts, all based on a secured channel between the API gateway and the backend.

Securing mobile infrastructure by gating access with API keys, preventing DOS attacks by using throttling, or using advanced security policies like JWT token validation.

API Management Components

API gateway: API Management is a gateway service that sits between apps and your API implementation. It performs following functions:

- Accepts API calls and routes them to your backends.
- Verifies API keys, JWT tokens, certificates, and other credentials.
- Enforces usage quotas and rate limits.
- Transforms your API on the fly without code modifications.
- Caches backend responses where set up.
- Logs call metadata for analytics purposes.

Publisher Portal: It is the administrative interface for the API Management. It performs following functions:

- Define or import API schema.
- Package APIs into products.
- Set up policies like quotas or transformations on the APIs.
- Get insights from analytics.
- Manage users.

Developer Portal: It performs following functions:

- Read API documentation.
- Try out an API via the interactive console.
- Create an account and subscribe to get API keys.
- Access analytics on their own usage.

Exercise 48: Step by Step Implementing API Management

Note: For this Exercise we will use is MS demo conference Application.

Step 1 Creating API Management Instance: Log on to Azure portal>Click +New>Click Enterprise Integration>click API Management>create API Management service blade opens> Fill as per your requirement and click create.

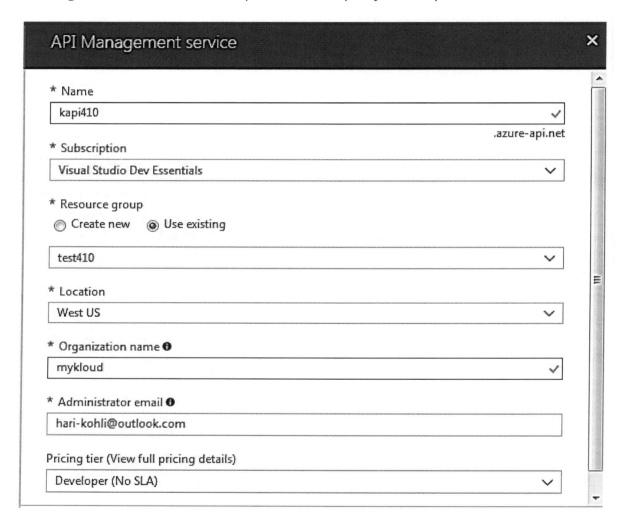

Step 2: Import API into API Management Instance

API represents a set of operations available to developers. Once the backend API is imported into API Management (APIM), the APIM API becomes a facade for the backend API. At the time you import the backend API, both the source API and the APIM API are identical. APIM enables you to customize the facade according to your needs without touching the backend API.

1. Figure below shows API Management Dashboard. See also the Tabs for Publisher and Developer Portal.

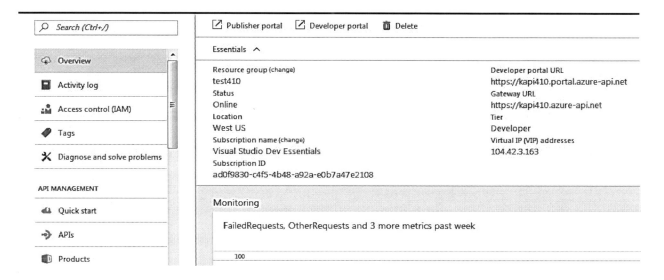

2. Click APIs in left pane>select Open API Specification>Create from OpenAPI Specification Blade opens. Specify the URL for Backend Application whose API are being exposed. The URL shown below is MS demo conference Application.

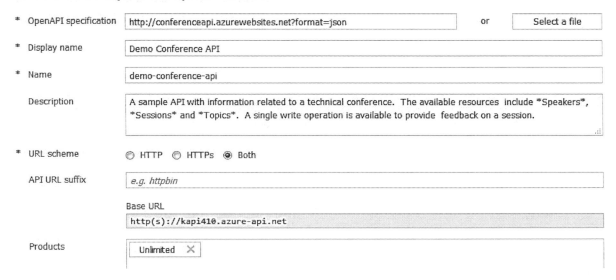

Step 3: Create and publish a product

In Azure API Management, a product contains one or more APIs as well as a usage quota and the terms of use. Once a product is published, developers can subscribe to the product and begin to use the product's APIs.
Products can be **Open** or **Protected**. Protected products must be subscribed to before they can be used, while open products can be used without a subscription.

1. Go to API Management Dashboard>Click Products in left pane>Click +Add>Select options as per your req and click create.

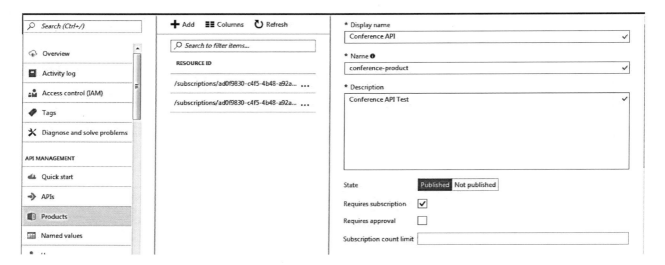

2. **Add API to your Product**>Click Products in left pane>Select your Product and click on it (In this case it is conference-product)> Click Add API>Select your API (In this case Demo Conference API) and click select.

Products are associations of one or more APIs. You can include a number of APIs and offer them to developers through the developer portal. Developers must first subscribe to a product to get access to the API. When they subscribe, they get a subscription key that is good for any API in that product.

Architecting Microsoft Azure Solutions Study & Lab Guide Part 2: Exam 70-535

Step 4: Test the newly created APIs

You can test APIs from the Azure Portal or Developer Portal.

1. API Management Dashboard> Click APIs in left pane>Select and click your API in left pane (In this case Demo Conference API)>Click Test Tab>Select Get speakers in left pane>Press send>**Backend responds** with 200 OK and some data.

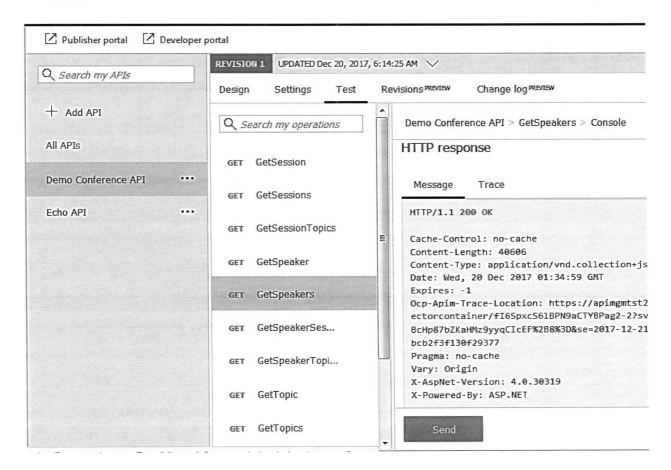

API Management Tiers

API Management is offered in four tiers—Developer, Basic, Standard, and Premium. Table below shows comparison of various tiers.

Features	Developer	Basic	Standard	Premium
Purpose	Non-production use cases and evaluations	Entry-level production use cases	Medium-volume production use cases	High-volume or Enterprise production use cases
Cache (per unit)	10 MB	50 MB	1 GB	5 GB
Scale-out (units)	1	2	4	10
SLA	No	99.9%	99.9%	99.95%
Azure Active Directory integration	Yes	No	Yes	Yes
Virtual Network support	Yes	No	No	Yes
Multi-region deployment	No	No	No	Yes
Estimated Maximum Throughput (per unit)	500 requests/sec	1000 requests/sec	2500 requests/sec	4000 requests/sec

SLA is only applicable when minimum of 2 units are deployed.

Caching

Caching can improve performance in Azure API Management. Caching can significantly reduce API latency, bandwidth consumption, and web service load for data that does not change frequently.
Caching is user response is stored in temp area. During subsequent response it is served from temp area.

Following table shows Cache storage available for Different API Management Tiers:

Features	Developer	Basic	Standard	Premium
Cache (per unit)	10 MB	50 MB	1 GB	5 GB

Virtual Network Support

Azure API Management can be deployed inside the virtual network (VNET), so it can access backend services within the network. The developer portal and API gateway, can be configured to be accessible either from the Internet or only within the virtual network.

Design Nugget: When deploying an Azure API Management instance to a Resource Manager VNET, the service must be in a dedicated subnet that contains no other resources except for Azure API Management instances.

Following table show VNET functionality supported by each tier:

Features	Developer	Basic	Standard	Premium
Virtual Network support	Yes	No	No	Yes

You can configure VNET support through API Dashboard. Click Virtual Network in left Pane>Select External or Internal>Select Location, Virtual Network & Subnet.

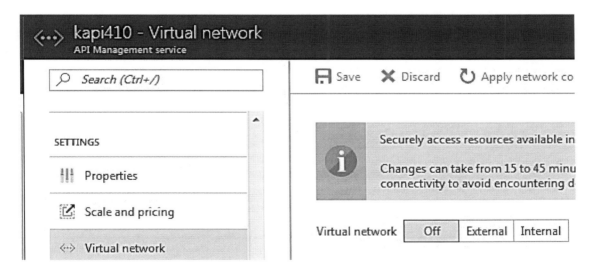

External Option: The API Management gateway and developer portal are accessible from the public internet via an external load balancer. The gateway can access resources within the virtual network.

Internal Option: The API Management gateway and developer portal are accessible only from within the virtual network via an internal load balancer. The gateway can access resources within the virtual network.

Architecting Microsoft Azure Solutions Study & Lab Guide Part 2: Exam 70-535

Scaling API Management

To meet the required performance you can Scale API Management Instance either by creating additional instances or upgrading to higher tier or both.

Following table shows number of instances supported by each API Management tier:

Features	Developer	Basic	Standard	Premium
Scale-out (units)	1	2	4	10

You can configure scale out through API Management Dashboard in Azure Portal. Click Scale and Pricing in left pane>If required upgrade your tier>Increase the number of units of API Management instance as per your requirement.

Design Nugget: SLA is only applicable when minimum 2 units are deployed.

API Management Pricing

Table below shows pricing of each tier.

Price	Developer	Basic	Standard	Premium
Price	$0.07/hour	$0.21/hour	$0.95/hour	$3.83/hour

Chapter 11 Azure Service Fabric

This Chapter covers following

- Azure Service Fabric

This Chapter Covers following Lab Exercises

- Deploying Service Fabric Cluster

Azure Service Fabric

Azure Service Fabric is a managed container orchestration platform for deploying and managing **Container & Microservices Applications** across a cluster of virtual machines.

As an orchestrator, Azure Service Fabric abstracts complex infrastructure problems of scalability, load balancing, discovery, deployment, reliability and manageability of Microservices and lets developers focus on implementation of workloads.

Azure Service Fabric can also be used to deploy traditional applications such as Web apps or Web services which can reap the same benefits of scalability, reliability and manageability as Microservices workloads, however, it is much better suited for hyperscale and Microservices based systems.

Service Fabric can deploy Microservices as processes or inside containers across the Service Fabric cluster. Service Fabric provides comprehensive runtime and lifecycle management capabilities to applications that are composed of these microservices. Containerized environment for Microservices enables Service Fabric to provide an increase in the density of deployment of workloads.

Azure Service Fabric orchestrates services across a cluster of machines. Each participant machine in a cluster is called a Node. Developers can use a variety of ways to build and deploy applications on Service Fabric such as, using the Service Fabric programming model, and deploying the application as guest executable. For each of the above application models, Service Fabric deploys the services as processes on nodes. Although, processes offer fastest activation and highest density, however, deploying the applications as processes can cause side effects such as resource starvation. Therefore, Service Fabric also supports deploying services in container images. Developers can also mix services deployed as processes and services deployed in container images in the same application.

Azure Service Fabric simplifies developing applications that use a microservice architecture, freeing developers to focus on building features that deliver customer value instead of managing infrastructure.

Service Fabric Deployment Options

Service Fabric is platform agnostic, so you can build your applications on Service Fabric and deploy them not just on Azure, but also on your local cloud or other public clouds.

Service Fabric can be deployed in Azure, on-Premises on a windows or Linux cluster and in Public Cloud like AWS. When deployed in Azure it is known as Azure Service Fabric. Figure below shows service fabric deployment options.

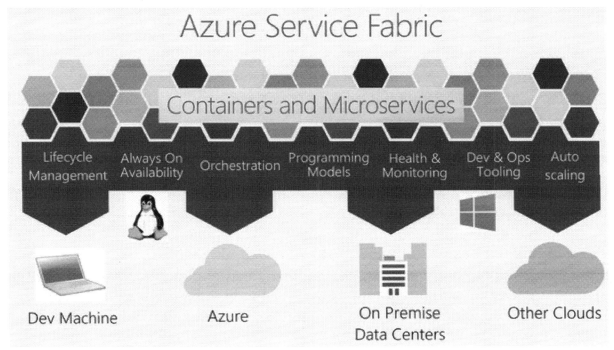

Advantages of running Service Fabric Clusters in Azure

Running Service Fabric clusters on Azure provides integration with other Azure features and services, which makes operations and management of the cluster easier and more reliable.

Auto-scaling: Clusters in Azure provide built-in auto-scaling functionality using Virtual Machine scale-sets.

Diagnostics: Clusters on Azure are integrated with Azure diagnostics and Log Analytics for easier management and troubleshooting.

Integration with Azure Infrastructure Service Fabric coordinates with the underlying Azure infrastructure for OS, network, and other upgrades to improve availability and reliability of your applications.

What Are Microservices

Microservices is an architectural style that structures an application as a collection of loosely coupled services which implement business capabilities. These services are independent of each other. Microservices enables each service to be developed independently by a team that is focused on that service.

Features of Microservices

1. A microservice application separates functionality into smaller services.
2. Services in a microservice architecture are independently deployable.
3. Services are organized around business capabilities.
4. Services are small in size, messaging enabled, autonomously developed, independently deployable, decentralized and built and released with automated processes.
5. Services in a microservice architecture (MSA) are processes that communicate with each other over well-defined interfaces and protocols.
6. Lends itself to a continuous delivery software development process. A change to a small part of the application only requires one or a small number of services to be rebuilt and redeployed.
7. Have unique names (URLs) used to resolve their location.

Comparison Between Monolithic and Microservices Application

A monolithic app contains domain-specific functionality and is normally divided by functional layers, such as web, App/Business and data tier. The figure below shows an e-commerce Monolithic App.

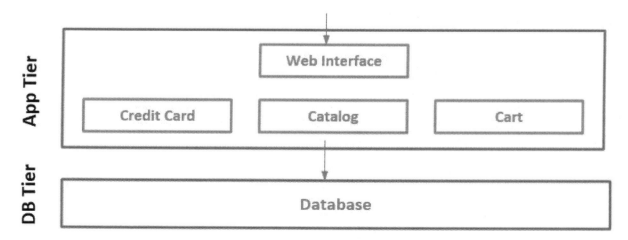

A Microservice Application separates application functionality into separate smaller services with each service having its own database. The figure below shows Microservices Application architecture.

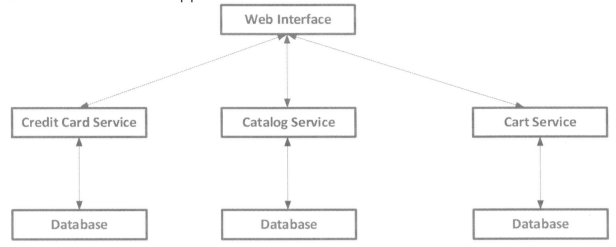

Benefits of Microservices Architecture

1. The **benefit** of decomposing an application into different smaller services is that it improves modularity and makes the application easier to develop and test. It also parallelizes development by enabling small autonomous teams to develop, deploy and scale their respective services independently.
2. Microservice architecture enables each microservice to be deployed independently. As a result, it makes continuous deployment possible for complex applications.

Example of Microservices application running on Service Fabric

Service Fabric powers many Microsoft services including Azure SQL Database, Azure Cosmos DB, Cortana, Microsoft Power BI, Microsoft Intune, Azure Event Hubs, Azure IoT Hub, Dynamics 365, Skype for Business and many core Azure services.

In **Summary**, the microservice approach is to decompose application into many smaller services. The services run in containers that are deployed across a cluster of machines. Teams develop a service that focuses on a scenario and independently test, version, deploy, and scale each service so that the entire application can evolve.

Microservices Types

Stateless Microservices: Either no state is maintained within the service or service state is maintained in an external Datastore.
Example of Stateless Microservices include Web Frontend, protocol gateways web proxies & calculations that don't require state.

Stateful Microservices: State is stored with the service. Allows for state to be persisted without the need for an external database. Data is co-located with the code that is running the service.
Example of Stateful Microservices include user accounts, gaming scenarios, data analytics, shopping carts, and queues.

Actor Microservices: An actor is a service which sends messages to other actors. The state persistence has three options – ***persisted, volatile*** and ***none***. The ***persisted*** option means that the state is written to a disk and replicated, while the ***volatile*** option causes that the state is kept in the memory only and replicated, whereas ***none*** state is in memory only and isn't replicated. The state is distinct to every actor. It is stored in a structure called Actor State Manager.
Figure below shows various Microservices states for loosely coupled services.

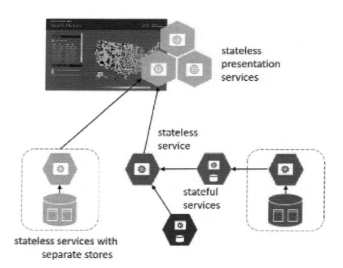

From above figure you can see that Stateless service either have no state maintained or state is maintained in external Store. Whereas Stateful services have data co-located with the service.

High level view of Service Fabric Cluster

Figure below shows 5 Node Service Fabric Cluster running both Management components and workloads on the same cluster.

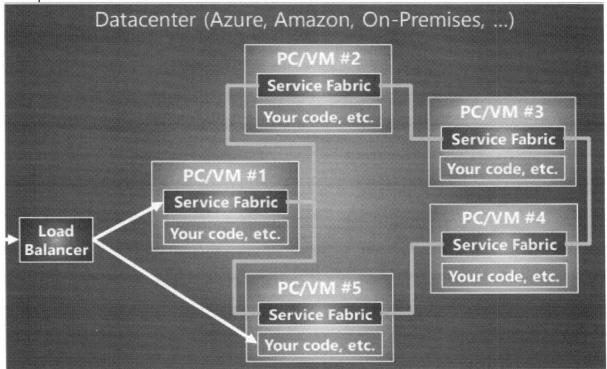

In Microservices Architecture an application is divided into multiple services. Figure below shows Placement of services across the cluster.

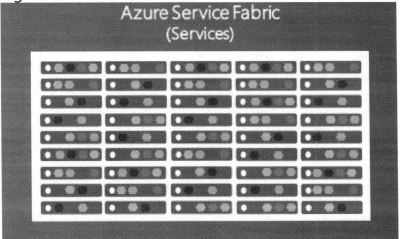

Multiple services can run in node. A Service can run in multiple nodes as secondary replica to provide high availability. Replication of services across nodes is done by Service Fabric orchestration platform.

Service Fabric Architecture

Service Fabric has a modular architecture in which there are several subsystems at play. Each subsystem is responsible for fulfilling a particular role in the overall system.

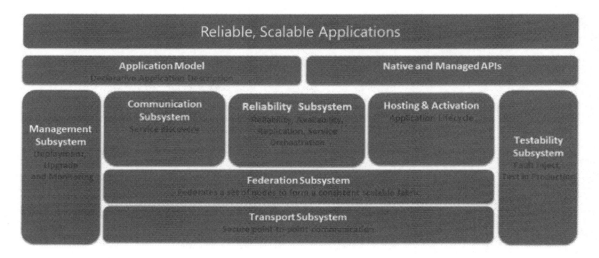

Transport subsystem: This subsystem is responsible for providing secure point-to-point communication channel both within the Service Fabric cluster (between nodes) and between Service Fabric cluster and application clients.

Federation subsystem: This subsystem provides services that unify the nodes to form a cluster. This subsystem provides failure detection, leader election, and routing services which are necessary to form a cluster from individual nodes.

Reliable subsystem: This subsystem adds reliability and high availability to the system by providing services for state replication, failover, and load balancing.

Management subsystem: This subsystem provides full ALM (Application Lifecycle Mangement) capabilities to Service Fabric. Service Fabric uses Management subsystem to manage application binaries, deploy, update, scale, and manage application health.

Hosting subsystem: The hosting subsystem manages performs the roles of Management subsystem, but at a node level.

Communication subsystem: In Microservices applications, service discovery is an important activity. The communication subsystem handles service discovery so that services can migrate freely between nodes.

Testability subsystem: Using the testability subsystem, developers can simulate various failure scenarios in Service Fabric cluster to find out any defects in the system.

Azure Service Fabric Cluster Architecture

A Service Fabric cluster is a network-connected set of virtual or physical machines into which your microservices are deployed and managed. Clusters can scale to thousands of machines.

Service Fabric can be deployed with single cluster or 2 Cluster or 3 Cluster option. **Each Cluster is deployed with Multiple Virtual Machines in a Virtual Machine Scale Set (VMSS).** A Load Balancer is also deployed with the VMSS for each cluster.

Service Fabric deployment with Single cluster (node type 1) is known as Primary Cluster. When Service Fabric is deployed with 2 cluster (Node Type 2) or 3 cluster (Node Type 3) option then the 1st cluster will be primary cluster. Each Cluster types is virtual machine scale sets, so Autoscaling functionality is built in.

Service Fabric Management component run in the primary cluster only. Whereas Container workloads can run both in Primary cluster as well as in Non-Primary clusters.

Supported operating systems for clusters on Azure

Service Fabric Cluster can be a windows Cluster or Linux cluster. You can create Service Fabric Cluster in Azure by using one of the following OS:

Windows Server 2012 R2 Datacenter
Windows Server 2016 Datacenter
Windows Server Datacenter 1709
Linux Ubuntu 16.04

Service Fabric Management Components (System Services)

Service Fabric Management component run in the primary cluster only.

Service Fabric Management component consist of set of system services that provides the underlying support for Service Fabric applications. The System Services are deployed in a redundant manner across multiple nodes so that they are highly available. Each Service is deployed as Primary replica and as multiple active secondary replicas.

Naming Service: A Node or a VM in Service Fabric Cluster can host multiple services, each with unique endpoints. **Naming Service** is a service discovery mechanism which can be used to resolve endpoint addresses.

The **Failover Manager** Service ensures that when nodes are added to or removed from the cluster, the load is automatically redistributed across the available nodes. If a node in the cluster fails, the cluster will automatically reconfigure the service replicas to maintain availability.

The **Cluster Manager** Service is the primary service that manages the lifecycle of the applications from provision to de-provision. It interacts with the Failover Manager to place the applications on the nodes based on the service placement constraints. It integrates with the health manager to ensure that application availability is not lost from a semantic health perspective during upgrades.

Image Store Service: Once your application is ready to be deployed, the application package files are versioned and copied to Service Fabric cluster's image store. The image store is made available to the cluster and other services through a hosted service called the image store service..

Upgrade Service: Azure cloud-based Service Fabric clusters are managed and upgraded by the Service Fabric Resource Provider(SFRP). The upgrade service coordinates upgrading the Service Fabric itself with the SFRP.
Health Manager service enables health monitoring of applications, services, and cluster entities. Cluster entities (such as nodes, service partitions, and replicas) can report health information, which is then aggregated into the centralized health store.

Service Fabric programming model overview

Service Fabric offers multiple ways to write and manage your services.

Guest Executables: A guest executable is an executable (written in any language) that can be run as a service in your application. Guest executables do not call the Service Fabric SDK APIs directly. However they still benefit from features the platform offers, such as service discoverability, custom health and load reporting by calling REST APIs exposed by Service Fabric.

Containers: Service Fabric can deploy services in containers. Service Fabric supports deployment of Linux containers and Windows containers on Windows Server 2016. Container images can be pulled from any container repository and deployed to the machine. You can deploy existing applications as guest executables, Service Fabric stateless or stateful Reliable services or Reliable Actors in containers, and you can mix services in processes and services in containers in the same application.

Reliable Services: Reliable Services is a light-weight framework for writing services that integrate with the Service Fabric platform and benefit from the full set of platform features. Reliable Services provide a minimal set of APIs that allow the Service Fabric runtime to manage the lifecycle of your services and that allow your services to interact with the runtime.
Reliable Services can be stateless or stateful. State is made highly-available through replication and distributed through partitioning, all managed automatically by Service Fabric.

ASP.NET Core: ASP.NET Core is open-source and cross-platform framework for building modern cloud-based Internet-connected applications, such as web apps, IoT apps, and mobile backends. Service Fabric integrates with ASP.NET Core so you can write both stateless and stateful ASP.NET Core applications that take advantage of Reliable Collections and Service Fabric's advanced orchestration capabilities.

Reliable Actors: Built on top of Reliable Services, the Reliable Actor framework is an application framework that implements the Virtual Actor pattern, based on the actor design pattern. It is fully integrated with the Service Fabric platform and benefits from the full set of features offered by the platform.

Application Deployment in Service Fabric Cluster

Service Fabric application consists of one or more microservices. A service performs a complete and standalone function and can start and run independently of other services. A service is composed of code, configuration, and data. For each service, code consists of the executable binaries, configuration consists of service settings that can be loaded at run time, and data consists of arbitrary static data to be consumed by the service.

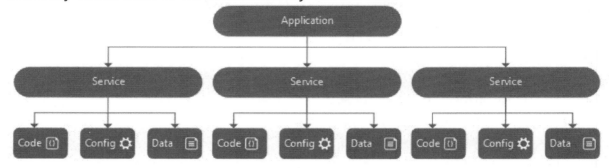

A Service Fabric Cluster can run multiple applications as shown below.

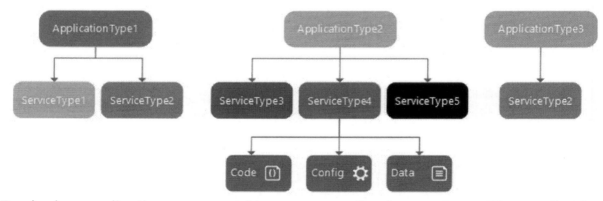

To deploy applications you need to create application package. The application package is a disk directory containing the application type's *ApplicationManifest.xml* file, which references the service packages for each service type that makes up the application type.

A service type is the name/version assigned to a service's code packages, data packages, and configuration packages. This is defined in a ServiceManifest.xml file, which is embedded in a service package directory.

The application package is copied to the Service Fabric cluster's image store. You can then create a named application from this application type, which then runs within the cluster.

You can use Service Fabric Template in Visual Studio to create application packages as executable or containers as shown below and then deploy to Azure Service Fabric Cluster.

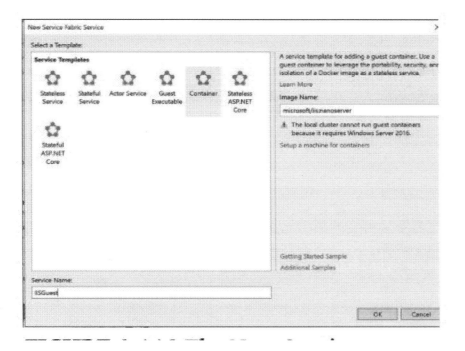

Service Fabric Application Scalability and Availability using Partitioning, Replicas & Instances.

Highly available services: Service Fabric services provide fast failover by creating multiple secondary service replicas. If a node, process, or individual service goes down due to hardware or other failure, one of the secondary replicas is promoted to a primary replica with minimal loss of service.

Scalable services: Individual services can be partitioned, allowing for state to be scaled out across the cluster. The replicas of each partition are spread across the cluster's nodes which allows your named service's state to scale. Services can be quickly and easily scaled out from a few instances on a few nodes to thousands of instances on many nodes, and then scaled in again, depending on your resource needs.

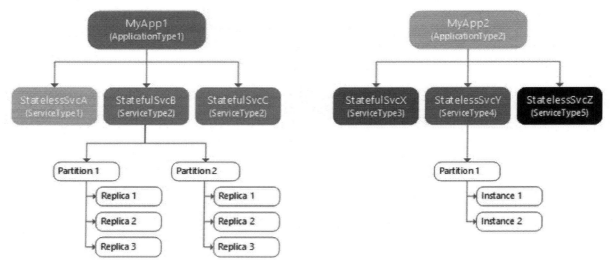

Within a partition, stateless named services have instances while stateful named services have replicas.

Stateful named services maintain their state within replicas and each partition has its own replica set. Read and write operations are performed at one replica (called the Primary). Changes to state from write operations are replicated to multiple other replicas (called Active Secondaries).

Stateless named services have one partition since they have no internal state. The partition instances provide for availability. If one instance fails, other instances continue to operate normally and then Service Fabric creates a new instance.

Exercise 49: Deploying Service Fabric Cluster

1. In Azure Portal click Create a resource>Containers>Service Fabric Cluster>
   Create Service Fabric Cluster blade opens> Enter as per your req and click ok.

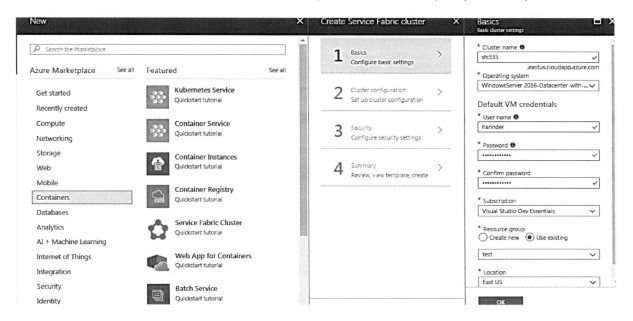

2. In Cluster configuration select Bronze tier and check mark Single node
   Cluster>Click Ok>Click Ok.

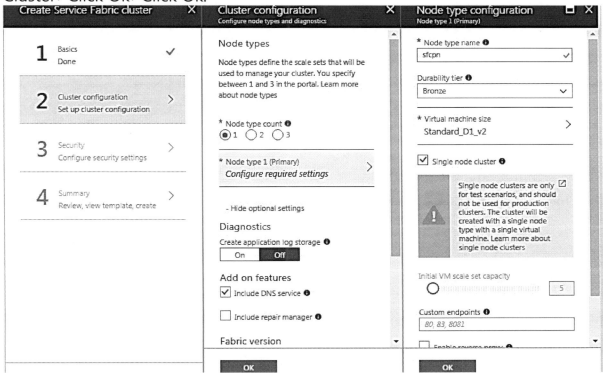

Architecting Microsoft Azure Solutions Study & Lab Guide Part 2: Exam 70-535

3. In Security Settings>Select Basic>Click Key Vault>select create new Key Vault>Create Key vault Blade opens>In name enter **sfc535**, select Resource group test and select location East US>click create.
    Note: With Basic option a certificate is created in key vault of your choice.

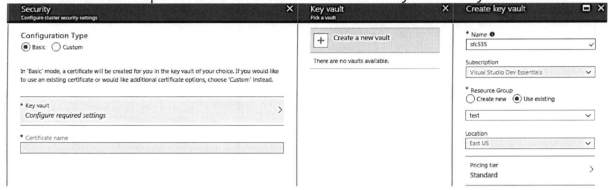

4. Click edit access Policies for Key Vault>Click show advanced access policies>Select all the advanced access policies as shown below>click save>Close the Access Policies blade.

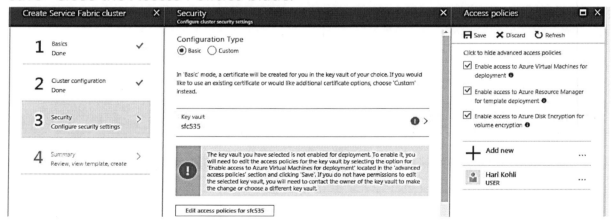

5. In Certificate name box enter sfc535-eastus>click Ok> In summary click create. It will take couple of minutes to create Cluster.

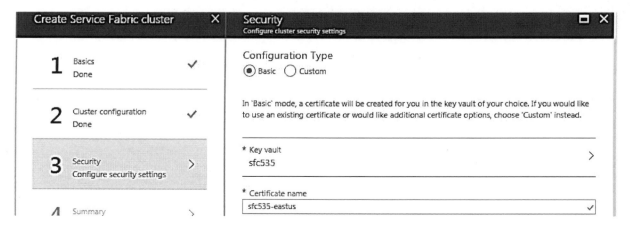

6. Figure below shows Dashboard of Service Fabric Cluster.

7. You can use Service Fabric Template in Visual Studio to create application packages as executable or containers and deploy them to Azure Service Fabric Cluster.

You can also deploy container images from Azure Container registery or Docker Hub to deploy your applications.

Chapter 12 Azure Cosmos DB

This Chapter covers following

- NoSQL Databases
- Cosmos DB Database
- Cosmos DB SQL API (Document) type Database
- Cosmos DB Table API (key-value pair) Database
- Cosmos DB Gremlin (Graph) API Database
- Cosmos DB Features
- Cosmos DB Pricing

This Chapter Covers following Lab Exercises

- Cosmos DB Account
- Create Cosmos DB SQL API (Document) Database
- Create Cosmos DB Table Storage (Key-Value) Database
- Create Cosmos DB Gremlin (Graph) Database
- Configuring firewall feature

NoSQL Database

NoSQL databases are non-relational databases optimized for scalable performance and schemaless data models. They use a variety of data models, including columnar, document, graph, and in-memory key-value stores.

A **NoSQL** database provides a mechanism for storage and retrieval of data that does not follow RDBMS model of placing data in tables.
NoSQL Database solves the problem of scalability, availability and latency which are inherent in traditional RDBMS Database when using large web scale applications.

Why we need NoSQL Database

Lets take an example of large e-commerce web scale application with a RDMBS backend used by millions of users. If a user is doing a transaction on e-commerce platform, the application will lock that particular product in the inventory database for other users till the transaction is over. This might work for a small set of users but not for millions of users accessing the application. **NoSQL Database solves this problem.**

NoSQL Database compromises consistency in favor of availability, partition tolerance, and speed. NoSQL databases offer a concept of "eventual consistency" in which database changes are propagated to all nodes "eventually" (typically within milliseconds) so queries for data might not return updated data immediately or might result in reading data that is not accurate.

ACID v/s BASE

Traditional RDBMS are based on ACID Principle (Atomicity, Consistency, Isolation and Durability).
Atomicity: Everything in a transaction succeeds lest it is rolled back.
Consistency: A transaction cannot leave the database in an inconsistent state.
Isolation: One transaction cannot interfere with another.
Durability: A completed transaction persists, even after applications restart.

NoSQL's basic idea is that for very large volumes of data, it is difficult to use the ACID principle.

Architecting Microsoft Azure Solutions Study & Lab Guide Part 2: Exam 70-535

NoSQL uses **BASE Principle**: basic accessibility (Basically Available), flexibility (Soft state), and the final alignment (Eventual consistency). This means that for every request guaranteed to finish (even unsuccessfully), the system state may change, even without the appearance of a data in the system, and that data will be compatible, although there still can be discrepancy.

Basic availability: Each request is guaranteed a response—successful or failed execution.

Soft state: The state of the system may change over time, at times without any input (for eventual consistency).

Eventual consistency: The database may be momentarily inconsistent but will be consistent eventually.

Therefore, if you are designing a Large Web Scale Solution that will load at the level of Amazon or Facebook or Twitter, you will have to use the **BASE** principles.

Features of NoSQL

Does not use Tables to store Data.
Does not use SQL as querying language.
Distributed Fault tolerant Architecture
Millisecond latency to support web scale operations.
No fixed schema.
No Joins. Joins are used in RDBMS for combining records from two or more tables. Joins require strong consistency and fixed schemas.

Comparing NoSQL with RDBMS

Capabilities	RDBMS	NoSQL	Cosmos DB
Global distribution	No	No	Yes
Horizontal scale	No	Yes	Independently scale storage & Throughput
Latency guarantees	No	Yes	Yes. 99% of reads in <10 ms and writes in <15 ms.
High availability	No	Yes	Yes
SLAs	Yes	No	Yes, comprehensive SLAs for latency, throughput, consistency, availability.

NoSQL Data Models

Key-Value Database: Key-Value Database stores data in pairs where you have Key with associated value. For Example take pair of Mobile 8625068410. Here Mobile is key and the number is value. Key- value database are typically used in session management and caching in web applications.

Document Database: Document Database stores semi-structured data in Documents format. Documents themselves act as records. Two Documents can have completely different set of records. **<u>Even though the documents do not follow a strict schema, indexes can be created and queried.</u>** Document databases are typically used in content management, User Profile Management and mobile application data handling.

Wide-Coumn Database: Wide-column stores organize data tables as columns instead of as rows. Wide-column stores can query large data volumes faster than conventional relational databases. A wide-column data store can be used for recommendation engines, catalogs, fraud detection and other types of data processing.

Graph Database: Graph data stores organize data as nodes, which are like records in a relational database, and edges, which represent connections between nodes. Because the graph system stores the relationship between nodes, it can support richer representations of data relationships. Graph databases are used to map relationships, such as reservation systems or customer relationship management.

Cosmos DB

Azure Cosmos DB is a Globally Distributed, Scalable, high throughput, low latency, multi-model managed NoSQL database service. Cosmos DB multi-model architecture natively supports document, key-value, graph, and column-family data models. Azure Cosmos DB supports following types of NoSQL Databases:

SQL (Document)
MongoDB (Document)
Azure Table (Key-Value)
Gemlin (Graph)
Apache Cassandra (Column Family)

Azure Cosmos DB Database is created under Cosmos DB Account. While creating Cosmos DB account you need to select one of the API. Each API supports one of the Data Model only (SQL, Mongo, Table Storage, Gemlin or Cassandra). Each Cosmos DB Account will support only one type of NoSQL Database.

Features of Cosmos DB

Globally Distributed: Azure Cosmos DB is globally distributed database. You can distribute your Cosmos DB data to any number of Azure regions.

Multiple data models: Azure Cosmos DB natively supports multiple data models including document, graph, key-value table, and column-family data models.

Storage: Azure Cosmos DB has SSD backed storage with low-latency response time in order-of-milliseconds. Database automatically scales when required.

Throughput: Easily scale database throughput anytime. You can independently scale Storage & Throughput.

Latency: Azure Cosmos DB guarantees end-to-end low latency in order of milliseconds.

Availability: Azure Cosmos DB offers 99.99% availability SLA for all single region database accounts, and all 99.999% read availability on all multi-region database accounts.

Consistency Models: Cosmos DB offer five consistency models from strong to eventual. Consistency levels enable you to make trade-offs between consistency, latency & cost.

Low cost of ownership: Five to ten times more cost effective than a non-managed solution or an on-premises NoSQL solution.

Cosmos DB use cases

Personalization: A personalized experience for a user to a website application requires lot of data– demographic, contextual, behavioral and more. Applications need to be able to retrieve personalized settings quickly and effectively to render UI elements and experiences quickly. Cosmos DB offers fast reads with low latency writes. Storing UI layout data including personalized settings as JSON documents in Cosmos DB is an effective means to get this data across the wire. Cosmos DB can scale elastically to meet the most demanding workloads and build and update visitor profiles on the fly, delivering the low latency required for real-time engagement with your customers.

Real Time Fraud Detection: Financial Service companies use Fraud detection extensively to minimize financial losses arising out of fraudulent deals and to comply with regulation. When customers pay with a credit or debit card, they expect immediate confirmation. Fraud Detection relies on data – detection algorithm rules, customer information, transaction information, location, time of day and more – applied at scale and in less than a millisecond. While relational databases struggle to meet this low latency requirement, elastically scalable NoSQL databases can reliably deliver the required performance.

Catalog in Retail and Marketing: Azure Cosmos DB can be used in e-commerce platform for storing Catalog Data. Catalog data is very dynamic and gets fragmented over period of time as new products and service are added and existing products specification gets changed. Cosmos DB NoSQL document database, with its flexible data model, enables enterprises to easily aggregate catalog data within a single database.

Additional Uses Cases

Gaming
User Profile
IOT Scenario
Social Applications
Mobile Applications
Big Data Applications

Exercise 50: Cosmos DB Account

Azure Cosmos DB Database is created under Cosmos DB Account. While creating Cosmos DB account you need to select one of the API. Each API supports one of the Data Model only

Creating Cosmos DB Account: Log on to Azure Portal>+New>Databases> Azure Cosmos DB> Cosmos DB New Account Blade opens. Give a unique name and Select your API (SQL, MongoDB, Cassandra etc) and click create.

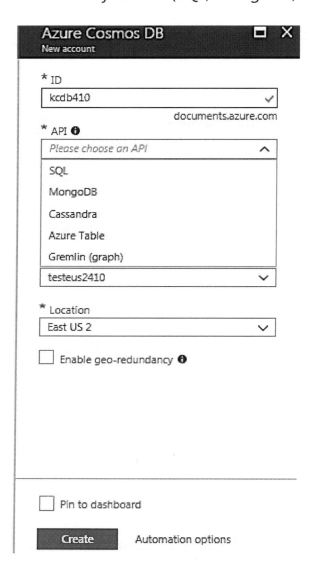

Note: When creating Cosmos DB Account you have the option to select one of the five types of Cosmos DB Database – SQL (Document), Mongo (Document), Cassandra (Column), Table (Key-Value) & Gremlin (Graph).

Architecting Microsoft Azure Solutions Study & Lab Guide Part 2: Exam 70-535

Cosmos DB SQL API (Document) type Database

Azure Cosmos DB SQL API (Document) is a Schema free NoSQL document database service designed from the ground up to natively support JSON and JavaScript directly inside the database engine. It's a schema-less JSON database engine with rich SQL querying capabilities.

SQL API (Document) databases stores semi-structured data in JSON Documents format. Documents themselves act as records. Two Documents can have completely different set of records. **Even though the documents do not follow a strict schema, indexes are automatically created and can be queried.**

Figure below shows 2 JSON documents with different records.

```
{
First Name: Deepti
Last Name: Sharma
Age        : 45
}

{

House Number: 140
Street         : 10th
Locality       : Dinsha Nagar
City           : Indore
District       : Indore
Pincode        : 452003

}
```

SQL API (Document) databases are logical containers for one or more collections. Collections are containers for JSON documents. Collections also contain stored procedures, user-defined functions and triggers.

SQL API Database stores data as collections of documents. Your application can use a variety of operation types supported by SQL API including CRUD, SQL and JavaScript queries, as well as stored procedures to work with documents. Figure below shows JSON documents stored in Cosmos DB SQL Database. You can query the document using familiar SQL Syntax. The SQL API provides full transactional execution of JavaScript application logic directly inside the database engine. This allows your application logic to operate over data without worrying about the mismatch between the application and the database schema.

You can connect Cosmos DB SQL API database to application platform of your choice including dot net, Java, Node.js & Xamarin.

SQL (Document) Database Use cases

Document databases are typically used in content management, User Profile Management and mobile application data handling.

Cosmos DB SQL API (document) Database Components

SQL API (Document) Database contains 4 components.

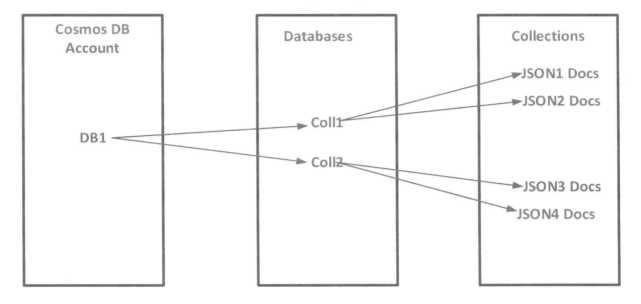

Cosmos DB Account: All Access to Cosmos DB Database happens through Cosmos DB account. Cosmos DB Account can contain one or more SQL API (Document) Databases.

Database: Databases are logical containers for one or more collections.

Collections: Collections are containers for JSON documents. Collections also contain stored procedures, user-defined functions and triggers.

Documents: Text based JSON Documents. A JSON Document contains multiple key-value pairs. Documents in a collection can have different records.

Exercise 51: Create Cosmos DB SQL API (Document) Database

1. **Create Cosmos DB account** using SQL API. The procedure was shown in Creating Cosmos DB Account on page.
2. **Add Collection**: Go to Cosmos DB account dashboard>Click Data Explorer in left pane>+ Add Collection> Add Collection Blade opens as shown below. Enter options as per your req and click ok. You get the option to select fixed 10 GB Storage capacity or unlimited Storage capacity. For fixed storage you can select throughput between 400 – 10000 RU/s. If you select unlimited Storage you can select throughput between 1000 – 100000 RU/s.

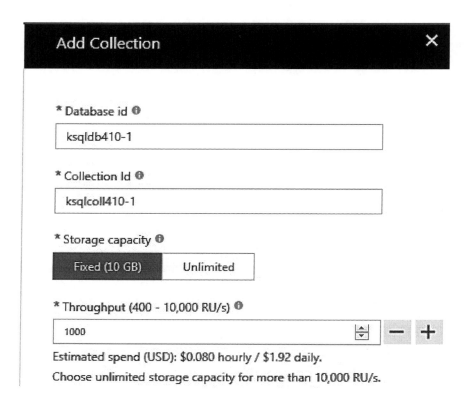

Note 1: You can choose between 10 GB or Unlimited Storage Capacity for Collection

Note 2: With 10 GB Storage you can choose Collection throughput between 400 to 10000 RU/s.

Note 3: With Unlimited Storage you can choose Collection throughput between 1000 to 100000 RU/s.

3. **Add documents** to collection created in step 2>In Cosmos DB Account Dashboard click Document Explorer in left pane> In right pane click upload > upload documents blade opens>Add your JSON Documents.

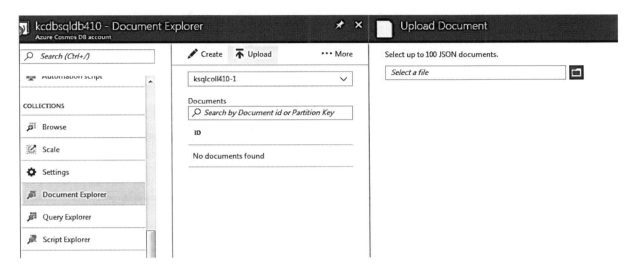

4. Copy **URL, keys and Connection strings** of the SQL (Document) Database. You need to add these in your application. Go to Cosmos DB Account Dashboard>Click Keys in left Pane.

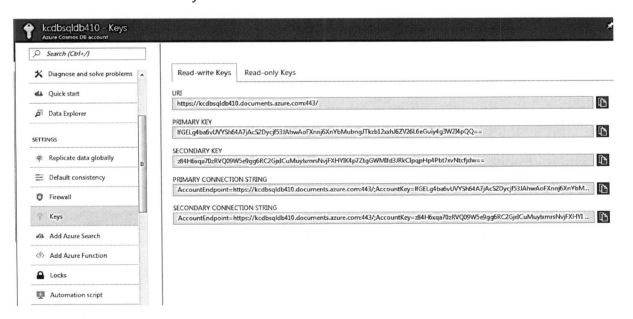

5. Connect your application to Azure Cosmos DB SQL (Document) Database by adding URL, keys and connection string generated in step 4.

6. You can also do **Query** on the JSON documents> Go to Cosmos DB Account Dashboard>Click query Explorer in left pane.

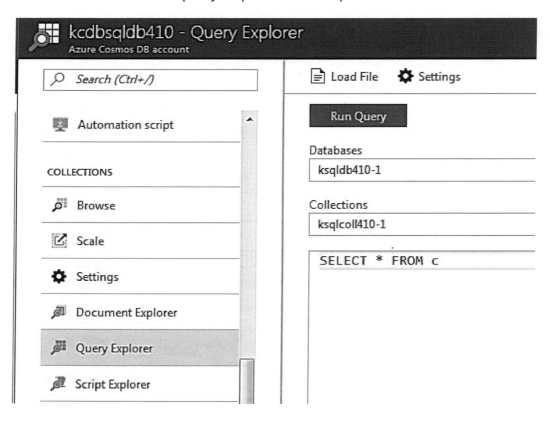

Cosmos DB Table API (key-value pair) Database

Tables are a structured Datastore based on **key-value pair** with a schemaless design. They are designed to store large amounts of data for massive scale where some basic structure is required, **but relationships between data don't need to be maintained**.

Cosmos DB Tables (Key-Value) Database stores data in pairs where you have a Key with associated value. For Example take Mobile 8625068410 Pair. Here Mobile is key and the number is value.

Advantage of Table is that Access to data is fast and cost-effective for all kinds of applications. Table storage is typically significantly lower in cost than traditional SQL for similar volumes of data.

Architecture

Cosmos DB Table API (key-value pair) Database is a collection of tables. A Table is a collection of entities. Tables don't enforce a schema on entities, which means a single table can contain entities that have different sets of properties.

Entity is a collection of Properties. A Property is a key-value pair. Each entity can include up to 252 properties (Key-value pair) to store data. Each entity also has 3 system defined properties that specify a partition key, a row key, and a timestamp. You need to specify the value of Partition and Row key.
An entity's row key is unique within a partition.
Entities can have different types of properties (String, Boolean Date, Time etc) even for the same partition key because there is no fixed schema.

Table Database Use Cases

Key-value databases are optimized for querying against keys. As such, they serve great in-memory caches. Following are some of the use cases:

Session management in Web Applications
Caching for Web Applications.
Diagnostic logs.

Table Storage Components

Table Storage Service contains 3 components.

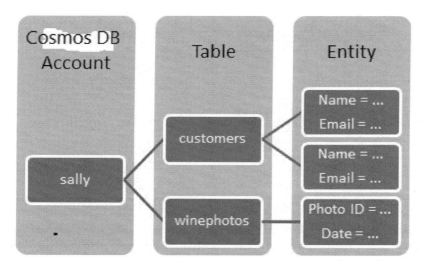

Cosmos DB Account: All Access to Cosmos DB Database happens through Cosmos DB account. Cosmos DB Account can contain one or more Table API (Key-Value) Database.

Table: A table is a collection of entities. Tables don't enforce a schema on entities, which means a single table can contain entities that have different sets of properties.

Entities: An entity is a set of properties with a Max size of 1MB. Each entity can include up to 252 properties to store data and 3 System Defined Properties.

Properties: A property is a **key-value pair**.

System Defined Properties: Each entity has three system defined properties that specify a partition key, a row key, and a timestamp. You specify value for Partition and Row key. Timestamp value is system generated. An entity's row key is unique within a partition.

Tables also contain stored procedures, user-defined functions, and triggers.

Exercise 52: Create Cosmos DB Table Storage (Key-Value) Database

1. **Create Cosmos DB account** using Table API. The procedure was shown in Creating Cosmos DB Account on page.
2. **Add Table**: Go to Cosmos DB account dashboard>Click Data Explorer in left pane>+ New Table> Add Table Blade opens as shown below. Enter options as per your req and click ok. You get the option to select fixed 10 GB Storage capacity or unlimited Storage capacity. For fixed storage you can select throughput between 400 – 10000 RU/s. If you select unlimited Storage you can select throughput between 1000 – 100000 RU/s.

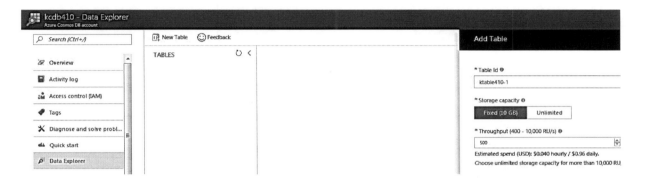

3. **Add Entities**. Go to Cosmos DB account dashboard>Click Data Explorer in left pane>Click on table you created in step 2 and it will enumerate>Click on entities>Click Add entity> Add Entity Blade opens> I have added 3 Properties (Email-test@test.com; Mobile-9998887777;LeapYear-true). Recall Properties are Key Value pair. Click Add entity.

   Important Note: There are already 3 system defined Properties: Partition key, Row key and Timestamp (Not shown). I have added a value of **1** for partition key and value of **a** for row key.

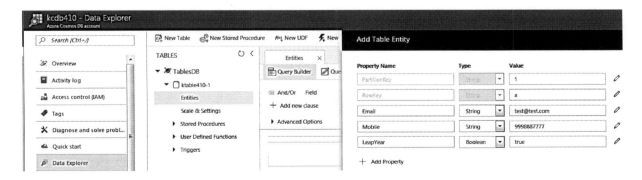

4. Figure below shows the entity that was created. It shows 6 Key-value pairs: PartitionKey, RowKey, Timestamp, Email, Mobile & LeapYear.

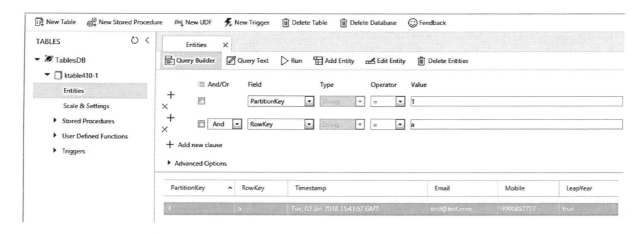

5. Copy **Endpoint, keys and Connection strings** of the Table Storage (Key-value)) Database. You need to add these in your application. Go to Cosmos DB Account Dashboard>Click Connection string in left Pane.

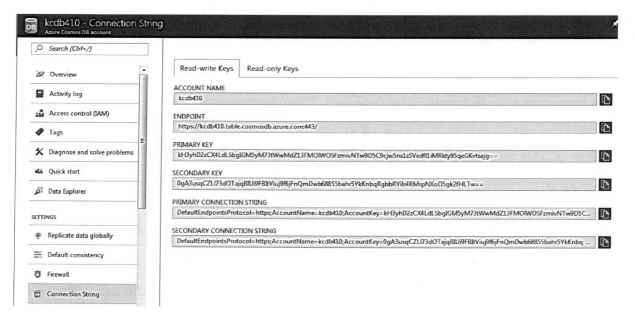

6. **Connect your application** to Azure Cosmos DB Table Storage (Key-value) Database by adding URL, keys and connection string generated in step 5. You will also need SDK specific to your application platform to connect your application to Azure Cosmos DB Table Storage Database.

Architecting Microsoft Azure Solutions Study & Lab Guide Part 2: Exam 70-535

7. You can also **query** the table or entity>Go to Azure Cosmos DB account Dashboard>click Data Explorer>select your table or entity and run your query.

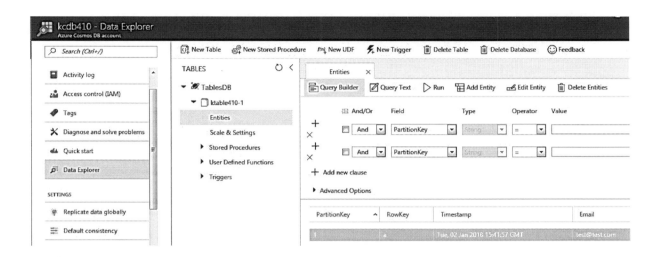

Cosmos DB Gremlin (Graph) API Database

Cosmos DB Gremlin (Graph) API Database is A Graph database that uses nodes and edges to represent and store data. It supports Open Graph APIs (based on the Apache TinkerPop specification, Apache Gremlin).

A graph is a structure that's composed of vertices/nodes and edges. Vertices/Nodes denote discrete objects such as a person, a place, or an event. Edges denote relationships between Vertices. For example, a person might know another person, be involved in an event and recently been at a location.

Properties express information about the vertices and edges. Example properties include a node that has a name, age, and edge, which has a time stamp and/or a weight.

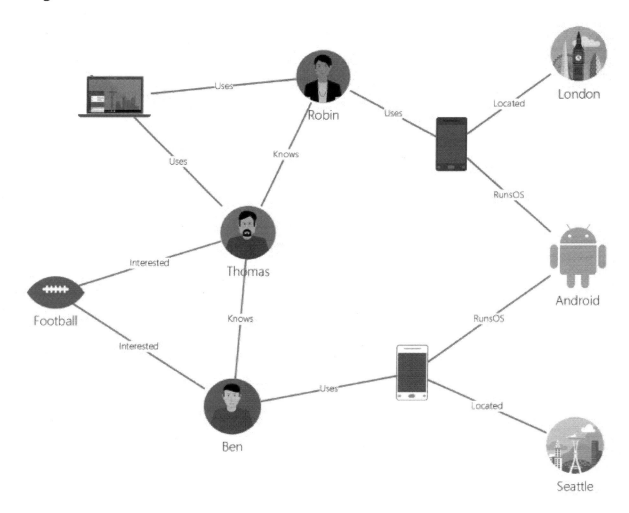

Architecture

Cosmos DB Gremlin (Graph) Database is created under Cosmos DB account. Gremlin (Graph) databases are logical containers for one or more Graphs. Graph are containers for Vertex. A Vertex is key Value pair. Graph can contain multiple Vertex.
Graphs also contain Scale & Settings, stored procedures, user-defined functions, and triggers.

Use Cases

Social networks: By combining data about your customers and their interactions with other people, you can develop personalized experiences, predict customer behavior, or connect people with others with similar interests. Azure Cosmos DB can be used to manage social networks and track customer preferences and data.

Recommendation engines: This scenario is commonly used in the retail industry. By combining information about products, users, and user interactions, like purchasing, browsing, or rating an item, you can build customized recommendations. The low latency, elastic scale, and native graph support of Azure Cosmos DB is ideal for modeling these interactions.

Geospatial: Many applications in telecommunications, logistics, and travel planning need to find a location of interest within an area or locate the shortest/optimal route between two locations. Azure Cosmos DB is a natural fit for these problems.

Internet of Things: With the network and connections between IoT devices modeled as a graph, you can build a better understanding of the state of your devices and assets. You also can learn how changes in one part of the network can potentially affect another part.

Cosmos DB SQL API (document) Database Components

Graph Database contains 4 components.

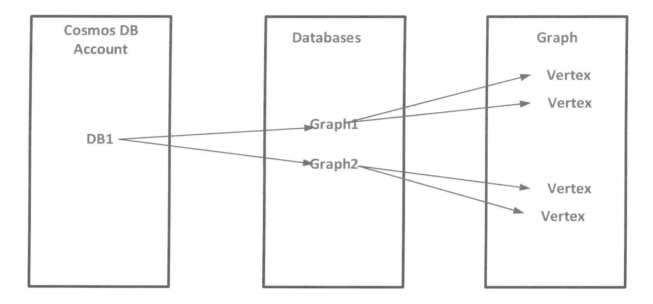

Cosmos DB Account: All Access to Cosmos DB Database happens through Cosmos DB account. Cosmos DB Account can contain one or more SQL API (Document) Databases.

Database: Databases are logical containers for one or more Graph Databases.

Graphs: Graphs are containers for Vertex & Edges. Graphs also contain stored procedures, user-defined functions and triggers.

Exercise 53: Create Cosmos DB Gremlin (Graph) Database

1. **Create Cosmos DB account** using Gremlin (Graph) API. The procedure was shown in Creating Cosmos DB Account on page.
2. **Add Graph**: Go to Cosmos DB account dashboard>Click Data Explorer in left pane>+ New Graph> Add Graph Blade opens as shown below. Enter options as per your req and click ok. You get the option to select fixed 10 GB Storage capacity or unlimited Storage capacity. For fixed storage you can select throughput between 400 – 10000 RU/s. If you select unlimited Storage you can select throughput between 1000 – 100000 RU/s.

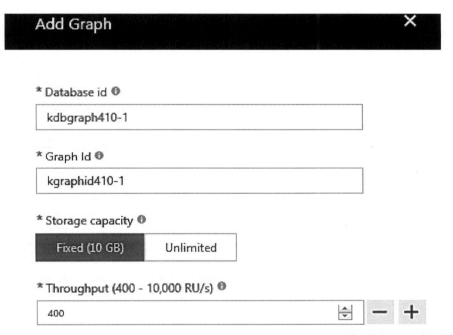

3. **Add Vertex**. . Go to Cosmos DB account dashboard>Click Data Explorer in left pane>Click on graph you created in step 2 and it will enumerate>Click on graph>Click New vertex in right pane> New vertex Blade opens. Fill as per your requirement.

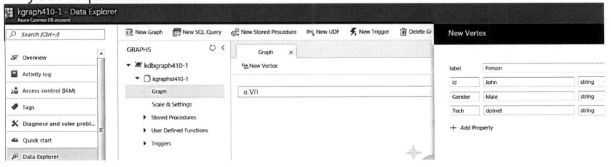

4. Copy **URL, keys and Connection strings** of the Graph Database. You need to add these in your application. Go to Cosmos DB Account Dashboard>Click Keys in left Pane.

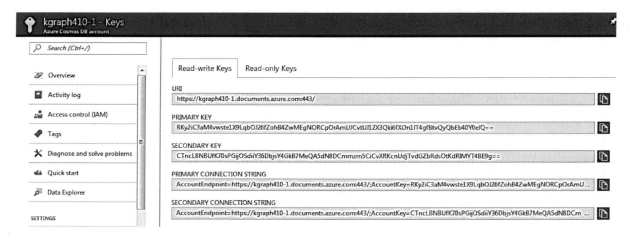

5. **Connect your application** to Azure Cosmos DB Graph Database by adding URL, keys and connection string generated in step 5. If you are developing your application on windows platform using Visual Studio you will also need Azure SDK to connect your application to Azure Cosmos DB Table Storage Database. If you are developing your application on Linux/Java platform then you will need Java SDK to connect your application to Azure Cosmos DB Table Storage Database.

Cosmos DB Firewall Feature (Applicable to all Database Types)

With Firewall feature you can limit access to Cosmos DB from selected IP Addresses only.

Exercise 54 Configuring firewall feature: Go to Cosmos DB Account Dashboard>Click Firewall in left Pane> Select ON for Enable IP Access control> Add IP's from where you would access Cosmos DB.

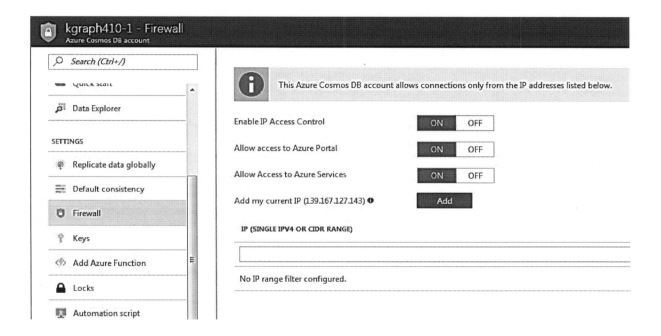

Cosmos DB Replication Feature (Applicable to all Database Types)

With Cosmos DB replication feature you can additional read replica regions.

With Cosmos DB you can have write in one region and multiple read regions. This enables you to put your data where your users are, ensuring the lowest possible latency to your customers.

In case of failure of write region one of the read region will be promoted as write region.

Adding Read Regions: Go to Cosmos DB Account Dashboard>Click Replicate Data Globally in left Pane>In Right Pane click Add New Region button to add a read regions.

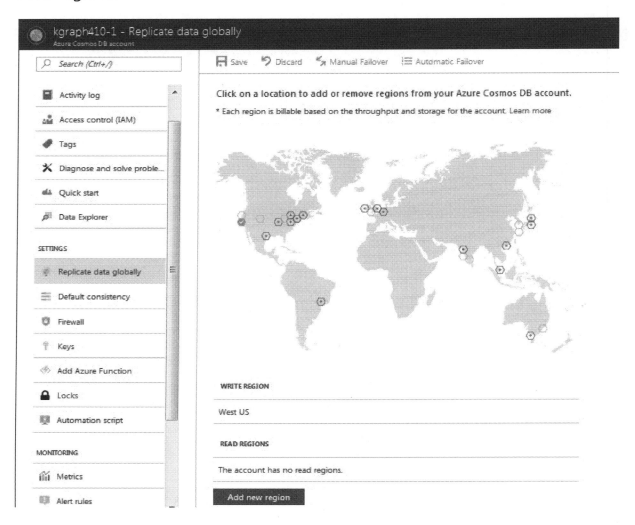

Add Azure Function (Applicable to all Database Types)

You can add a Azure function which uses Cosmos DB as a trigger from Cosmos DB account Dashboard. The biggest advantage of this option is that you don't need to add a software code to connect Cosmos DB to Azure Function

Add Azure Function: Go to Cosmos DB Account Dashboard>Click Add Azure function in left Pane> Add Azure Function Blade opens.

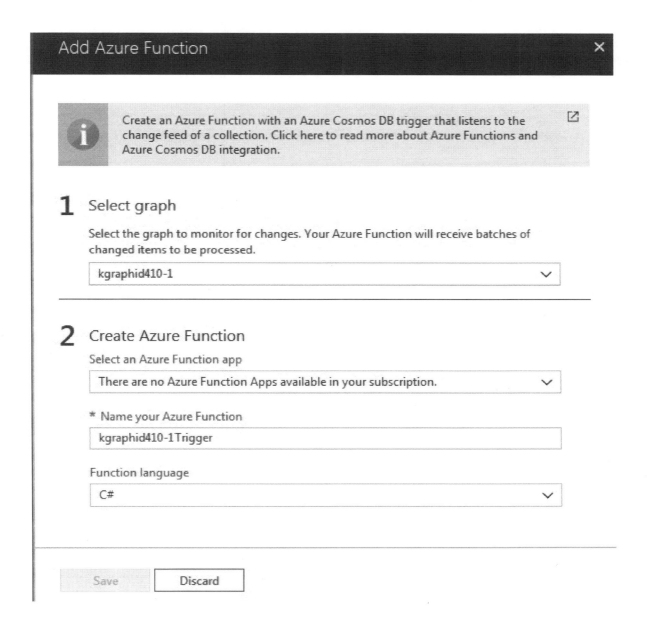

Consistency levels in Azure Cosmos DB

Consistency levels enable you to make trade-offs between consistency, availability, and latency.

Azure Cosmos DB provides five consistency levels: strong, bounded-staleness, session, consistent prefix, and eventual. Strong offers the most strong read consistency and Eventual the least read consistency.

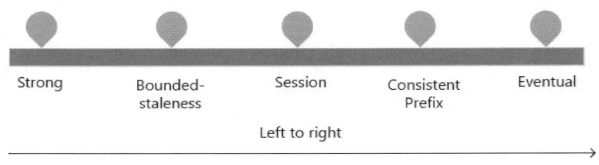

| Strong | Bounded-staleness | Session | Consistent Prefix | Eventual |

Left to right

Lower read Consistency, Lower latency, Higher Availability, Better Read Scalability

Configuring Consisitency Level: Go to Cosmos DB Account Dashboard>Click Default Consistency in left Pane>Select the consistency level in right pane from one of the 5 Tabs>Click Save.

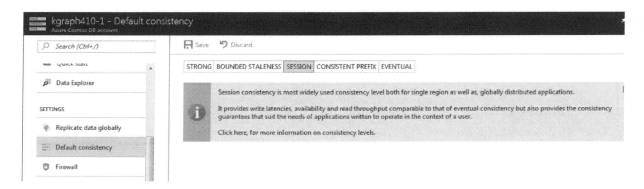

Strong Consistency: Strong consistency offers reads guarantee to return the most recent version of an item. Strong consistency guarantees that a write is only visible after it is committed durably by the majority quorum of replicas. Strong consistency is scoped to a single azure Region only. The cost of a read operation (in terms of request units consumed) is higher than session and eventual, but the same as bounded staleness.

Bounded Staleness: Bounded staleness consistency guarantees that the reads may lag behind writes by at most K versions or prefixes of an item or t time-interval. Azure Cosmos DB accounts that are configured with bounded staleness consistency can associate any number of Azure regions with their Azure Cosmos DB account. The cost of a read operation (in terms of RUs consumed) with bounded staleness is higher than session and eventual consistency, but the same as strong consistency.

Bounded staleness is great for applications featuring group collaboration and sharing, stock ticker, publish-subscribe/queueing etc.

Figure below shows the configuration options for Bounded Staleness:

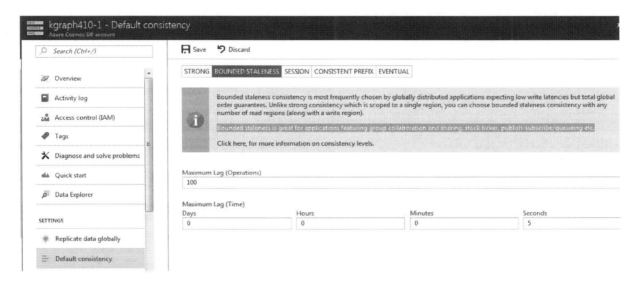

Session Consistency: Session Consistency provides write latencies, availability and read throughput comparable to that of eventual consistency but also provides the consistency guarantees that suit the needs of applications written to operate in the context of a user. Azure Cosmos DB accounts that are configured with session consistency can associate any number of Azure regions with their Azure Cosmos DB account. The cost of a read operation (in terms of RUs consumed) with is less than strong and bounded staleness, but more than eventual consistency.

Consistent Prefix: Consistent prefix level guarantees that reads never see out of order writes. If writes were performed in the order `A, B, C`, then a client sees either `A`, `A,B`, or `A,B,C`, but never out of order like `A,C` or `B,A,C`. Consistent Prefix provides write latencies, availability and read throughput comparable to that of eventual consistency, but also provides the order guarantees that suit the needs of scenarios where order is important. Azure Cosmos DB accounts that are configured with consistent prefix consistency can associate any number of Azure regions with their Azure Cosmos DB account.

Eventual Consistency: Eventual consistency is the weakest form of consistency wherein a client may get the values which are older than the ones it had seen before, over time. In the absence of any further writes, the replicas within the group will eventually converge. Azure Cosmos DB accounts that are configured with eventual consistency can associate any number of Azure regions with their Azure Cosmos DB account. The **cost** of a read operation (in terms of RUs consumed) with the eventual consistency level is the lowest of all the Azure Cosmos DB consistency levels.

Eventual consistency is ideal where the application does not require any ordering guarantees. Examples include count of Retweets, Likes or non-threaded comments.

Azure Cosmos DB Container Storage & Throughput

Cosmos DB provides containers (Collections, Graphs or Tables) for storing data. You can provision containers with required storage & throughput.

Storage: Azure Cosmos DB has SSD backed storage with low-latency in order-of-millisecond response times. Storage for container is either fixed 10 GB or unlimited Storage. Storage auto-scales and you are charged for storage used.

Throughput in RU/s: For each container you can specify throughput in terms of **Request Units per second (RU/s)**. For fixed storage you can select throughput between 400 – 10000 RU/s. For unlimited Storage you can select throughput between 1000 – 100000 RU/s and specify a partition key.

For example, a read operation on a 1KB document requires 1 RU. You can adjust reserved RU/s for each container programmatically or via the portal at any time regardless of the amount of the data stored.

Estimating number of request units per second (RU/s)

To estimate the number of request units (RU/s) to provision for Azure Cosmos DB container, take the following variables into consideration:

Item size. As size increases the number of request units consumed to read or write the data also increases.

Item property count. Assuming default indexing of all properties, the units consumed to write a document/node/entity increase as the property count increases.

Data consistency. When using data consistency models such as Strong or Bounded Staleness, additional request units are consumed to read items.

Indexed properties. An index policy on each container determines which properties are indexed by default. You can reduce your request unit consumption by limiting the number of indexed properties or by enabling lazy indexing.

Document indexing. By default each item is automatically indexed. You consume fewer request units if you choose to not index some of your items.

Query patterns. The complexity of a query impacts how many request units are consumed for an operation. The number of predicates, nature of the predicates, projections, number of UDFs, and the size of the source data - all influence the cost of query operations.

Script usage. As with queries, stored procedures and triggers consume request units based on the complexity of the operations being performed.

Partitioning

Azure Cosmos DB provides containers (Collections, Graphs or Tables) for storing data. Containers are logical resources and can span one or more physical partitions or servers. Each physical partition is replicated to provide high availability for your container data.

A **physical partition** is a fixed amount of reserved SSD-backed storage. Each physical partition is replicated for high availability. One or more physical partitions make up a container. Physical partition management is fully managed by Azure Cosmos DB.

A **logical partition** is a partition within a physical partition that stores all the data associated with a **single partition key value**. Multiple logical partitions can end up in the same physical partition. In the following diagram, a single container has three logical partitions. Each logical partition stores the data for one partition key, LAX, AMS, and MEL respectively. Each of the LAX, AMS, and MEL logical partitions cannot grow beyond the maximum logical partition limit of 10 GB.

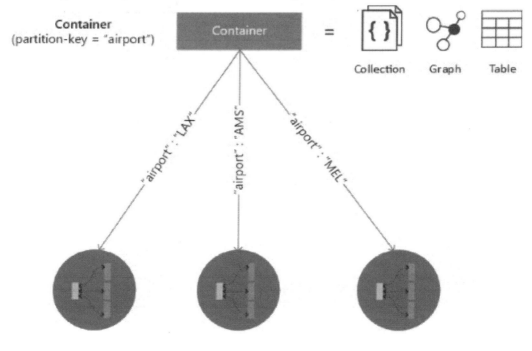

Design Nugget: For containers to auto-scale or auto split into **p1** and **p2** **physical partitions,** you must create containers with at least 1,000 RU/s of throughput and a partition key is also specified.

Cosmos DB Pricing

Cosmos DB Pricing is based on 2 components: Reserved Throughput and SSD Storage.

Reserved Throughput is billed as Request Units per second or RU/s. You assign Reserved throughput to containers.

SSD Storage is Data Stored in containers per GB per month.

Containers are Collection Documents, table or Graph. Each container is billed on an hourly basis for throughput provisioned in units of 100 RU/second, with a minimum of 400 RU/second, and data stored (in GBs).

Unit	Pricing
SSD Storage (per GB)	$0.25 GB/month
Reserved RUs/second (per 100 RUs, 400 RUs minimum)	$0.008/hour

Chapter 13 Azure Redis Cache

This Chapter covers following

- Azure Redis Cache

This Chapter Covers following Lab Exercises

- Create and use Azure Redis Cache

Azure Redis Cache

Azure Redis Cache is Managed service in Azure and is based on open source Redis Cache.

Azure Redis cache is in-memory key-value No SQL data store and cache. Azure Cache improves the performance of applications by allowing you to retrieve information from fast, managed, in-memory data stores, instead of relying entirely on slower disk-based databases.

All Redis data resides in its server's main memory, in contrast to most database management systems that store data on disk or on SSDs. By eliminating the need to access disks, in-memory databases such as Redis avoid seek time delays and can access data with simpler algorithms that use fewer CPU instructions. Typical operations require less than a millisecond to execute.

Redis is a fast, open source, in-memory key-value data structure store. Redis comes with a set of versatile in-memory data structures which enable you to easily create a variety of custom applications.

Redis Cache Use Cases

Caching: Redis placed in "front" of another database creates a highly performant in-memory cache to decrease access latency, increase throughput, and ease the load off a relational or NoSQL database.

Session management: Redis is highly suited for session management tasks. Simply use Redis as a fast key-value store with appropriate TTL on session keys to manage your session information. Session management is commonly required for online applications, including games, e-commerce websites and social media platforms.

Real-time Leaderboards: Using the Redis Sorted Set data structure, elements are kept in a list, sorted by their scores. This makes it easy to create dynamic leaderboards to show who is winning a game, or posting the most-liked messages, or anything else where you want to show who's in the lead.

Rate Limiting: Redis can measure and, when needed, throttle the rate of events. By using a Redis counter associated with a client's API key, you can count the number of access requests within a certain time period and take action if a limit is exceeded. Rate limiters are commonly used for limiting the number of posts on a forum, limiting resource utilization and containing the impact of spammers.

Queues: The Redis List data structure makes it easy to implement a lightweight, persistent queue. Lists offer atomic operations as well as blocking capabilities, making them suitable for a variety of applications that require a reliable message broker or a circular list.

Chat and Messaging: Redis supports the PUB/SUB standard with pattern matching. This allows Redis to support high performance chat rooms, real-time comment streams, and server intercommunication. You can also use PUB/SUB to trigger actions based on published events.

Azure Redis Cache Features and tiers

Basic: Basic cache is a single node cache which is ideal for development/test and non-critical workloads. There is no SLA on Basic tier. Basic and Standard caches are available in sizes up to 53 GB Memory. Maximum number of Client connections is 20000.

Standard: A replicated cache in a two node Primary/Secondary configuration managed by Microsoft, with a high availability SLA of 99.9%. Microsoft manage automatic replication between the two nodes. Basic and Standard caches are available in sizes up to 53 GB. Maximum number of Client connections is 20000.

Premium: Enterprise ready tier which can be used as a cache and persist data. Designed for maximum scale and enterprise integration. Premium caches are available in sizes up to 530 GB Memory. Maximum number of Client connections is 40000.

Premium Tier Additional Feature

Better Performance: Better performance over Basic or Standard-tier Caches for similar size VM, bigger workloads, disaster recovery and enhanced security.

Redis data persistence: The Premium tier allows you to persist the cache data in an Azure Storage account. In a Basic/Standard cache all the data is stored only in memory. In case of underlying infrastructure issues there can be potential data loss. We recommend using the Redis data persistence feature in the Premium tier to increase resiliency against data loss.

Redis cluster: With Redis cluster you can create caches larger than 53 GB. Each node consists of a primary/replica cache pair managed by Azure for high availability. Premium caches are available in sizes up to 530 GB Memory. Redis clustering gives you maximum scale and throughput. Throughput increases linearly as you increase the number of nodes in the cluster.

Enhanced security and isolation with VNET: Caches created in the Basic or Standard tier are accessible on the public internet. Access to the Cache is restricted based on the access key. With the Premium tier you can further ensure that only clients within a specified network can access the Cache. You can deploy Premium Redis Cache in an Azure Virtual Network (VNET). You can use all the features of VNET such as subnets, access control policies, and other features to further restrict access to Redis.

Geo-replication links two Premium tier Azure Redis Cache instances. One cache is designated as the primary linked cache, and the other as the secondary linked cache. The secondary linked cache becomes read-only, and data written to the primary cache is replicated to the secondary linked cache. This functionality can be used to replicate a cache across Azure regions.

Reboot: The premium tier allows you to reboot one or more nodes of your cache on-demand. This allows you to test your application for resiliency in the event of a failure.

Comparing Different Redis Cache Tiers

Features	Basic	Standard	Premium
Cache	Yes	Yes	Yes
Compute Nodes	1	2 (Active-Passive)	Multiple
Replication and Failover		Yes	Yes
SLA		99.9%	99.9%
Redis Data Persistence			Yes
Redis Cluster			Yes
Scale Out to multiple Cache units			Yes
Azure Virtual Network			Yes
Memory Size	250 MB - 53 GB	250 MB - 53 GB	6 GB - 530 GB
Maximum number of Client connections	256 - 20,000	256 - 20,000	7,500 - 40,000

Exercise 55: Create and use Azure Redis Cache

Creating and using Azure Redis Cache is a 2 step process. First you create Redis Cache and then add Redis Cache connection string in your application.

1. **Create Redis Cache**: In Azure Portal Click **Create a resource > Databases > Redis Cache> Enter information as per your requirement and click create.**

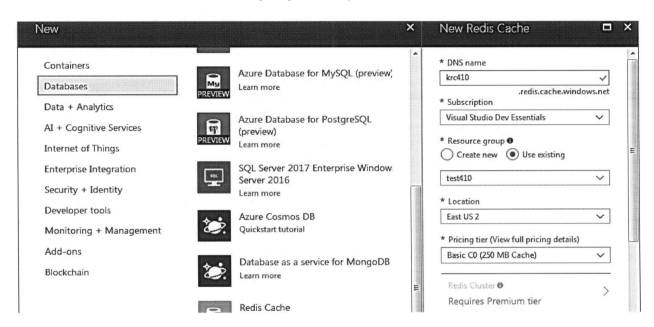

2. **Copy Redis Cache connection String**. Go to newly created Redis Cache Dashboard>click Access Keys and copy the Primary Connection String.

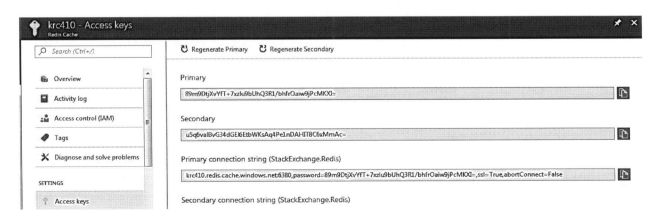

3. In your application add Primary connection string. Also configure your application to use Azure Redis Cache.

Architecting Microsoft Azure Solutions Study & Lab Guide Part 2: Exam 70-535

Chapter 14 High Performance Computing (HPC)

This Chapter covers following

- High Performance Computing
- Azure Virtual Machines with HPC support
- Microsoft HPC Pack
- Azure Batch

High Performance Computing (HPC)

High-performance computing (HPC) aggregates computing power from multiple computers to run parallel processing Workloads or Applications.

Parallel Workloads are those where the applications can run independently on Cluster of computers and each instance completes part of the work.

In Azure You can implement HPC in following 3 ways:

High Performance Computing Virtual machines: Azure Virtual Machines such as H Series & N Series can run HPC Workloads. You need to deploy HPC Software on Azure VMs to run HPC workloads.

Microsoft HPC Pack: Microsoft Free HPC Software Pack is used to create Linux or Windows High Performance Computing (HPC) Cluster. ARM templates are used to deploy the HPC Pack on Azure VMs. HPC Pack creates Single or Multiple **Head Nodes** and Cluster of **Compute Nodes** which run Parallel Processing Workloads. All Resources are deployed in Azure Virtual Network. **HPC Cluster Manager** is used to configure and manage HPC Cluster.

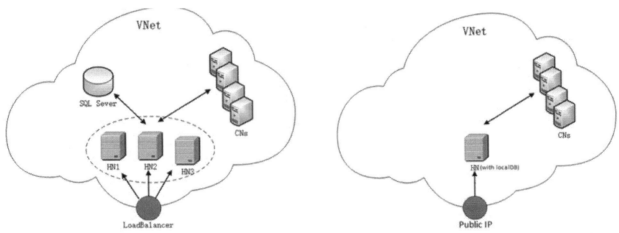

Cluster with Multiple Head Nodes and External Database Server

Cluster with Single Head Node and Local Database

Both of the above solutions are not managed solutions and have high operational and Administrative overheads.

Azure Batch provides on-demand managed compute & software resources that enable you to run and high-performance computing (HPC) workloads.

High Performance Computing with Azure Batch

Azure Batch provides on-demand managed compute & software resources that enable you to run large-scale parallel HPC workloads.

Azure Batch creates and manages a pool of compute nodes (virtual machines), installs the applications you want to run, and schedules jobs to run on the nodes. Azure Batch provides job scheduling and cluster management, allowing applications to run in parallel and at scale.

Azure Batch is a platform service that schedules compute-intensive work to run on a managed collection of virtual machines, and can automatically scale compute resources to meet the needs of your jobs.

Advantages of Azure Batch

1. Azure Batch creates and manages a pool of compute nodes (virtual machines), installs the applications you want to run, and schedules jobs to run on the nodes.
2. Advantage of running HPC with Azure Batch that there is no cluster or job scheduler software to install & manage. Cluster and Job Scheduler software comes as a managed service with Azure Batch.

Azure Batch Use cases (Intrinsically Parallel Workloads)

Intrinsically parallel workloads are those where the applications can run independently, and each instance completes part of the work. When the applications are executing, they might access some common data, but they do not communicate with other instances of the application. Example of Parallel workloads include:

Financial risk modeling
VFX and 3D image rendering
Image analysis and processing
Media transcoding
Genetic sequence analysis
Optical character recognition (OCR)
Data ingestion, processing, and ETL operations

Azure Batch Use cases (Tightly coupled Workloads)

Tightly coupled workloads are those where the applications you run need to communicate with each other, as opposed to run independently. Tightly coupled applications normally use the Message Passing Interface (MPI) API. You can run your tightly coupled workloads with Batch using Microsoft MPI or Intel MPI. Some examples of tightly coupled workloads:

Finite element analysis
Fluid dynamics
Multi-node AI training

Azure Batch Architecture & Working

Figure below shows Architecture of Azure Batch Solutions running a parallel workload on cluster of compute nodes.

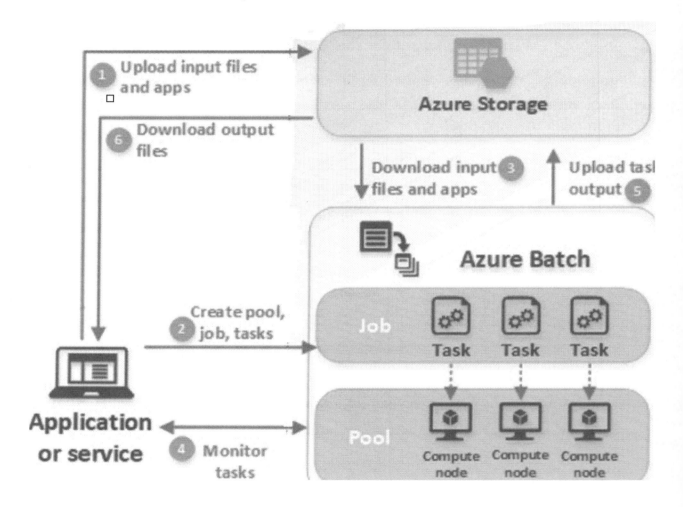

Components of Azure Batch Solutions

Storage Account contains Batch Application and Data which will be downloaded to Cluster of compute nodes.

Batch Account provides pool of **Compute nodes** which will run Batch applications and Job Scheduling software to schedule **jobs** and run **tasks**. It also monitors the progress of the application running on the compute Cluster.

Client Application connects to Batch service to query and monitor tasks running on compute node.

Implementation Steps for Deploying Azure Batch Computing

1. Create Batch Account with associated Storage Account.
2. Create a pool of compute nodes.
3. Create a job.
4. Create a task.
5. View task output.

Azure Batch Pricing

There is no charge for Batch itself. You only pay for the underlying compute, storage and Application licenses (If used) consumed to run your batch jobs.

For Compute & Storage Pricing refer to Virtual Machine and Storage Chapter.

For compute you can use normal VMs or Low Priority VMs.

Low-priority VMs in Batch

Low Priority VMs are priced at 20% of Normal VMs. Low Priority VMs are allocated from Azure unutilized capacity and can be taken back by Azure. The availability SLA for normal VMs does not apply to low-priority VMs.

Low-priority VMs can significantly reduce the costs of running workloads or allow much more work to be performed at a greater scale for the same cost.

If applications can tolerate interruption, then use of low-priority VMs can significantly lower compute costs. Suitable workloads include batch processing and HPC jobs, where the work is split into many asynchronous tasks. If VMs are pre-empted, then tasks can be interrupted and rerun—job completion time can also increase if capacity drops

If low-priority VMs are pre-empted, then any interrupted tasks will be re-queued, and the pool will automatically attempt to replace the lost capacity.

Graphics and rendering application licensing

Azure Batch pools can optionally be configured with graphics and rendering applications installed, where the application licensing is handled by Batch and the application costs are billed by Batch alongside the VM costs.

APPLICATION	Price
Autodesk Maya	$0.625/VM/hour
Autodesk 3ds Max	$0.625/VM/hour
Autodesk Arnold	$0.025/core/hour
Chaos Group V-Ray	$0.025/core/hour

Chapter 15 Azure Search

This Chapter covers following

- Azure Search

This Chapter Covers following Lab Exercises

- Azure Search Provisioning and Working

Azure Search

Azure Search is a managed cloud search service that helps you build a powerful search experience into custom apps, and then monitor service, index and query activity through Azure portal views.

Azure Search makes it easy to add powerful and sophisticated search capabilities to your website or application.

Azure Search is a search-as-a-service cloud solution that gives developers APIs and tools for adding a rich search experience over your content in web, mobile, and enterprise applications.

Azure Search advantage

Azure Search removes the complexity of setting up and managing your own search index. This fully managed service helps you avoid the hassle of dealing with index corruption, service availability, scaling and service updates. Create multiple indexes with no incremental cost per index. Easily scale up or down as the traffic and data volume of your application changes.

Why Azure Search

Many applications use search as the primary interaction pattern for their users. When it comes to search, user expectations are high. They expect great relevance, suggestions, near-instantaneous responses, multiple languages, faceting and more. Azure Search makes it easy to add powerful and sophisticated search capabilities to your website or application. Azure search can give your service a competitive advantage in the marketplace.

How Application Access Azure Search

Your applications can access Azure search functionality through a simple REST API or .NET SDK. In addition to APIs, the Azure portal provides administration and content management support, with tools for prototyping and querying your indexes.

Azure Search Features, Tiers & Pricing

Azure search can be provisioned with Free, Basic or Standard Tier. **Standard** Tier is available in multiple configurations and capacities.
If a tier's capacity turns out to be too low, you will need to provision a new service at the higher tier and then reload your indexes. There is no in-place upgrade of the same service from one SKU to another.

Free: A shared service, at no charge, used for evaluation, investigation, or small workloads. Because it's shared with other subscribers, query throughput and indexing varies based on who else is using the service. Capacity is small (50 MB or 3 indexes with up 10,000 documents each).

Basic: Small production workloads on dedicated hardware. Highly available with capacity up to 3 replicas and 1 partition (2 GB).QPS is approximately 3 queries per second.

Standard S1: Standard S1 supports flexible combinations of partitions (12) and replicas (12), used for medium production workloads on dedicated hardware. You can allocate partitions and replicas in combinations supported by a maximum number of 36 billable search units. At this level, partitions are 25 GB each and QPS is approximately 15 queries per second.

Standard S2: Standard 2 runs larger production workloads using the same 36 search units as S1 but with larger sized partitions and replicas. At this level, partitions are 100 GB each and QPS is about 60 queries per second.

Standard S3: Standard 3 runs proportionally larger production workloads on higher end systems, in configurations of up to 12 partitions or 12 replicas under 36 search units. At this level, partitions are 200 GB each and QPS is more than 60 queries per second.

Standard S3 High Density (HD): Standard 3 High Densisty is designed for a large number of smaller indexes. You can have up to 3 partitions, at 200 GB each. QPS is more than 60 queries per second.

Table below shows the comparison between various search tiers.

Features	Free	Basic	Standard S1	Standard S2	Standard S3
Storage	50 MB	2 GB	25 GB/Partition	100 GB/Partition	200 GB/Partition
Max Indexes	3	5	50	200	200 or 1000
Documents Hosted	10000	1 Million	15 Million/Partition	60 Million/Partition	120 Million/Partition
Scale Out Limits	N/A	Up to 3 units per service (Max 1 partition; max 3 replicas)	Up to 36 units per service (Max 12 partitions; max 12 replicas)	Up to 36 units per service (Max 12 partitions; max 12 replicas)	Up to 36 units per service (Max 12 partitions; max 12 replicas) Up to 12 Replicas in High Density mode
Price per unit	Free	$0.101/hour	$0.336/hour	$1.344/hour	$2.688/hour

Exercise 56: Azure Search Provisioning and Working

Step 1 Provisioning: logon to Azure Portal> click create a resource>Web + Mobile>Azures Search> Enter information as per your req and click Create.

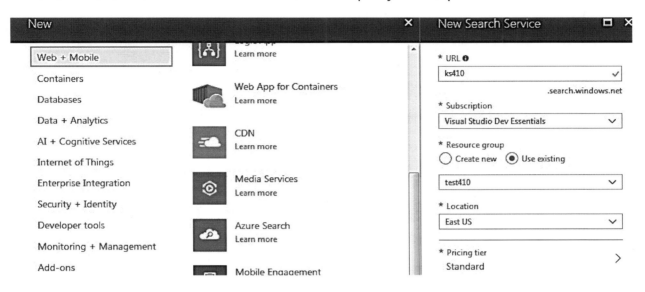

Step 2: Copy Azure Search URL from Search Dashboard. Also copy primary key of the search service. This information will be added in your application to access the Azure search service.

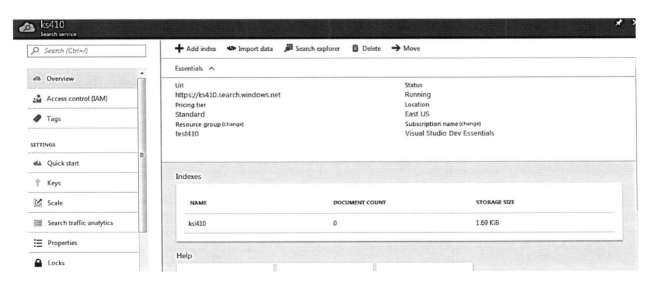

Step 3 Create index: Before you can upload searchable content, you must first define an Azure Search index. An index is like a database table that holds your data and can accept search queries. You define the index schema to map to reflect the structure of the documents you wish to search, similar to fields in a database.

In Search dashboard> Click +Add Index> Add Index blade opens> Enter information as per your req and click ok.

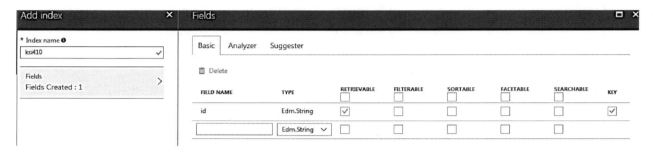

Step 4 Upload Content: Once you have defined an index, you're ready to upload content. You can use either a push or pull model to upload the content.

The **pull model** retrieves data from external data sources to your Azure Search index and let Azure Search automatically pull your data into the search service.

The **push model** manually pushes your data into the index using the Azure Search REST API or .NET SDK. You can push data from virtually any dataset using the JSON format.

In Search dashboard> Click import data> Import Data Blade opens> Here we will select sample data source included with Azure search. A default index is included with sample data source. You can edit default index as per your req.

Step 5 Search: In your application add Search URL and Primary copied in step 2. You can issue search queries to your service endpoint from your application using simple HTTP requests with REST API or the .NET SDK.

Architecting Microsoft Azure Solutions Study & Lab Guide Part 2: Exam 70-535

Scale your Search Service

You can scale your search service in 2 ways - Partitions and Replicas.
1. Add Replicas to grow your capacity to handle heavy query loads.
2. Add Partitions to grow storage and I/O for faster document search.

In Azure Portal go to Search Dashboard>Click Scale in Right Pane. You can add Partitions and Replica to your service.

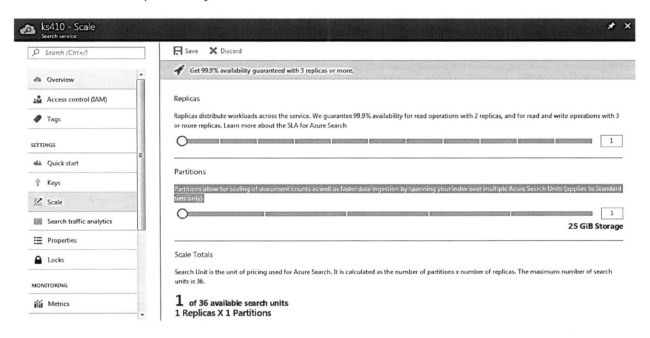

Scale your Service in Basic SKU: In Basic tier you can only add replicas.

Scale your Service in Standard SKU: In Standard tier you can scale search service in two dimensions: replicas and partitions.

Replica: Replicas are instances of the search service, used primarily to load balance query operations. Each replica always hosts one copy of an index. If you have 12 replicas, you will have 12 copies of every index loaded on the service. Replicas allow your service to handle a higher load of search queries - a service requires 2 replicas to achieve a read-only SLA and requires 3 replicas to achieve a read/write SLA.

Partition: Partitions provide index storage and I/O for read/write operations. Partitions allow search service to store and search through more documents.

Architecting Microsoft Azure Solutions Study & Lab Guide Part 2: Exam 70-535

Increase query performance with replicas

Query latency is an indicator that additional replicas are needed. Generally, a first step toward improving query performance is to add more of this resource. As you add replicas, additional copies of the index are brought online to support bigger query workloads and to load balance the requests over the multiple replicas.

On average, a replica at Basic or S1 SKUs can service about 15 QPS, but your throughput will be higher or lower depending on query complexity (faceted queries are more complex) and network latency. Also, it's important to recognize that although adding replicas will definitely add scale and performance, the result is not strictly linear: adding three replicas does not guarantee triple throughput.

Increase indexing performance with partitions

Search applications that require near real-time data refresh will need proportionally more partitions than replicas. Adding partitions spreads read/write operations across a larger number of compute resources. It also gives you more disk space for storing additional indexes and documents.

Larger indexes take longer to query. As such, you might find that every incremental increase in partitions requires a smaller but proportional increase in replicas. The complexity of your queries and query volume will factor into how quickly query execution is turned around.

General recommendations for high availability

Two replicas for high availability of read-only workloads (queries)
Three or more replicas for high availability of read/write workloads (queries plus indexing as individual documents are added, updated, or deleted)

Chapter 16 Operations Management Suite (OMS)

This Chapter covers following

- Operations Management Suite (OMS)

This Chapter Covers following Lab Exercises

- Monitoring IIS Web Server with Log Analytics

Operations Management Suite (OMS)

Operations Management Suite (OMS) is a collection of cloud-based services for managing your on-premises and cloud environments.

Microsoft OMS is the IT management solution for the hybrid cloud. With OMS, you can manage any instance in any cloud, including on-premises, Azure, AWS, Windows Server, Linux, VMware, and OpenStack, at a lower cost than competitive solutions.

The advantage of OMS is that it is implemented as a cloud based service, you can have it up and running quickly with minimal investment in infrastructure services. New features are delivered automatically, saving you on-going maintenance and upgrade costs.

OMS Solution Components

It Consist of following Four cloud based services plus Management Solutions.

Log Analytics
Automation & Control
Protection and Disaster Recovery (Backup & ASR)
Security and Compliance

Management solutions extend the functionality of Operations Management Suite (OMS) by providing packaged management scenarios that customers can add to their environment. Management solution packs have Pre Built rules and Algorithms that perform analysis. Management solutions can be installed from the Solutions Gallery in the OMS portal or through Azure Portal.

You can manage all four services and Management Solutions through OMS portal @ https://<OMS workspace>.portal.mms.microsoft.com

Before you can access OMS portal you must first create OMS workspace. OMS workspace is a combination of Log Analytics service and OMS repository.

Log Analytics

Log Analytics is a service in Operations Management Suite (OMS) that helps you collect and analyze data generated by resources in your cloud and on-premises environments.

It gives you real-time insights using integrated search and custom dashboards to readily analyze millions of records across all of your workloads and servers regardless of their physical location.

Log Analytics Architecture

Log Analytics has 2 components – OMS Workspace & OMS Monitoring Agent.

<u>The combined solution of Log Analytics service and OMS repository is known as OMS Workspace.</u> OMS repository is hosted in the Azure cloud.

OMS Monitoring Agent is installed on the connected source. Data is collected into the repository from connected sources.

Figure below shows Log Analytics collecting and analyzing data generated by resources in Azure, on-premises and other Clouds.

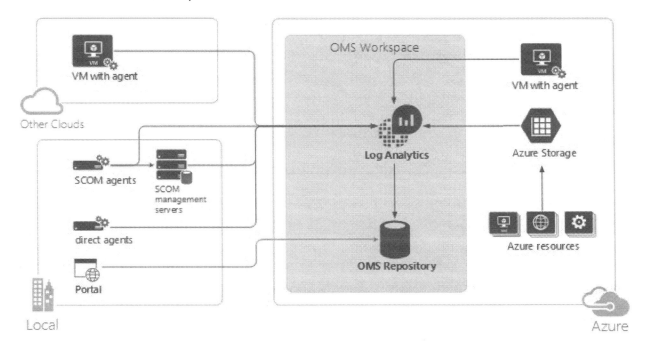

Data Collection from Connected Sources & Azure Managed Resources

Connected Sources can be on-premises or Cloud Resources. All Resources which you have created in your Subscription will appear in Log Analytics Dashboard under various Data Sources. You can add following Connected Sources in Log Analytics Services.

1. On-Premises Windows & Linux Servers with MS Monitoring Agent Installed.
2. Azure VMs with Microsoft Monitoring Agent virtual machine extension.
3. Azure Storage Accounts.
4. Azure Activity Logs
5. Azure Resources: You can add Azure Resources to Log Analytics which you have created in your subscription. For example following Azure Resources I have created in My Subscription and they appear under Azure Resources in Log Analytics Dashboard. You can enable all of them or enable as per your requirement to send Monitoring Data to Log Analytics Services.

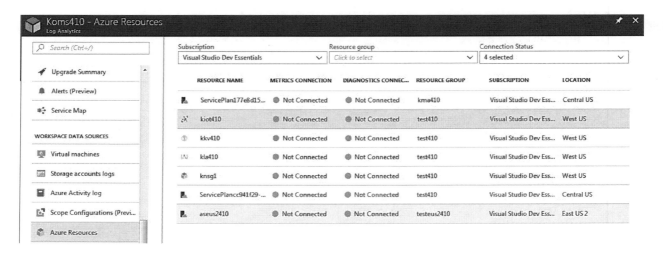

Data Sources

Data sources are configured on connected sources. Data sources can be IIS Logs, Performance Counters, Syslog, windows security events, windows firewall log, Network Security group.

Design Nuggets: You can create multiple workspaces in Azure Subscription. Workspaces are independent of each other and that data collected from each workspace cannot be viewed in another workspace.

Log Analytics Working, Reporting and Analyzing data

Log Analytics collects data from managed resources into a central repository. This data could include events, performance data, or custom data provided through the API. Once collected, the data is available for alerting, analysis, and export.

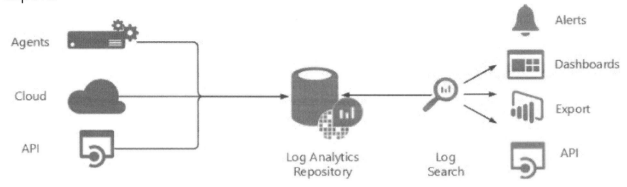

Log Analytics includes a powerful query language to extract data stored in the repository. The result of the query can be viewed in following ways:

Dashboard: You can view the result of the query in Log Analytics Dashboard.
Export: You can export the results of any query to analyze it outside of Log Analytics. You can schedule a regular export to Power BI which provides significant visualization and analysis capabilities.
Log Search API. Log Analytics has a REST API for collecting data from any client. This allows you to programmatically work with data collected in the repository or access it from another monitoring tool.

Alerting

You can create Alerts on the Log search data. In addition to creating an alert record in the Log Analytics repository, alerts can take the following actions.

Email. Send an email to proactively notify you of a detected issue.

Runbook. An alert in Log Analytics can start a runbook in Azure Automation. This is typically done to attempt to correct the detected issue. The runbook can be started in the cloud in the case of an issue in Azure or another cloud, or it could be started on a local agent for an issue on a physical or virtual machine.

Webhook. An alert can start a webhook and pass it data from the results of the log search. This allows integration with external services such as an alternate alerting system, or it may attempt to take corrective action for an external web site.

Exercise 57: Monitoring IIS Web Server with Log Analytics

There are 4 steps involved in this: Creating OMS workspace, Add Connected source, Add data source and Query IIS Log data using log search.

Note: In this example we will monitor Azure VM running IIS server.

Step 1: Creating OMS workspace (This will create Log Analytics service and OMS Repository)

1. https://portal.azure.com

2. Click + Create a resource > Monitoring > Log Analytics> Log Analytics create OMS workspace blade opens>specify following and click ok.

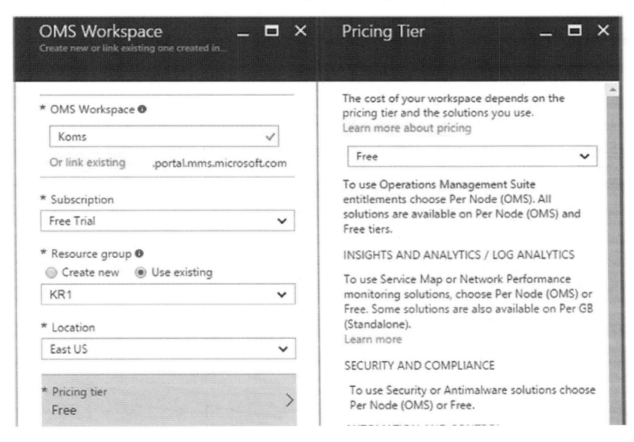

This creates OMS Workspace with name Koms.

Step 2: Add Connected Source (Azure Virtual Machines KWeb1 running IIS Web Server) by installing Log Analytics VM Extension

1. Go to Log Analytics KOMS Dashboard>Click Virtual Machines> On the right side it shows the Web Server Virtual Machine KWeb1 and the status of OMS Connection. Which in this case is not connected.

2. Click Web Server Virtual Machine KWeb1 >KWeb1 VM Blade opens> Click Connect. This will also install Log Analytics Agent VM Extension.

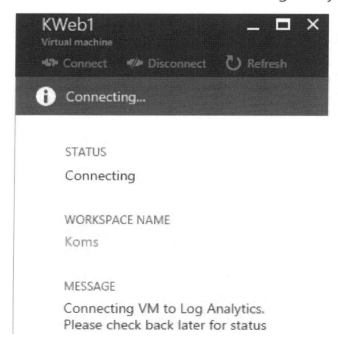

Note: Readers are advised to add wvm535 created in Compute Chapter.

Step 3: Add Data Source – IIS log

1. Log on to OMS portal by going to https://koms.portal.mms.microsoft.com
2. Click Setting>Data>IIS Logs>Select Collect W3C format IIS log files.

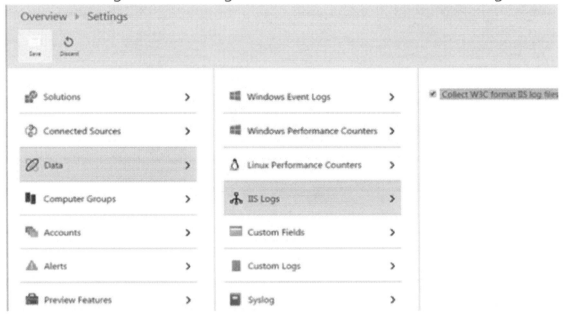

Step 4: Query Log Data for Website on virtual machine KWeb1 using Log search

1. Log on to OMS portal by going to https://koms.portal.mms.microsoft.com

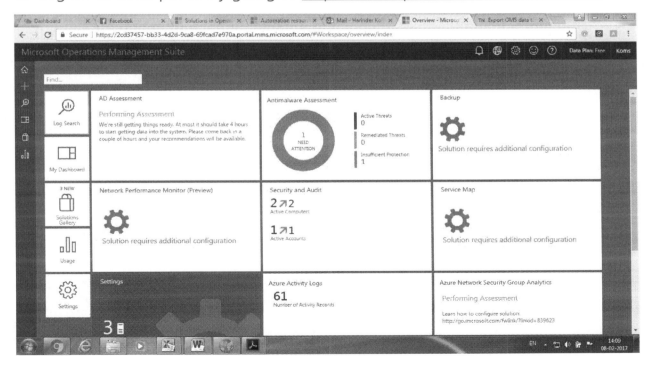

2. Click Log search tile in OMS Portal> Log search Blade opens>Click All Collected Data>Click W3IISLog in left pane.

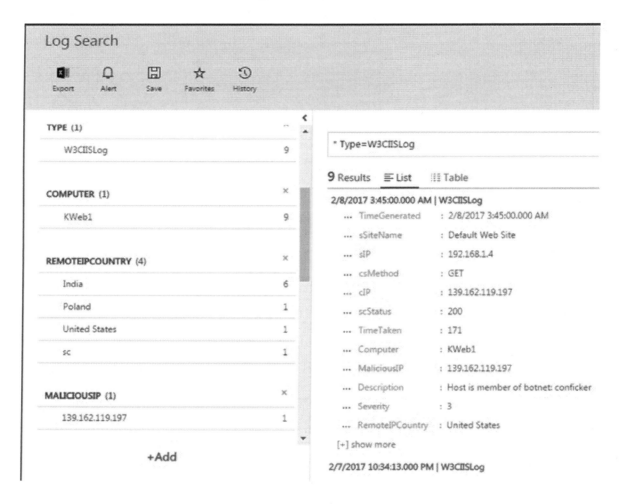

From the above figure following can be inferred.

1. The website on Virtual Machine KWeb1 has been accessed from 4 countries.
2. There is malicious IP 139.162.119.197 and the origin is United Sates.
3. Just Scroll down the left pane and you will see IP addresses of hosts who have accessed this website.

Similar way you can monitor Performance counters, Event Logs of the connected source using Log analytics.

Management solutions

Management solution packs have Pre Built rules and Algorithms that perform analysis leveraging one or more OMS services. Management solutions are added to Log Analytics Workspace.

Management solutions are available both from Microsoft and partners.

Management solutions can be installed from the Solutions Gallery in the OMS portal or through Azure Portal. Figure below some of the Management solutions which can be added to Log Analytics service.

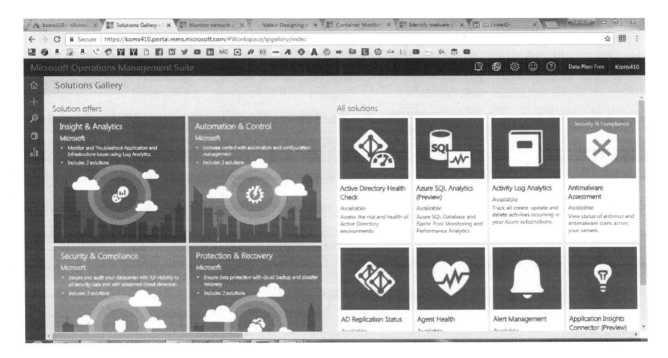

Active Directory Health Check : Active Directory Health Check solution assesses the risk and health of your server environments (Domain Controllers) on a regular interval. The solution provides a prioritized list of recommendations specific to your deployed server infrastructure.

AD Replication Status : The AD Replication Status solution pack regularly monitors your Active Directory environment for any replication failures.

Alert Management Solution : The Alert Management solution helps you analyze all of the alerts in your Log Analytics repository.

Network Performance Monitor (NPM): The Network Performance Monitor management solution is a network monitoring solution that monitors the health, availability and reachability of networks.

Network Security Group analytics solution: Network Security Group analytics management solutions collect diagnostics logs directly from Network Security Groups for analyzing them in Log analytics.

Container Monitoring Solution: Container Monitoring Solution shows which containers are running, what container image they're running, and where containers are running. You can view detailed audit information showing commands used with containers.

Key Vault Analytics solution: Azure Key Vault solution in Log Analytics reviews Azure Key Vault logs.

Office 365 management solution: Office 365 management solution allows you to monitor your Office 365 environment in Log Analytics.

Service Fabric Analytics: Identify and troubleshoot issues across Service fabric Clusters.

Service Maps: Automatically discovers and Maps servers and their dependencies in real-time. Service Map automatically discovers application components on Windows and Linux systems and maps the communication between services. It also consolidates data collected by other services and solutions to assist you in analyzing performance and identifying issues. Service Map shows connections between servers, processes, and ports across any TCP-connected architecture, with no configuration required other than the installation of an agent.

SQL Server Health Check: SQL Health Check solution assesses the risk and health of your SQL Server environments on a regular interval.

Update Management: Identifies and orchestrates the installation of missing system updates. This solution requires both Log Analytics and Automation account.

Change Tracking: Tracks configuration changes across your servers. This solution requires both Log Analytics and Automation account.

Antimalware Assessment: OMS Antimalware Assessment solution helps you identify servers that are infected or at increased risk of infection by malware.

Azure Site Recovery: Monitor's Virtual Machine replication status for your azure Site Recovery Vault.

IT Service Management (ITSM) connector: Connects Log Analytics with ITSM Products such as servicenow.

Log Analytics Tiers & Pricing

Log Analytics is offered in two tiers—free and paid.

Log analytics is billed per gigabyte (GB) of data uploaded into the service. The free tier has a limit on the amount of data collected daily. The paid tier does not have a limit on the amount of data collected daily.

	Free	Paid
Daily limit	500 MB	No Limit
Retention period	7 Days	1 Month
Customise longer retention periods	No	Yes
Price	Free	$2.30/GB
Additional retention beyond 1 month	NA	$0.10/GB/month

Chapter 17 Network Watcher

This Chapter covers following

- Network Watcher

This Chapter Covers following Lab Exercises

- Enabling Network Watcher
- Network Watcher Capabilities

Network Watcher

Before going into details of Network watcher, let's discuss what happens without Network Watcher.

Without Network Watcher: Azure provides monitoring, troubleshooting, diagnostics and logging at individual resource level such as Virtual Network, Load Balancers, NSG, Application Gateway & ExpressRoute etc.

With Network Watcher: Network Watcher provides end to end Monitoring, Diagnostics and logging across Resource levels or network topology level.

Exercise 58: Enabling Network Watcher

1. In Azure Portal Click All Services in left pane>Under Networking Click Network Watcher> Network watcher Dashboard opens>Enable Network Watcher for all regions or in the region of your choice>Here we will enable for EastUS> Click 27 Region icon>Select and click EastUS>Click Enable Network Watcher.

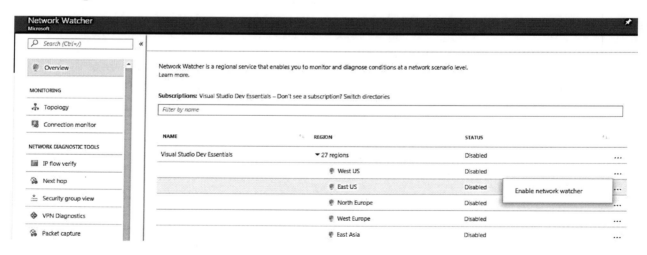

Exercise 59: Exploring Network Watcher Capabilities

Topology: Provides a network level topology diagram showing the various interconnections and associations between network resources in a RG.
Click Topology in left pane>in right pane select your Resource Group and VNET.

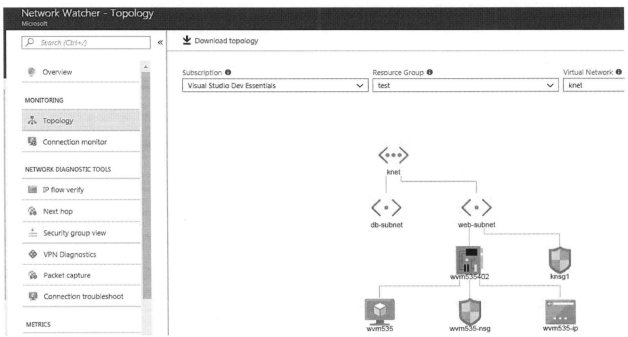

Next Hop: Traffic from the source to destination has a next hop. Next Hop feature finds or verifies the next hop for packets being routed in the Azure Network Fabric, enabling you to diagnose any misconfigured user-defined routes.

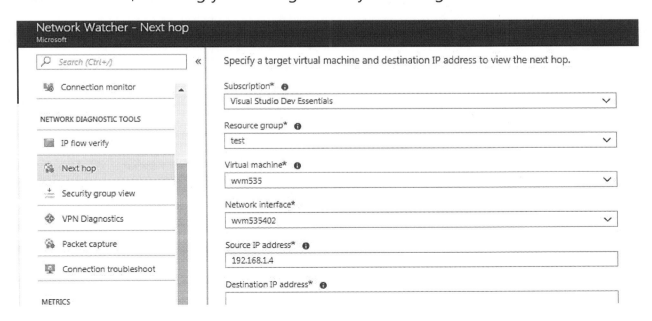

IP flow verify: IP Flow Verify helps to verify if a virtual machine can talk to another machine. If the packet is denied by a security group, the rule and group that denied the packet is returned. You can choose the source and destination to diagnose connectivity issue.

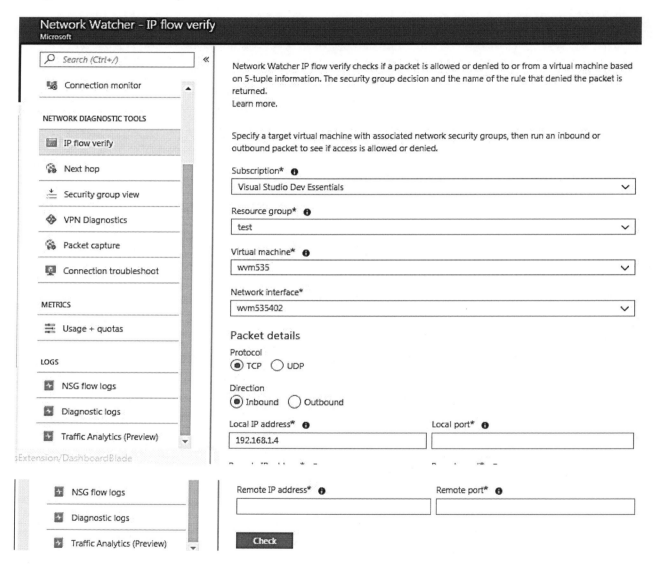

Packet Capture: Packet Capture creates packet capture sessions to track traffic to and fro from a virtual machine. Requires packet capture extension enabled at VM level.

Connection Monitor: Monitors and Diagnoses communication problems between 2 Virtual Machines. Network Watcher Connection Monitor enables you to configure and track connection reachability, latency, and network topology changes. If there is an issue, it tells you why it occurred and how to fix it.

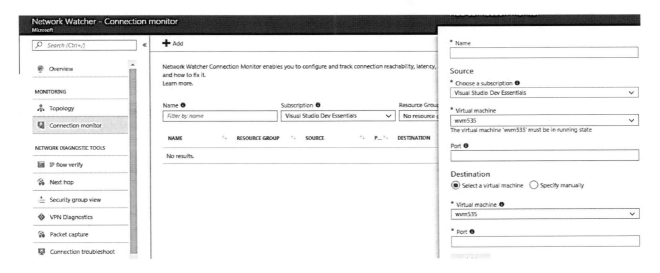

VPN Diagnostics: Virtual Network Gateways provide connectivity between on-premises and virtual networks. Network Watcher provides the capability to monitor and troubleshoot Virtual Network Gateways and Connections.

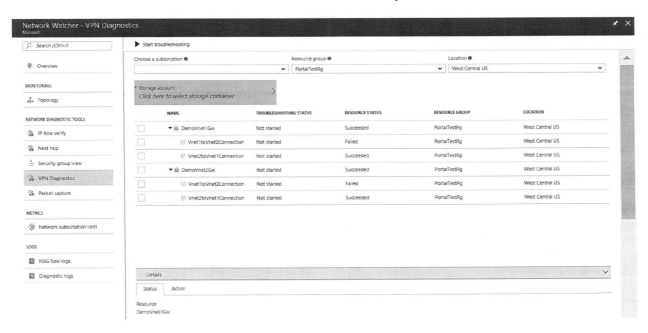

Network Watcher Pricing

Feature	Monthly Allotment (Free)	Overage Charges
Network Logs Ingested	5 GB	$0.50 per GB
Network Diagnostic Tools	1,000 checks	$1 per 1000 checks
Connection Monitoring		$3 per connection per month
Ping Mesh	10 connection metrics per month	10-2,40,010 connections — $0.30 per connection metric per month

Network logs are stored within a storage account. Corresponding charges will apply for storage, Log Analytics and event hubs respectively.

Network Watcher Diagnostic Tools (Packet capture, IP Flow Verify etc) and Topology features are billed for the number of Network Diagnostic checks initiated via Azure Portal, PowerShell, CLI, or Rest.

Chapter 18 Security Center

This Chapter covers following

- Security Center

This Chapter Covers following Lab Exercises

- Accessing Security Center Dashboard
- Enabling Detection and Remediation

Azure Security Center

Azure Security Center is an Azure Managed Service that **detects** threats against your Azure resources and Non Azure Resources and helps you to **remediate** those threats.

Security Center collects security data and events from your resources and services to help you prevent, detect, and respond to threats.

Azure Security Center can be used to monitor your infrastructure as a service (IaaS) resources such as Azure Virtual Machines, Non Azure Resources like on-premises server and PaaS resources such as Azure SQL Database.

Security Center Dashboard

With Azure Security Centre Dashboard, you get a central view of the security state of all of your Azure resources. At a glance, verify that the appropriate security controls are in place and configured correctly. And quickly identify any resources which require attention.

Exercise 60: Accessing Security Center Dashboard

In Azure Portal Click Security Center in left Pane> Security Center Dashboard opens.

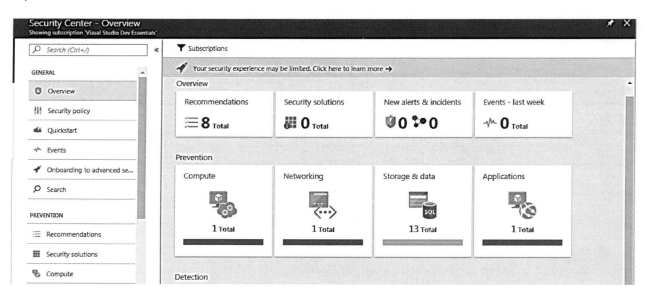

Exercise 61: Enabling Detection and Remediation (4 Steps)

1. Enabling Data Collection
2. Choose Security Policy Components to enable or disable threat detection
3. Detecting threats
4. Remediating threats

Step 1 Enabling Data Collection: This enables the automatic installation of the Microsoft Monitoring Agent (MMA) on all the VMs in your subscription. If enabled, any new or existing VM without an installed agent will be provisioned.

In Security Center dashboard click security Policy in left pane>Select your subscription>In Data collection select **on** under Auto Provisioning>Select Log Analytics workspace option.

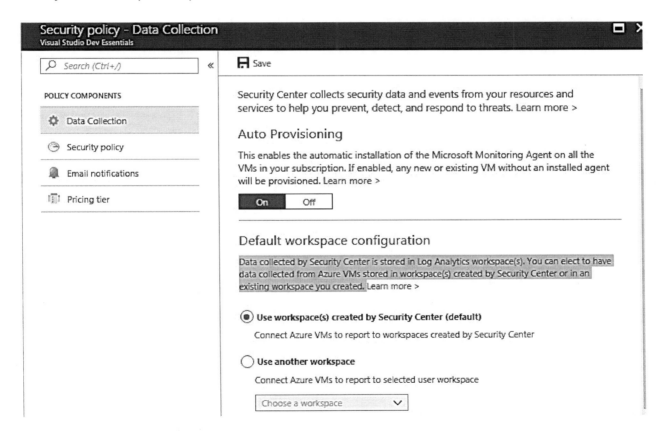

Note: Data collected by Security Center is stored in Log Analytics workspace(s). You can elect to have data collected from Azure VMs stored in workspace(s) created by Security Center or in an existing workspace you created.

Step 2 Choose Security Policy Components to enable or disable threat detection: Click Security Policy under Policy Componentson>Select your components. **By Default all Policy components are on.**

Security Center detects threats for which security policy components are enabled in the security policy.

These threats are classified into following areas.
Compute | Networking | Storage & Data | Applications

Step 3: Detecting Threats

Based on Security Policy components configured, Security Center detects threats against Azure and Non-Azure resources and shows those threats in **Security Center (SC) recommendation dashboard** as shown below.

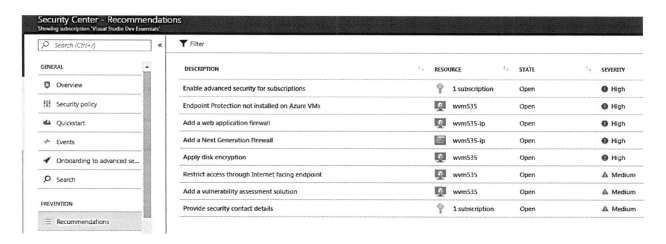

Step 4: Remediating Threat

In the Security Center recommendation dashboard if you click a recommendation it will help remediate that threat. In the above figure if we click Endpoint Protection not installed on Azure VM recommendation then following screen will open and you can install Endpoint protection on Azure VM wvm35.

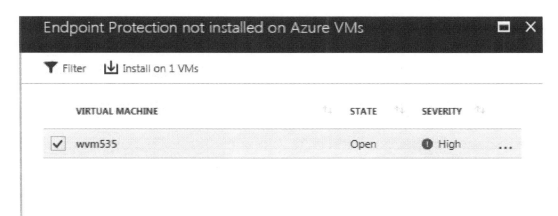

Just in time (JIT) VM access

Just in time (JIT) virtual machine (VM) access can be used to lock down inbound traffic to management port on Azure VMs, reducing exposure to attacks while providing easy access to connect to VMs when needed.

When just in time is enabled, Security Center creates <u>Network Security Group</u> (NSG) rules, which restrict access to management ports so they cannot be targeted by attackers. **JIT VM access feature requires SC Standard Tier.**

Figure below shows attacker targeting management ports of Azure VM.

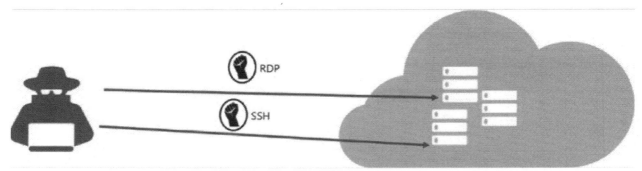

You can Specify rules for how users can connect to virtual machines. When needed, access can be requested from Security Center or via PowerShell. As long as the request complies with the rules, access is automatically granted for the requested time.

Enabling JIT VM Access: In Security Center Dashboard click Just in time VM in left pane>Select VMs in Right Pane and click Enable JIT on VMs.

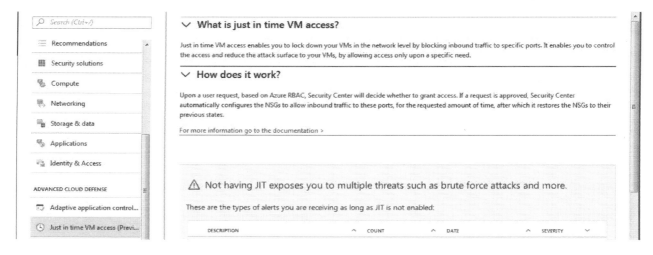

Adding Non-Azure Windows Computers

You can enable Security Center for resources running outside of Azure, for example on-premises or in other clouds, by provisioning the Microsoft Monitoring Agent (MMA).

Requirement for adding Non Azure Windows Computers

1. You require Security Center Standard pricing tier to add Non-Azure Windows computers.
2. Microsoft Monitoring Agent (MMA) to be installed on Target resource: Non-Azure Windows computers.
3. A Log Analytics workspace is required in order to onboard non-Azure computers to Security Center.

On-Boarding Non-Azure Computer to Security Center

1. In Security Center Dashboard click **onboarding to advanced security** in left pane> onboarding to advanced security dashboard opens.

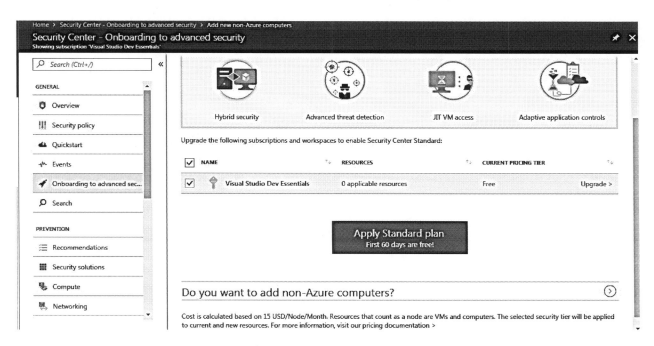

2. Click Do you want to add non-Azure computers>Add new Non-Azure dashboard opens>Click + Add Computers> In Direct Agent Dashboard Click Download agent. Copy the workspace id and Primary Key.

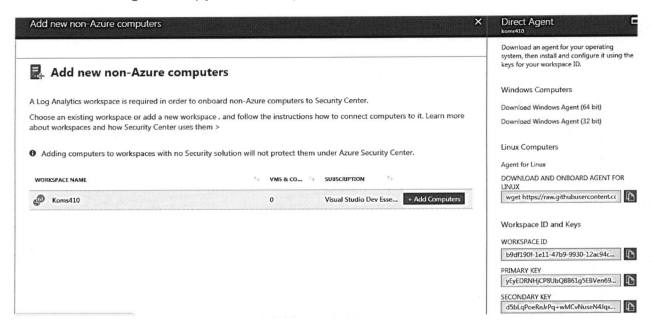

3. Install the MMA agent which was downloaded in step 2 on the computer which is to be monitored through Security Center. During installation enter workspace id and the primary key.

4. You can monitor Non-Azure computer in SC Recommendation dashboard.

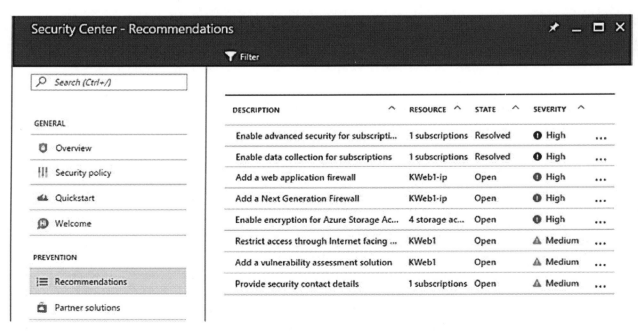

Adaptive Application Control

Application control helps you deal with malicious and/or unauthorized software, by allowing only specific applications to run on your VMs.

Adaptive Application Control feature requires Security Center Standard Tier.

Security Center analyzes data of applications to find VMs for which there is a constant set of running applications. Security Center creates whitelisting rules for each group of VMs and presents the rules in the form of a recommendation. Once the recommendation is resolved, Security Center configures it by leveraging Applocker capabilities.

Enabling Adaptive Application Control on VM or Group of VMs

1. In Security Center Dashboard click **adaptive application control** in left pane> Select group of VMs and open the **Create application control rules** option> Whitelist the application you want run by Selecting the applications.

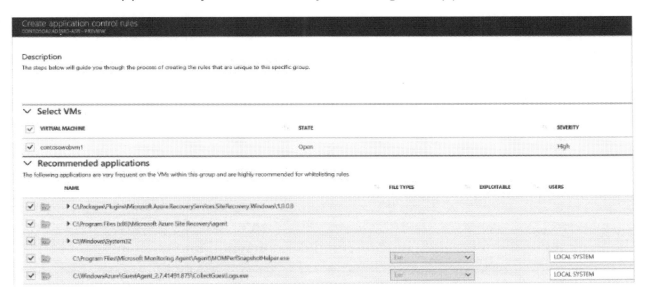

Application control policy is always configured in *Audit* mode or Enforce mode. Default is Audit mode.
In **Audit mode**, the application control solution does not enforce the rules, and only audits the activity on the protected VMs.
In **Enforce mode**, the application control enforces the rules, and makes sure that applications that are not allowed to run are blocked.

Security Center Tiers and Pricing

Azure Security Center is offered in two tiers: Free and Standard. The Standard tier is free for the first 60 days. Any usage beyond 60 days will be automatically charged as per the pricing scheme below.

Feature	Free	Standard
Security policy, assessment and recommendations	✓	✓
Connected partner solutions	✓	✓
Security event collection and search	NA	✓
Just in time VM Access	NA	✓
Adaptive application controls	NA	✓
Advanced threat detection for networks, VMs/servers and Azure services	NA	✓
Built-in and custom alerts	NA	✓
Threat intelligence	NA	✓
Included Data	NA	500 MB/Day
Price	Free	$15 / node/ month
Additional data uploaded over included daily data	NA	$2.30 per GB
Additional retention beyond one month	NA	$0.10/GB/month

Free tier offers limited security for your Azure resources only. Standard tier extends these capabilities to on-premises and other clouds.

Security Center Standard helps you find and fix security vulnerabilities, apply access and application controls to block malicious activity, detect threats using analytics and intelligence, and respond quickly when under attack. You can try Security Center Standard at no cost for the first 60 days.

Chapter 19 Monitoring Solutions

This Chapter covers following

- Azure Monitoring Solutions
- Application Insights
- Activity Log
- Diagnostic Logs
- Diagnostic Logs (Compute Resource)
- Azure Monitor
- Azure Advisor
- Azure Service Health

This Chapter Covers following Lab Exercises

- Create Application Insight Service in Azure
- Accessing Activity Log from a Monitor Dashboard
- Accessing Activity Log from a Resource Dashboard
- Accessing Diagnostic Log from the Resource Dashboard
- Accessing Diagnostic Log from the Monitor Dashboard
- Accessing Monitor Dashboard
- Accessing Advisor Dashboard
- Accessing Service Health Dashboard
- Configuring Alerts for Service Health

Azure Monitoring Solutions

Azure includes multiple services that individually perform a specific role or task in the monitoring space. Together, these services deliver a comprehensive solution for collecting, analyzing, and acting on telemetry from your application and the Azure resources that support them.

The figure below shows a conceptual view of the components that work together to provide monitoring of Azure resources.

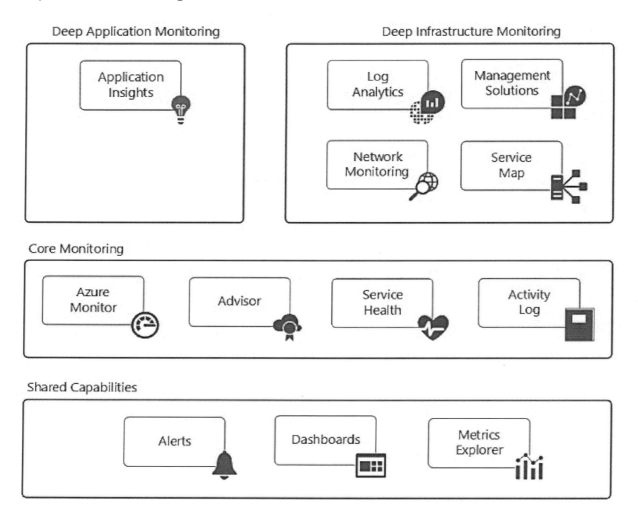

Application Insights

Application Insights is a Managed Application Performance Management (APM) service for web applications running on Web Apps, Virtual Machines or Physical Servers in the cloud or on-premises.

Azure Application Insight monitor's live Web Application for **availability, performance, and usage**. You can also identify and diagnose errors in your application without waiting for a user to report them.

It works for apps on a wide variety of platforms including .NET, Node.js and J2EE, hosted on-premises or in the cloud. It integrates with DevOps process, and has connection points to a variety of development tools. It can monitor and analyze telemetry from mobile apps by integrating with Visual Studio App Center.

Parameters Monitored by Application Insights

Request rates, response times, and failure rates - Find out which pages are most popular, at what times of day, and where your users are. See which pages perform best. If your response times and failure rates go high when there are more requests, then perhaps you have a resourcing problem.

Dependency rates, response times, and failure rates - Find out whether external services are slowing you down.

Exceptions - Analyse the aggregated statistics, or pick specific instances and drill into the stack trace and related requests. Both server and browser exceptions are reported.

Page views and load performance - reported by your users' browsers.

AJAX calls from web pages - rates, response times, and failure rates.

User and session counts.

Performance counters from your Windows or Linux server machines, such as CPU, memory, and network usage.

Host diagnostics from Docker or Azure.

Diagnostic trace logs from your app - so that you can correlate trace events with requests.

Custom events and metrics that you write yourself in the client or server code, to track business events such as items sold or games won.

Architecture, Components and Working of Application Insight

The Figure below shows the Architect & Components of Application Insight (Shown in Purple Color) for Monitoring and Availability of Web Applications.

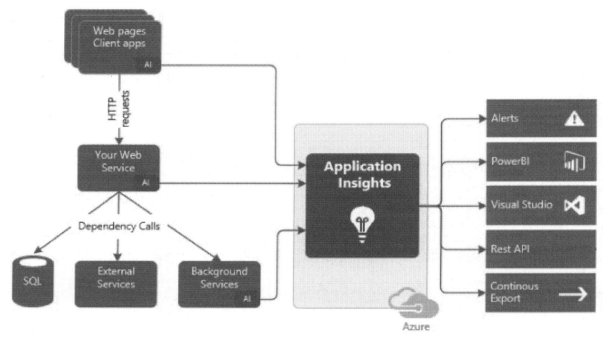

Components of Application Insight

Application Insight Agent in your application code
Application Insight Managed Service in Azure.

Brief Working

1. Setup Application Insight Service in Azure.
2. Install Application Insight Agents in Applications running in Cloud or on-premises.
3. The Application Insight Agent monitors application and sends telemetry data to the portal.
4. You can Graphically view Application performance data in real time .
5. You can apply analytic and search tools to the raw data in Application Insight service in Azure.
6. You can setup alerts on the metrics which can trigger a response when threshold is breached.
7. You can export your data to Business Intelligence tools like Power BI.

Exercise 62: Create Application Insight Service in Azure

1. Log on to Azure Portal> Click +Create a resource> Management Tools> Application Insights> Create Application Insights Blade opens>Enter required information>Click Create.

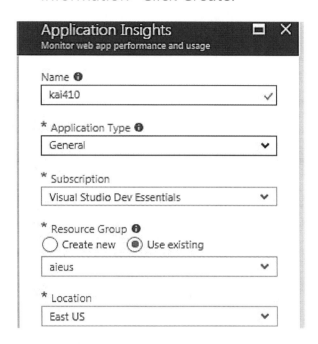

2. Figure below shows the dashboard of Application Insight.

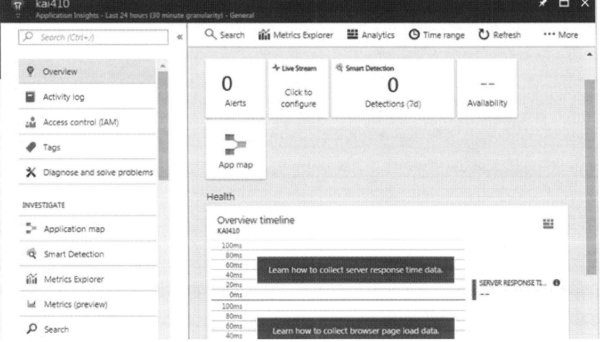

Options to Enable Application Insights monitoring on your web application server

1. Add the Application Insights SDK to your app in Visual Studio to collect performance and usage telemetry.
2. Download and Install Application Insights Status Monitor on your server.
3. Application Insight is natively integrated with Azure Web Apps and Azure Functions. You can enable it from the dashboard.

Figure below shows the option to add Application Insight in our application.

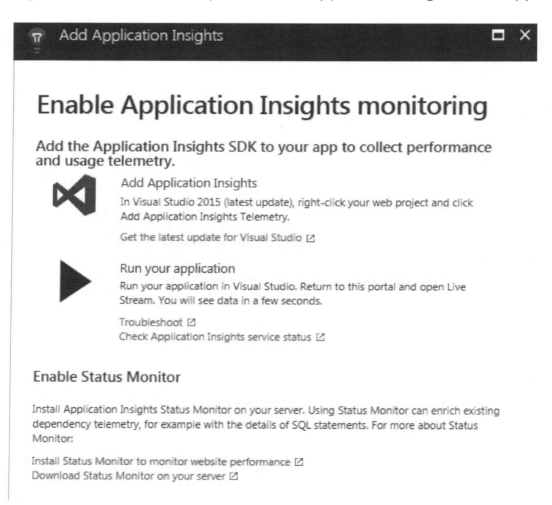

Smart Detection

Smart Detection automatically warns you of potential performance problems in your web application. It performs proactive analysis of the telemetry that your app sends to Application Insights. If there is a sudden rise in failure rates, or abnormal patterns in client or server performance, you get an alert. This feature needs no configuration. It operates if your application sends enough telemetry.

You can access Smart Detection alerts both from the emails you receive, and from the Smart Detection blade.

Accessing Smart Dashboard: In Application Insight Dashboard click Smart detection in left pane> click settings> Smart Detection setting blade opens.

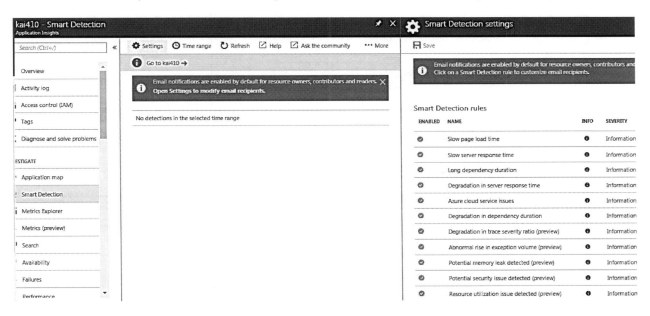

Application Insight Tiers and Pricing

Application Insights comes in two pricing tiers—Basic and Enterprise.

Basic Tier pricing is based on volume of telemetry data your application sends. With Basic Tier you get 1 GB free allowance per month. You are charged after you have sent 1 GB Data to Application Insight in Azure Portal.

Enterprise pricing is based on number of nodes that host your application and volume of telemetry data your application sends. You get a daily free allowance of 200 MB of Data Per node. Additional data beyond the daily allowance is charged per GB.

A "node" is a server, or Platform-as-a-Service instance that runs application, and from which Application Insight Portal in Azure receives telemetry Data.

	Basic	Enterprise
Base monthly price	Free (unlimited nodes)	$15 per node
Included data	1 GB/month	200 MB/node/day
Additional data	$2.30 per GB	$2.30 per GB
Data retention (raw and aggregated data)	90 days	90 days
Application Performance Management (APM) and Analytics features	Included	Included
Continuous export	$0.50 per GB	Unlimited
Connector for Operations Management Suite Log Analytics	Not Included	Included
Multi-step web tests	$10/test/month	$10/test/month

Activity Log

The **Azure Activity Log** provides insight into subscription-level events that have occurred in Azure.

Activity Logs provide data about the operations on a resource from the outside. The Activity Log reports control-plane events for your subscriptions. For Example Azure Activity log will log an event when a virtual machine is created or a logic app is deleted. But any Activity performed by virtual Machine will not be reported by Activity Log.

Using the Activity Log, you can determine the 'what, who, and when' for any write operations (PUT, POST, DELETE) taken on the resources in your subscription. You can monitor Activity log for Compute as well as non-compute Resources.

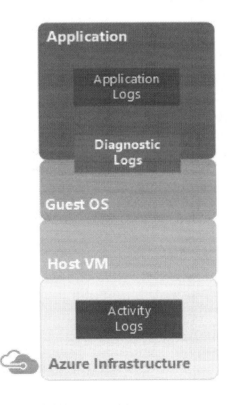

Compute resources only   **Non-Compute resources only**

Activity Log is a Platform level Service. You don't require any agents to be installed and nor you require any Azure Level service to be created. Compare this with Application Insight where you need to install agent and create Application insight service in Azure.

Activity Log Architecture

The Figure below shows the Architecture of Activity Log.

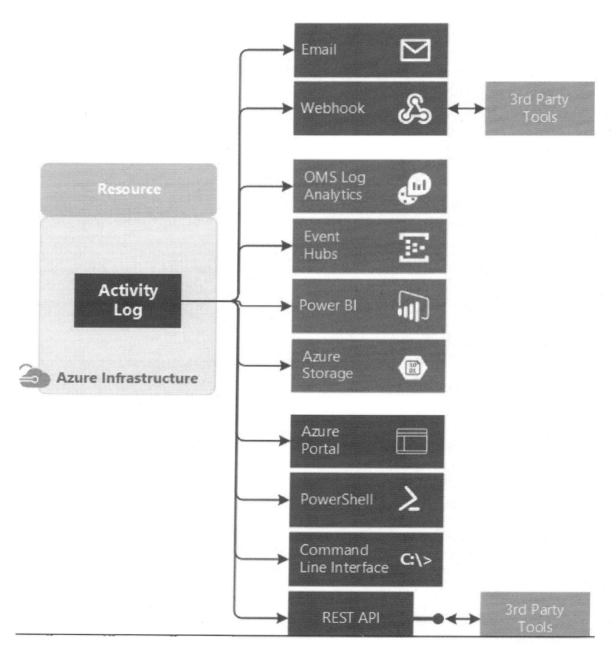

Activity Log is a Platform level Resource which logs subscription level Events. Events can be seen in Azure Portal. Events Logs can be exported to Azure Storage, Event Hubs, Power BI and OMS Log Analytics. You can create alerts on Events generated in Activity Log.

Architecting Microsoft Azure Solutions Study & Lab Guide Part 2: Exam 70-535

Exercise 62: Accessing Activity Log from a Monitor Dashboard

In Azure Portal click Monitor in Left pane> Monitor Dashboard opens> Click Activity Log. This will report events at subscription level for all the resources.

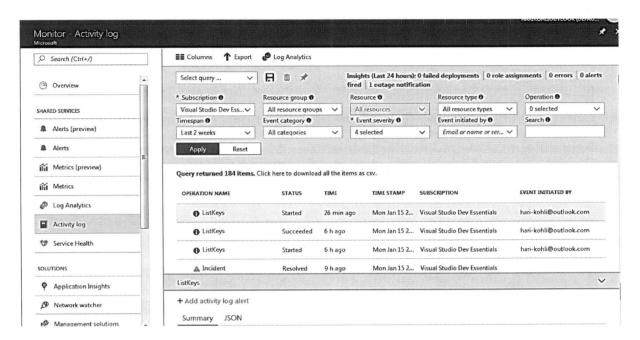

Exercise 63: Accessing Activity Log from a Resource Dashboard

Log on to Azure Portal>Go to Resource (Resource Group) Dashboard> Click Activity Log in left Pane. This will report events at Resource Group level.

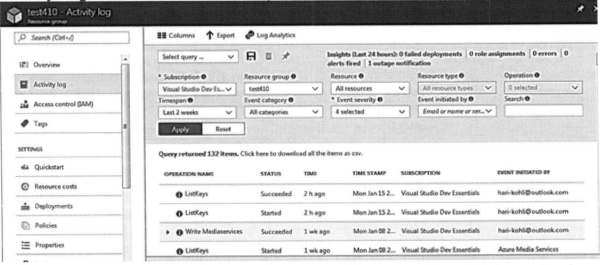

You can export events to Storage Account or Stream to Event Hubs or Analyze in Log analytics. You can create an alert on an event.

Diagnostic Logs (Non Compute Resources)

Azure resource-level diagnostic logs are logs emitted by a resource about the operation of that resource. Diagnostic logs provide insight into operations that were performed within that resource itself, for example, getting a secret from a Key Vault.

Difference between Activity and Diagnostic Logs: Activity Logs provide data about the operations on a resource from the outside (the "control plane"). Diagnostics Logs are emitted by a resource and provide information about the operation of that resource (the "data plane").
You can monitor Diagnostic log for Compute as well as non-compute Resources.

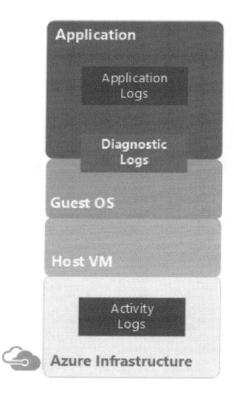

Compute resources only

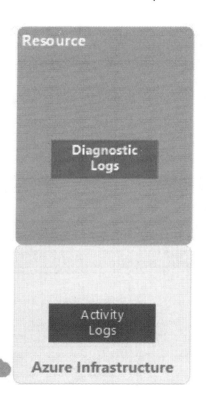

Non-Compute resources only

Diagnostic log is a Platform level Service. **You don't require any agents to be installed** and nor you require any Azure Level service to be created. **You just need to enable diagnostic logs for the resource**. Compare this with Application Insight where you need to install agent and create Application insight service in Azure.

Architecting Microsoft Azure Solutions Study & Lab Guide Part 2: Exam 70-535

Diagnostic Log Architecture

The Figure below shows the Architecture of Diagnostic Log.

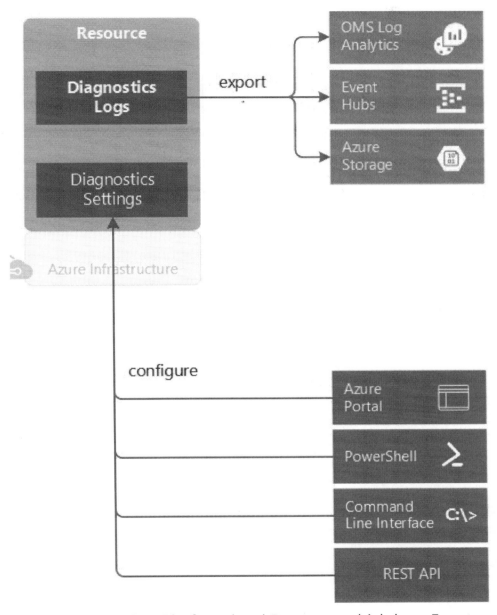

Diagnostic Log is a Platform level Resource which logs Events generated by the resource. Events Logs can be seen in Azure Portal.

Diagnostic Logs can be streamed to Event Hubs for ingestion by a third-party service or custom analytics solution such as PowerBI. You can Analyze logs with OMS Log Analytics.

Exercise 64: Accessing Diagnostic Log from the Resource Dashboard

The figure below shows accessing Diagnostic Log from a Resource Dashboard (Resource is Key Vault in this Example). You need to just enable the diagnostic Logs. It will show you what data will be collected when you enable it. In the case of Key Vault, it shows it will collect AuditEvent and AllMetrics.

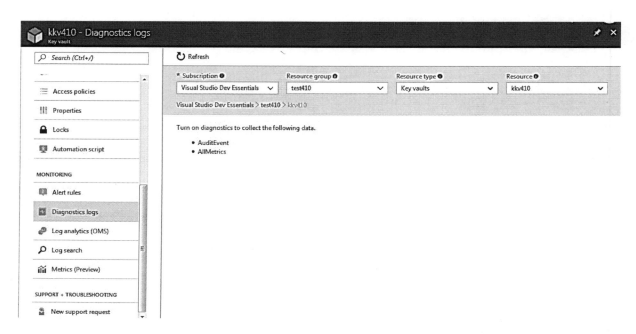

Exercise 65: Accessing Diagnostic Log from the Monitor Dashboard

In Monitor Dashboard click Diagnostic settings in left pane> Right pane shows diagnostic logs status for all the Azure resources in the subscription.

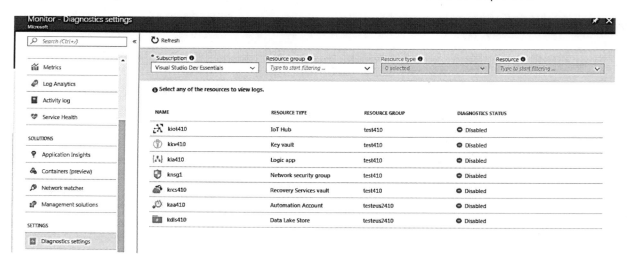

Diagnostic Logs (Compute Resource)

Compute resource diagnostic logs are collected by an agent running inside of a virtual machine or other supported resource type.

Guest OS-level diagnostic logs capture data from the operating system and applications running on a virtual machine. Guest OS-level diagnostic logs collect following types of Metrics and Logs:

Performance counters
Application Logs
Windows Event Logs
.NET Event Source
IIS Logs
Manifest based ETW
Crash Dumps
Customer Error Logs

Enabling Guest OS Diagnostic: You can enable Guest OS Diagnostics during VM creation time or afterwards from VM Dashboard. Click Diagnostic settings in VM wvm35 dashboard>Enable Guest Level Monitoring.

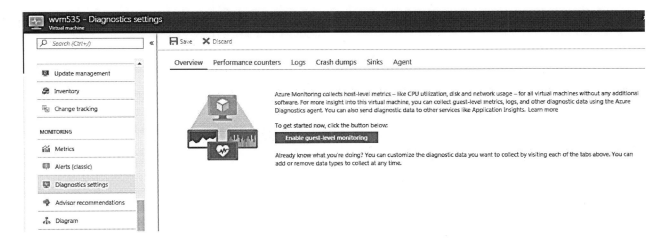

Compare this with Resource Level diagnostics logs which require no agent and capture resource-specific data from the Azure platform itself

Azure Monitor

Azure Monitor provides centralized dashboard for viewing Logs, metrics & alerts for Azure resources.

Azure Monitor provides mini-dashboards for Metrics, Activity Log, Diagnostic logs, alerts, Service Health, Network Watcher & Application Insights etc. Data can be exported to Log Analytics and Power BI for further Analysis.

Exercise 66: Accessing Monitor Dashboard

In Azure Portal click Monitor in Left pane> Monitor Dashboard opens> In the left pane you can see Alerts, Metrics, Log analytics, Activity Log, Service Health, Application Insights, Containers, Network Watcher, Management solution and Diagnostic settings etc.

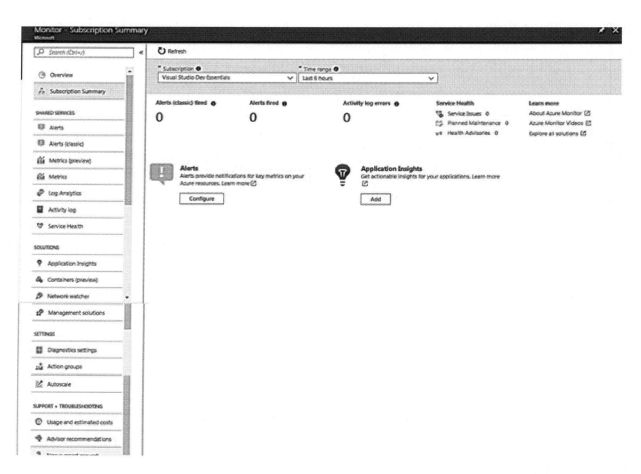

Viewing Diagnostic Logs for Azure Resources: In Monitor Dashboard click Diagnostic settings in left pane> Right pane shows diagnostic logs status for all the Azure resources in the subscription.

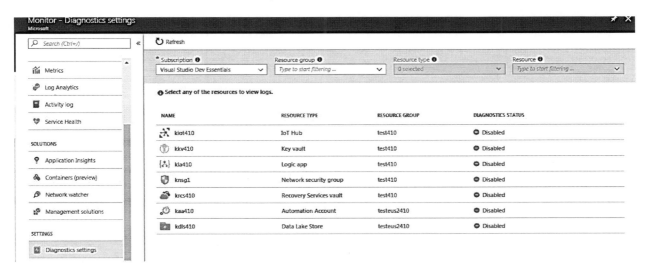

Enabling Diagnostic Log for IOT Hub: Click IOT Hub resource line in Right pane>You can turn on the diagnostic to collect data for the metrics mentioned in the right pane.

View Activity Logs for Azure Resources: In Monitor Dashboard click Activity log in left pane> Right pane shows Activity logs for all the Azure resources in the subscription.

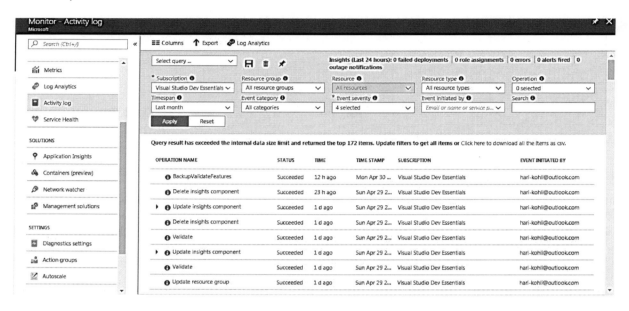

View Metrics and Create Alert: In Monitor Dashboard click Metrics log in left pane> In Right pane select your resource (wvm535) from drop down boxes> click click to add an alert>Add Rule blade opens>Select your metric (I selected % CPU)>select email or webhook when condition is met or Take Action to run a runbook or run a logic app.

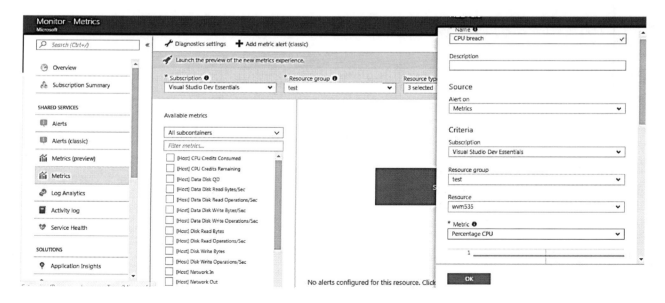

Azure Advisor

Azure Advisor is a personalized recommendation engine that provides proactive best practices guidance for optimally configuring your Azure resources.

Azure Advisor gives recommendation to optimize across **four** different areas – high availability, performance, security, and cost – with all recommendations accessible in one place on the Azure portal.
Azure Advisor is a free service.

Working

It analyzes your resource configuration and usage telemetry. It then recommends solutions to help improve the performance, security, and high availability of your resources while looking for opportunities to reduce your overall Azure spend.

Exercise 67: Accessing Advisor Dashboard

You can access Advisor Dashboard either through Azure Portal or through Monitor Dashboard. In Azure Portal click Advisor in Left pane> Advisor Dashboard opens. It shows recommendation in 4 areas - High availability, Performance, Security and Cost.

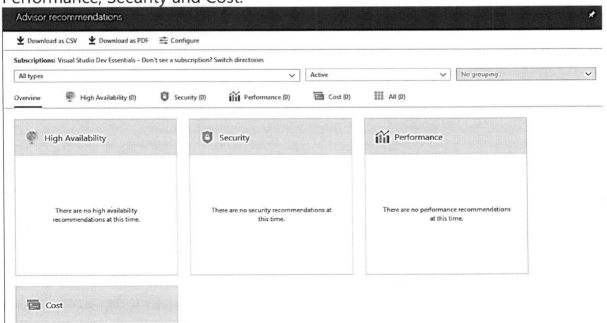

You can download recommendations in CSV or PDF.

Implementing Advisor recommendations

1. Click one of the tabs: High Availability, Security, Performance, or Cost in the Advisor Dashboard.
2. Click a recommendation that you want to review in detail.
3. Review the information about the recommendation and the resources that the recommendation applies to.
4. Click on the Recommended Action to implement the recommendation.

Azure Service Health

Azure Service Health provides status of Azure services which can affect your business critical applications. It also helps you prepare for upcoming planned maintenance. Azure Service Health alerts you and your teams via targeted and flexible notifications.

Service Health Events

Service Health tracks following three types of health events that may impact your resources:

1. **Service issues** - Problems in the Azure services that affect you right now.
2. **Planned maintenance** - Upcoming maintenance that can affect the availability of your services in the future.
3. **Health advisories** - Changes in Azure services that require your attention. Examples include when Azure features are deprecated or if you exceed a usage quota.

Exercise 68 Accessing Service Health Dashboard: Click Service Health Tile in Azure Portal> Service Health Dashboard Opens.

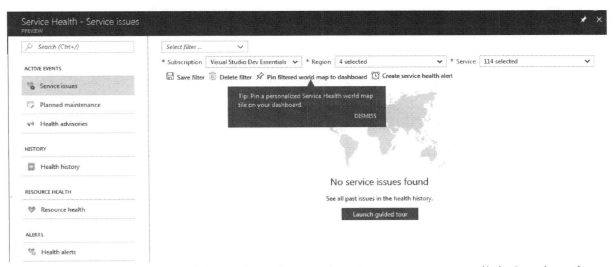

From Service Health Dashboard under Active Events you can click Services issues, Planned maintenance and Health advisories to get more information on the status of Azure Services, upcoming Maintenance schedule in your region.

Architecting Microsoft Azure Solutions Study & Lab Guide Part 2: Exam 70-535

Exercise 69: Configuring Alerts for Service Health

1. Click Service Health Tile in Azure Portal> Service Health Dashboard Opens>click health alerts in left pane> Click +Create Service Health Alert in Right pane>Add Activity Log Blade opens>Enter Information as per requirement and click ok.

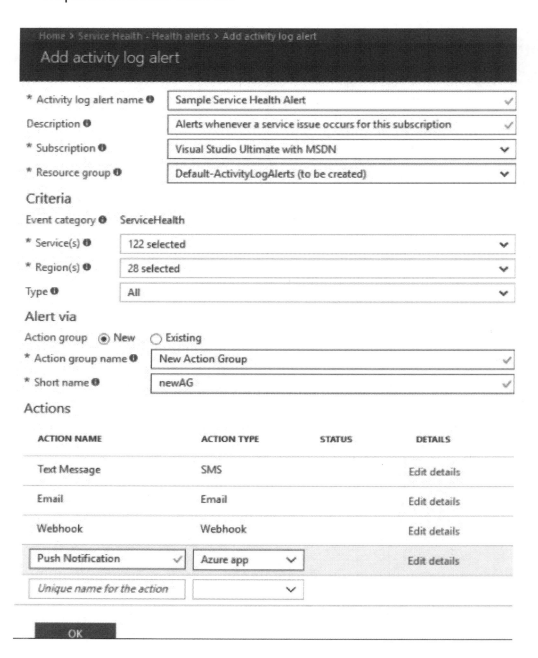

Chapter 20 Azure Automation

This Chapter covers following

- Azure Resource Manager (ARM) Template
- Azure Automation
- Process Automation with Runbooks
- Desired State Configuration (DSC)
- Change Tracking & Inventory Functionality
- Update Management

This Chapter Covers following Lab Exercises

- View Template of an Existing Resource Group
- View the existing template of a resource and then deploy it to create a new resource
- Process Automation using Runbooks
-

Azure Resource Manager (ARM) Template

ARM Templates are used to deploy resources using Infrastructure as a Code.

ARM Template is a text based JavaScript Object Notation (JSON) file that defines one or more resources to deploy to a resource group. It also defines the dependencies between the deployed resources. The template can be re-used to deploy the resources consistently and repeatedly.

Templates are also created by MS and 3rd parties. Figure below shows a sample ARM Template for Storage account creation.

```
1  {
2      "$schema":
   "https://schema.management.azure.com/schemas/2015-01-01/deploymen
   tTemplate.json#",
3      "contentVersion": "1.0.0.0",
4      "parameters": {
5          "storageAccounts_arm4100201_name": {
6              "defaultValue": "arm4100201",
7              "type": "String"
8          }
9      },
10     "variables": {},
```

Why we need ARM Template

Take an Example that you need to deploy a 3 tier application (Web/App/DB) in a new Virtual network. Internet user will connect to Web Tier, Web Tier will connect to App and App will connect to DB tier.

Using Azure Portal or Powershell we can deploy these resources one by one. To deploy we first need to create Virtual network and 3 subnets. Deploy VMs to these 3 subnets. Configure NSG on Subnets and VM NICs. There are following disadvantages to this approach:

1. It is time consuming to deploy and configure the resources.
2. It is error prone
3. You require skilled resources for deployment.

Instead of above option of deploying resources individually we can create an ARM template once, specifying multiple resources and other configurations parameters for deployment. Using this ARM template you can now deploy multiple resources (VNET, Subnet, NSG & Virtual Machines) simultaneously. The ARM template can be re-used multiple times.

Advantages of Template

1. We can deploy, manage, and monitor all the resources for our solution as a group, rather than handling these resources individually.
2. We can re-use the ARM template any number of times.
3. Saves time.
4. We can define the dependencies between resources so they are deployed in the correct order.

Exercise 70: View Template of an Existing Resource Group

In Azure Portal click any Resource group (We selected test)>In test Dashboard dashboard click **Automation script** in left pane> In right pane you can see the configuration of ARM template of all the resources deployed in the resource group test.

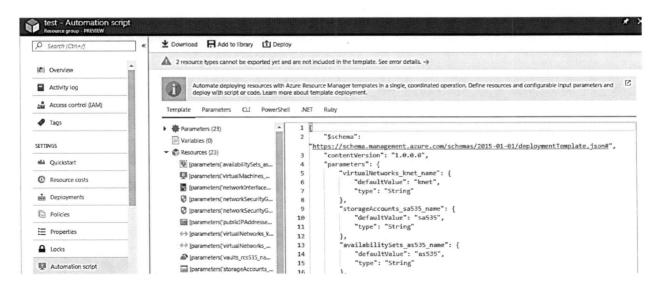

Creating ARM template options

1. Create an ARM Template from scratch using JSON file
2. Download a template of a resource from Azure Portal and Edit it as per your requirement and then deploy it.

ARM Template Deployment Options

1. Powershell
2. CLI
3. Azure Portal

Exercise 71: View the existing template of a resource and then deploy it to create a new resource

In this exercise we will view the template of a Storage Account (arm41002) and then deploy that template to create a new storage account (arm41003). For this exercise I created a storage account arm41002 in ARM1 resource group.

1. In Azure Portal go to storage Account sa1arm Dashboard>Click Automation script in left pane> In right pane you can see template of the storage account.

In Right pane at top you can see download & deploy option buttons.

Architecting Microsoft Azure Solutions Study & Lab Guide Part 2: Exam 70-535

2. Click Deploy in right pane> Custom Deployment Blade opens as shown below> Change the storage Account name to arm41003>click Purchase.

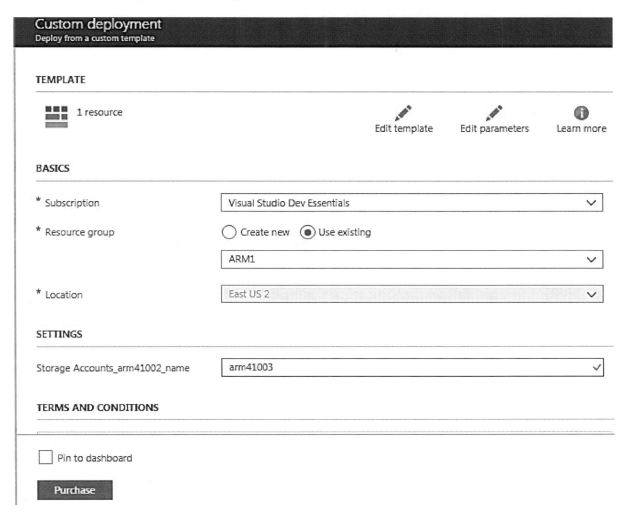

3. Go to ARM1 resource group Dashboard> you can see arm41003 storage account deployed.

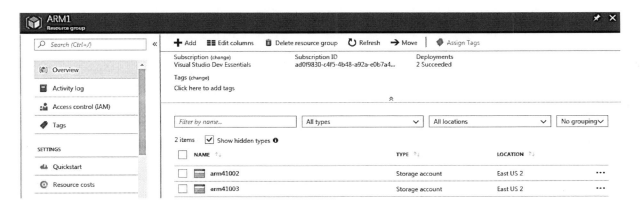

Architecting Microsoft Azure Solutions Study & Lab Guide Part 2: Exam 70-535

Azure Automation

Azure Automation is a managed service that provides **process automation**, **configuration management** and **update management**. It automates manual processes (Process Automation) and enforces configurations for physical and virtual computers (Desired State Configuration).

Figure below shows the architecture of Azure Automation. Azure Automation provides it functionality to both Azure and on-premises resources.

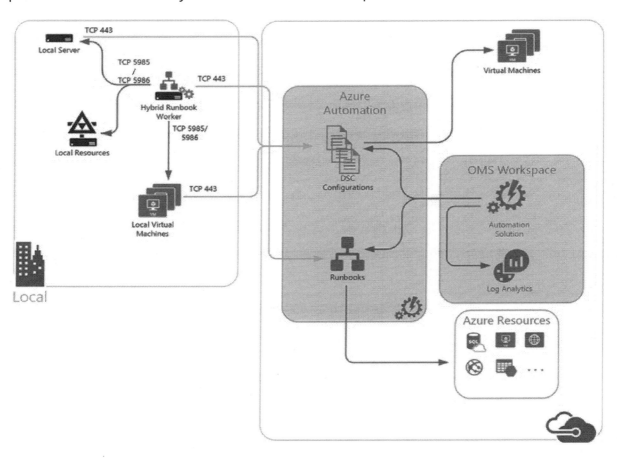

Azure automation provides capabilities to do process automation, update management, desired state configuration, track changes and collect inventory.

Log analytics workspace is required if you want to offer Update Management, change & Inventory tracking functionality and Hybrid worker solution. It also collects Runbook job status and receives configuration information from your Automation account.

Process Automation Working and Architecture

Azure Process Automation automates manual processes using Runbooks against Azure Resources. Runbooks are containers for custom scripts and workflows. You can invoke and run runbooks on demand or according to schedule by using Automation Schedule assets or based on alerts in OMS Log Analytics.

Figure below shows Architecture of Process Automation.

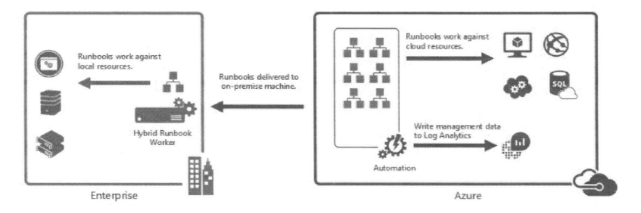

Runbooks are created in Azure Automation Account and work against Azure Resources such as VMs, Azure SQL, Web Apps etc to automate manual process.

Runbooks can also run on-premises where-in you can install one or more Hybrid Runbook Workers in your data center which run runbooks against local resources. Each Hybrid Runbook Worker requires Microsoft Management Agent to be installed and an Automation account. The agent must have a connection to an Azure Log Analytics workspace.

Example of Process Automation

You want your Azure VMs to run only during office hours only (8 AM – 5 PM). To save money an administrator shuts down VMs at 5 PM and Re-Starts at 8 AM. Using Azure Process Automation you can Automate shutdown and re-start activity. You can use Azure Process Automation to create Runbooks (containing Powershell scripts) to shutdown VMs and Re-start VMs which run against your Azure VMs at Schedule time daily.

Runbooks

Runbooks are containers for custom scripts and workflows which run set of tasks that perform an automated process in Automation based on Windows PowerShell. You run Runbooks against Azure and on-premises resources to automate frequent, time-consuming and error-prone tasks.

Runbooks in the cloud don't run under any credentials, but they can leverage Automation assets such as credentials, connections, and certificates to authenticate to resources they access.

Types of Runbooks

Types	Description
Graphical	Based on Windows PowerShell and created and edited completely in graphical editor in Azure portal.
Graphical PowerShell Workflow	Based on Windows PowerShell Workflow and created and edited completely in the graphical editor in Azure portal.
PowerShell	Text runbook based on Windows PowerShell script.
PowerShell Workflow	Text runbook based on Windows PowerShell Workflow.
Python	Text runbook based on Python.

Running Runbooks

Azure Portal: You can start runbooks from Azure Automation Dashboard in Azure Portal. In addition to starting runbooks, you can import them or author your own.

Scheduled: You can schedule runbooks to start at regular intervals. This allows you to automatically repeat a regular management process or collect data to Log Analytics.

PowerShell and API: You can start runbooks and pass them required parameter information from a PowerShell cmdlet or the Azure Automation REST API.

Webhook: A webhook can be created for any runbook that allows it to be started from external applications or web sites.

Log Analytics Alert. An alert in Log Analytics can automatically start a runbook to attempt to correct the issue identified by the alert.

Automation Assets (To be used with Runbooks)

Azure automation assets are resources (settings) that are to be used with a runbook. There are currently six Automation asset categories: **Schedules, Credentials, Certificates, Variables, Connections and Modules.**

A runbook can be linked to multiple Automation assets and an Asset can have multiple runbooks linked to it.

Automation Schedules Assets are used to schedule runbooks to run automatically once or Schedule runbooks to run recurringly multiple times. A runbook can be linked to multiple schedules, and a schedule can have multiple runbooks linked to it.

Automation Credential Assets holds a PSCredential object which contains security credentials such as Azure login username and password. Runbooks and DSC configurations can use the Get-AzureAutomationCredential cmdlet to authenticate applications and services.

Automation Certificates assets can be stored securely in Azure Automation so they can be accessed by runbooks or DSC configurations using the **Get-Automation Certificate** activity.

Automation Variable assets are persistent values that are available to all runbooks and DSC configurations in your automation account. Variables can be String, Boolean, DateTime, Integer, or Not Specified.

Automation Connection assets define the information required to connect to a service or application. The different types of connections you can create are defined by the modules imported into Automation.

Automation module asset is a PowerShell module that optionally contains a metadata file specifying an Azure Automation connection type to be used with the module. Certain module assets are shipped as "global module assets" in the Automation service. You can add additional modules by browsing the gallery.

Note: Readers are advised to go through all Automation assets and there properties in the Automation Account dashboard under shared resources.

Exercise 72: Process Automation using Runbooks

1. Create Automation Account
2. Create/use existing & Run Runbook

Step 1 Create Automation Account: In Azure Portal click create a resource> Monitoring + Management> Automation>Create Automation account blade opens> Enter information as per your requirement and click create.

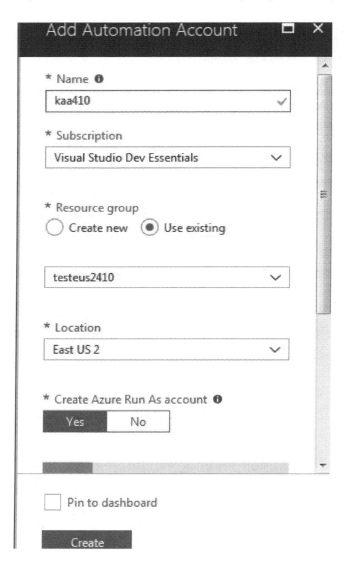

Azure Automation account can be created in following 2 ways:
Standalone Azure Automation Account.
Azure Automation account along with Log Analytics workspace.

Dashboard of Automation account

Note the Configuration Management, Update Management, Process Automation and shared resources functionality offered by Automation Account.

Step 2 Create/Run a Runbook: Here we will run an existing Runbook which is automatically created as part of Automation account. Click Runbooks in Azure Automation Account Dashboard. Run **AzureAutomationtutorialScript** runbook. This Runbooks lists all resources under Resource groups created in your subscription.

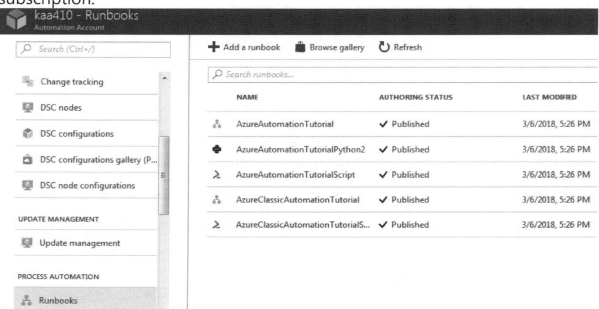

Manually Run the RunbooK: Select AzureAutomationtutorialScript runbook>Click start>In Job page click Output>It will show all resources in the Resource Groups in your subscription.

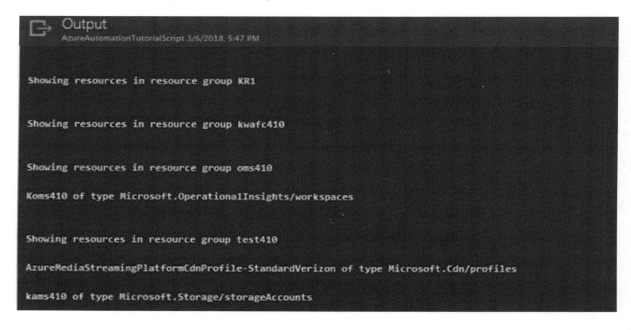

Architecting Microsoft Azure Solutions Study & Lab Guide Part 2: Exam 70-535

Desired State Configuration Architecture and Working

Desired State Configuration (DSC) is a management platform in Windows PowerShell that deploys and enforces the configuration on physical and VMs. Figure below shows Architecture of Desired State Configuration (DSC).

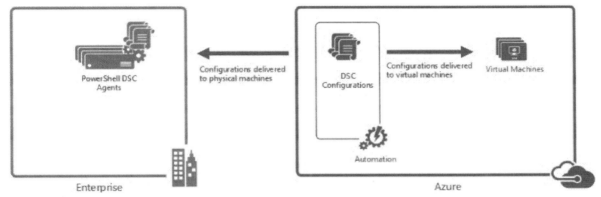

Brief Working

Azure Automation provides a pull server in the cloud that manages DSC configurations which agents can access to retrieve required configurations.

PowerShell DSC configurations are PowerShell scripts that apply Desired configurations to DSC Nodes from a DSC Pull Server in the Azure cloud. If DSC nodes deviate from there desired configuration then you can manually or automatically update desired machine configuration on DSC nodes.

DSC Management Platform & Agents

DSC Management Platform can manage both Azure VMs and Non Azure VMs & Servers. It can manage following types of Machines:

1. Azure Virtual Machines running Windows or Linux.
2. Amazon Web Services (AWS) Virtual Machines running Windows or Linux.
3. Physical and Virtual Windows & Linux computers that are on-premises or in a cloud other than Azure or AWS.

Azure VMs require Desired State Configuration agent extension. It is automatically deployed to Azure VMs when you add them as DSC nodes in Automation Account Dashboard. Non Azure VMs & Servers require Powershell DSC agents.

Change Tracking & Inventory Functionality

The Change Tracking and Inventory solution in Azure Automation provides the ability to track changes and inventory on your virtual machines. The solution tracks changes to Windows and Linux software, Windows and Linux files, Windows registry keys, Windows services, and Linux daemons.

Changes to installed software, Windows services, Windows registry and files, and Linux daemons on the monitored servers are sent to the Log Analytics service in the cloud for processing.

Change Tracking Functionality requires Log analytics workspace.

Enabling Change Tracking & Inventory: In Automation Account Dashboard click change tracking in left pane>Select the Log Analytics workspace>Click enable.

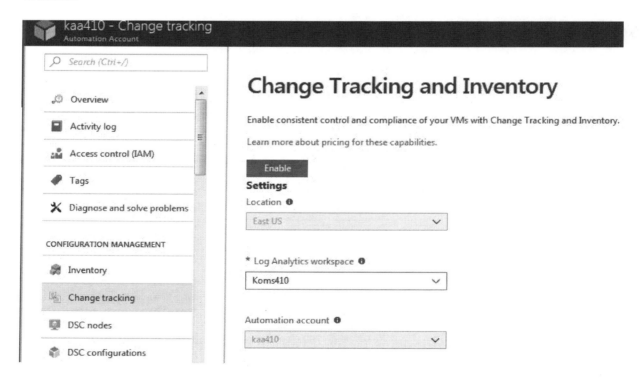

After the solution is enabled, you can view the summary of changes for your monitored computers by selecting **Change Tracking** under **CONFIGURATION MANAGEMENT** in your Automation account or in Log Analytics Workspace.

Update Management

The Update Management solution in Azure automation allows you to manage operating system security updates for your Windows and Linux computers deployed in Azure, on-premises environments, or other cloud providers.

Update Management Functionality requires Log analytics workspace.

Azure Process Automation Pricing

Process automation includes runbook jobs and watchers. Billing for jobs is based on the number of job run time minutes used in the month and for watchers is based on the number of hours used in a month. Charges for process automation are incurred whenever a job or watcher runs.

	FREE UNITS INCLUDED (PER MONTH)	PRICE
Job run time	500 minutes	$0.002/minute
Watchers	744 hours	$0.002/hour

Azure Automation DSC Configuration management Pricing

Configuration management includes the configuration pull service and change tracking capabilities. Billing is based on the number of nodes that are registered with the service and the log data stored in the Azure Log Analytics service.

Charges for configuration management start when a node is registered with the service and stop when the node is unregistered from the service. A node is any machine whose configuration is managed by configuration management. This could be an Azure virtual machine (VM), on-premises VM, physical host or a VM in another public cloud. Billing for nodes is pro-rated hourly.

	FREE UNITS INCLUDED (PER MONTH)	PRICE
Azure node	NA	Free
Non-Azure node	5 nodes	$6/node/Month

Azure Automation Update Management Pricing

Update management includes visibility and deployment of updates in your environment. There are no charges for the service, you only pay for log data stored in the Azure Log Analytics service.

	FREE UNITS INCLUDED (PER MONTH)	PRICE
Any node	NA	Free

Architecting Microsoft Azure Solutions Study & Lab Guide Part 2: Exam 70-535

Chapter 21 Case Studies Consolidated

This Chapter Covers following Case Studies

1. Design a Business Continuity Solution for Web/App tier and Database Tier
2. Choosing a Database tier
3. Azure Web App High Availability
4. Real Time Prediction of breakdown of Industrial Machinery using Stream Analytics and Machine Learning
5. Visualize real-time IoT Device Data using Power BI
6. Visualize real-time IoT Device Data using Azure Web App

Design Case study 1: Design a Business Continuity Solution for Web/App tier and Database Tier.

An Automobile giant is running a 2-tier Dealer application – web/app tier running on Azure Web App and Database Tier running on Azure SQL Database. Recently they had a regional outage and had to face a downtime of 3 hours. They want to have a Disaster recovery solutions hosted in different region which can be activated in case of an outage or a regional disaster. They want DR site should be up and running within 30 minutes of outage or disaster at primary site.

They have constraint that Cross-region connectivity between the application and the Primary database is not acceptable due to latency. This was confirmed during a pilot test.

Design a solution which satisfies the above requirement.

Solution

Designing Web/App Tier

For web/app tier we will have active-passive deployment of Azure Web App as cross region connectivity between the application and the Primary database is not acceptable due to latency. Web App in Primary Region will be active and Web App in secondary will be passive.

Azure Traffic Manager (TM) will be used to Load balance traffic between web apps in Primary and secondary regions. As it is Active-Passive deployment, Traffic Manager should be set up to use failover routing.

Web App in each region will be connected to Azure SQL Database in there region only.

Designing Database Tier

Primary Region already has Azure SQL Database running. Using Active Geo-Replication a secondary Database will be created in secondary Region. Database in each region will be paired to the Web App in there region only.
Azure SQL Database in Primary Region is active and is Primary Database.

Active Traffic and Disaster Recovery to Secondary Site

All Traffic will be served through primary region. In case of outage Traffic will be shifted to Secondary Region. Secondary Database will be promoted to Primary Database manually or automatically using a monitoring app.

Figure below shows the Business Continuity solution for 2-tier Dealer Application.

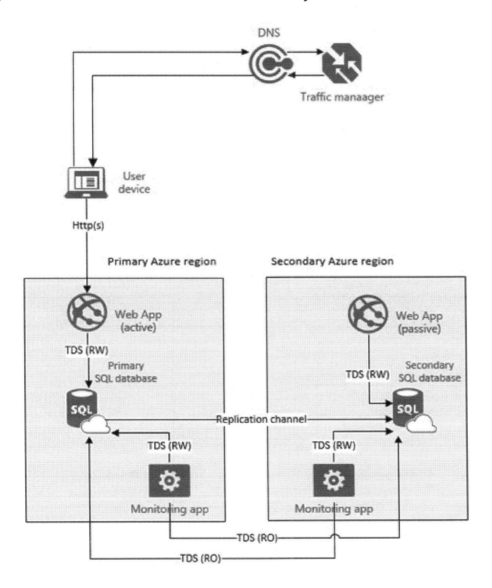

Design Case study 2: Choosing a Database tier

A corporate company is deploying a 2 tier application - Web/App tier and Database tier in Azure. They have chosen Azure SQL Database as there backend.

The application team has given there requirement for Database tier. Database size will be 400 GB and they want Database performance DTU of upto 50.

Based on above Requirement choose the appropriate Database tier.

Solution

Standard S2 Tier gives a DTU of 50. Maximum Database size in S2 is 250 GB. Premium P1 Tier gives a DTU of 125. Maximum Database size in P1 is 500 GB.

Premium P1 Tier will be chosen as it satisfies both DTU and Size requirements. Whereas Standard S2 Tier satisfies only DTU Requirement.

Case Study 3: Azure Web App High Availability

A Global Multinational company is running dealer management application in Azure Web App. Azure Web App uses Azure SQL Database as backend.

They want to have a High Availability and DR solution in a different region. All traffic would be served from primary region. In case of outage in Primary region, Application traffic will be re-directed to Secondary region.

They want to minimize the cost of the HA & DR Setup. They have given a RTO of 30 minutes -60 minutes. There should be no data loss in Azure SQL Database. They want secondary region to be activated without any complicated procedures or operational & administrative overheads. Suggest a solution which satisfies the above requirement.

Solution

Options for High Availability across Primary and Secondary Regions

Active/passive with hot standby: Traffic goes to one region, while the other waits on hot standby. Hot standby means the Web App in the secondary region are running at all times.

Active/passive with cold standby: Traffic goes to one region, while the other waits on cold standby. Cold standby means the Web App in the secondary region are not running until needed for failover. This approach costs less to run, but will generally take longer to come online during a failure.

Active/active: Both regions are active, and requests are load balanced between them. If one region becomes unavailable, it is taken out of rotation.

We will choose **Active/passive with cold standby option** as cost of HA& DR setup is one of the main requirements given by the company.

Web App Setup: One Web App will be setup in each region. Primary Region Web App will be active and will serve all traffic. Secondary region Web App will be in **powered off mode** to save cost. In case of outage Web App in Secondary will be activated and will serve the application traffic. Each Web App will be connected to Azure SQL Database in their region only.

Architecting Microsoft Azure Solutions Study & Lab Guide Part 2: Exam 70-535

Azure SQL Database: Azure SQL Database in Primary region will be Geo-Replicated to Secondary region in read only mode. Each Azure SQL Database will be connected to Azure Web App in their region only. In case of outage in primary region, Azure SQL Database will be promoted as Primary Database.

Azure Traffic Manager: Traffic Manager will route incoming requests to the primary region. For the above scenario we will use **Priority** routing. With this setting, Traffic Manager sends all requests to the primary region unless the endpoint for that region becomes unreachable.

Steps to be taken for activating secondary region

3. Power-on Azure Web App in Secondary Region.
4. Promote Secondary region SQL Database as primary database.

Figure below shows the Architecture of the solution.

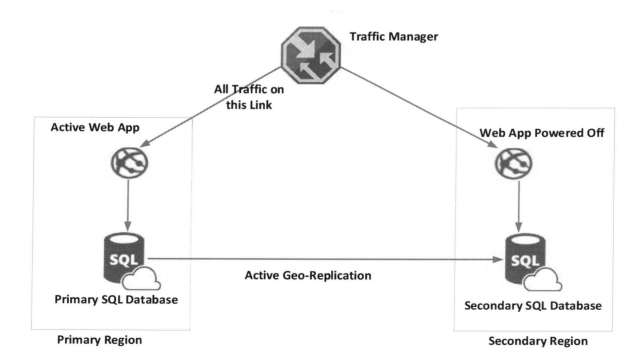

Important Note: Make sure to use Web App Standard Tier and above because Traffic Manager does not Basic/Shared/Free tier as endpoint.

Case Study 4: Real Time Prediction of breakdown of Industrial Machinery using Stream Analytics and Machine Learning

Machine learning is a technique of data science that helps computers **learn from existing data** in order to **forecast future behaviors, outcomes, and trends.**

Azure Machine Learning is a fully managed cloud based predictive analytic service. Azure Machine Learning can make use of streaming data to enable real-time prediction.

Combining the real-time analytic capabilities of Azure Stream Analytics with the real-time predictive analytics capabilities of Azure Machine Learning can help businesses rapidly deploy data solutions to support complex information challenges.

Figure below shows Machine health Sensor Data from Industrial Machinery being ingested into Event Hub.

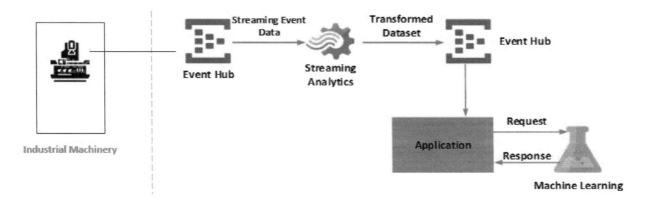

Solution Working

Event Sensor will send maintenance data from Industrial machines in real-time to Event Hub. Azure Streaming Analytics will analyze and transform the Sensor data in real-time. This transformed and filtered data will be consumed by application through event hub. Machine learning will analyze this data in real time to predict the breakdown of the Machine.

Case Study 5: Visualize real-time IoT Device Data using Power BI

Power BI is a Business Intelligence tool from Microsoft. Power BI give graphical view of the data.

Figure below shows Architecture of the setup.

Device   Azure IoT Hub   Stream Analytics   Power BI

Brief Working of the Setup

IoT devices in the field will inject data generated by devices into IoT Hub. In IoT Hub create consumer Groups or use default consumer group. Consumer groups are used by applications to pull data from Azure IoT Hub.

Create Stream Analytic Job and add Iot Hub as input to Stream Analytics Job. Stream Analytics will read data from IoT Hub using consumer groups. Consumer Groups are added in IoT Hub and are used by applications like Stream Analytics to pull data from Azure IoT Hub.
Add Power BI as output to Stream Analytics job and specify Power BI workspace name and Dataset name.
Run the Stream Analytics Job.

Sign in to your Power BI account. Go to the group workspace that you set when you created the output for the Stream Analytics job. Visualize your IoT Data graphically in Power BI.

Case Study 6: Visualize real-time IoT Device Data using Azure Web App

Web Apps is a fully managed compute platform that is optimized for hosting websites and web applications. Web Apps is a managed VM with pre-installed web server and an option to choose application framework (You can choose from Dot Net, PHP, Node.js, Python & Java).

Figure below shows Architecture of the setup.

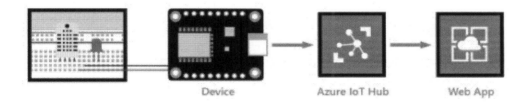

Device   Azure IoT Hub   Web App

Brief Working of the Setup

IoT devices in the field will inject data generated by devices into IoT Hub. In IoT Hub add consumer Groups or use default consumer group. Consumer groups are used by applications to pull data from Azure IoT Hub.

Create Web App. In Web App Dashboard click Application settings and in Right pane under App settings add following Key Value Pairs:

Key	Value
Azure.IoT.IoTHub.ConnectionString	From IoT Device Pane
Azure.IoT.IoTHub.ConsumerGroup	The name of the consumer group that you add to your IoT hub

Upload IoT Data Monitoring Application to Web App. Web Application will read real time data from IoT Hub using consumer group. Web application will process the data and will show the result in the Web Browser.

77643175R00236

Made in the USA
Middletown, DE
23 June 2018